AF560257

# Food, Nutrition and Cookery

# Food, Nutrition and Cookery

Mayank Parkash

RANDOM PUBLICATIONS
NEW DELHI (INDIA)

**Food, Nutrition and Cookery**

---

ISBN 978-93-5111-842-8



Published in 2016 in India by

**RANDOM PUBLICATIONS**

4376-A/4B, Gali Murari Lal, Ansari Road
New Delhi-110 002
Phone : +9111-43580356, 011-23289044, 011-43142548
e-mail: sales@randompublications.com,
info@randompublications.com, randomexports@gmail.com

Reprinted 2019

*Type Setting by* : Friends Media, Delhi-110089
*Digitally Printed at* : Replika Press Pvt. Ltd.

# Preface

Food is any substance consumed to provide nutritional support for the body. It is usually of plant or animal origin, and contains essential nutrients, such as fats, proteins, vitamins, or minerals. The substance is ingested by an organism and assimilated by the organism's cells to provide energy, maintain life, or stimulate growth. Historically, people secured food through two methods: hunting and gathering and agriculture. Today, the majority of the food energy required by the ever increasing population of the world is supplied by the food industry. Food safety and food security are monitored by agencies like the International Association for Food Protection, World Resources Institute, World Food Programme, Food and Agriculture Organization, and International Food Information Council. They address issues such as sustainability, biological diversity, climate change, nutritional economics, population growth, water supply, and access to food. The right to food is a human right derived from the International Covenant on Economic, Social and Cultural Rights (ICESCR), recognizing the "right to an adequate standard of living, including adequate food," as well as the "fundamental right to be free from hunger."

– ***Author***

# Contents

# 1

# Food Security

## ESTIMATES OF HUMAN NUTRIENT REQUIREMENTS

Estimates of human nutrient requirements were first codified during the latter half of the nineteenth century. From the time of their establishment, FAO and WHO have sponsored many meetings, committees and working groups to study and recommend desirable nutrient intakes, each meeting re-estimating recommended levels based on new knowledge. At least 50 national, regional and international agencies recommend what they consider desirable intakes of essential nutrients. Recommendations are customarily cited as specific amounts of each essential nutrient to be ingested daily. Some authorities name them Recommended Daily Allowances [RDAs], others Recommended Daily or Dietary Intakes [RDIs], others Recommended Nutrient Intakes [RNIs]. The evolution of recommended dietary standards was reviewed by several authors. The purpose of RDAs is to encourage healthy eating habits and to prevent diseases attributable to nutrient deficiencies. Earliest motivations for government dietary standards arose in times of severe stress and distress; to feed nations at war or when suffering economic depressions, widespread poverty and malnutrition.

Recommended Daily Allowances [RDAs] the preferred American designation, are intended to serve several purposes: (a) to assess adequacy of food intake among selected population groups; (b) for national food and agricultural policy formulation; (c) to balance food nutritional quality with human need; (d) to provide adequate food during emergencies, particularly for the poor and disadvantaged; (e) to prescribe and enact standards for nutrient labelling of packaged foods. RDAs were first designed to meet the needs of the majority, often embodying margins of safety to allow for variable needs among people of different ages, activities and conditions of health. It is now customary to prescribe specific RDAs for citizens of different sexes, ages and levels of activity.

RDAs were first calculated by estimating the average physiological requirements for each absorbed nutrient, a value then modified to compensate for incomplete absorption and utilisation, variability among persons, bioavailability among different food sources. RDAs are based on foods consumed in normal diets, not on pure substances or concentrates, and take account of nutrient variability within and among particular foods. At high levels of intake some nutrients, such as vitamin A, may be toxic so that upper limits of safe intake are prescribed. It is difficult to prescribe precise RDAs for all conditions of men, women and children and their variable activities. Experiments on human beings are expensive, time consuming and only small groups of volunteer subjects can be studied in confined controlled conditions. Using humans as experimental animals also raises ethical objections. RDAs are intended for people as they go about their normal daily activities but food intakes and nutrient balance are difficult to determine where subjects move freely and are not confined in a metabolic research facility.

Data based on *ex post facto* recall by subjects going about their normal lives are at best approximate. Despite a vast accumulation of nutritional data, with more sensitive analytical tools available, nutrition remains a relatively imprecise and speculative science. Concepts change as more evidence comes to light. Thirty years ago it was believed military men working in Arctic climates needed more food than those working in temperate zones so Canadian troops in the Arctic north were given packaged rations that provided 5,000 kg Cals/day. It was later realised that with insulated clothing and the need to move slowly to avoid heavy perspiration that could freeze, caloric requirements were no higher in cold than in temperate climates. Since caloric intake must balance energy expenditure, people who perform heavy work or strenuous exercise need higher caloric intakes than sedentary persons.

People who change from energy-intensive activities to a sedentary life-style tend to eat more than they need. Overeating with resultant obesity is disturbingly evident among the richer nations and affluent persons in less developed economies.

It is reported that between 25 and 30 per cent of Europeans and North Americans are excessively obese, at risk of cardiovascular diseases, diabetes and other related disabilities. The obese among the affluent reflect Nerissa's comment in Shakespeare's *Merchant of Venice*: "They are as sick who surfeit with too much as those who starve with nothing." The nutrient content of every food crop varies among genotypes and conditions of cultivation. Among the world's wheat collection on a dry weight basis, protein contents range from 6 to 23 per cent, lysine (as per cent of protein) from 2 per cent to 4.3 per cent. A review of over 1,300 sorghum analyses reported protein contents (N × 5.7 DWB) to range from 7.1 to 14.2 per cent, lysine (mg/g nitrogen) from 71 to 212, iron (mg/100g) from 0.9 to 20.0, niacin [mg/100g] from 2.9 to 6.4. Significant variability was reported among samples of pearl millet (*Pennisetum typhoides*), chickpea (*Cicer arietinum*), faba bean (*Vicia faba*), and lentils (*Lens esculenta*).

Accurate chemical and biochemical analyses are difficult and demand professional competence and experience. Inexperienced technicians are unaware of many sources of error among standard analytical methods. Some 16 sources of error were identified in the classical Kjeldahl method of determining protein nitrogen.

Responsible nutritional scientists seek to encourage rational eating habits based on the best available knowledge. The alchemist's pursuit of the *Elixir vitae* is far from moribund among publicists who proclaim all manner of diets guaranteed to ensure good health and longevity. The penchant for nutritional panaceas has been evident for the past 50 years. During the 1950s vitamins were in favour, in the 1960s proteins and amino acids were in fashion, from the 1970s cholesterol and cardiovascular dysfunctions obsessed public attention, next came the health benefits promised by dietary fibre. The present passion is for nutriceuticals, proclaimed in principle some 4,000 years ago by the Chinese, and for 'functional foods' (which beg the question: what are non-functional foods?), neither of which are specifically defined. RDAs, RDIs and RNIs can be useful as general guides for cognisant officials responsible for formulating national health, food and agricultural policies. For most consumers, RDAs have little practical meaning. Consumers are better advised by illustrated guides to healthy eating based upon mixed diets of foods that are familiar, acceptable and seasonably available.

Human nutritional requirements, criteria used to arrive at recommended levels of intake, consequences of serious deficiencies, food intolerances and allergic responses are discussed in greater detail in other publications. Predictions of the size to which the world population will grow, and for how many persons the planet can provide sustainable food security 50 or 100 years from now, though intellectually diverting, are of little practical utility. One can estimate with reasonable certainty what could be produced with present resources. What may be feasible 50 or 100 years from now is indeterminable.

Of more pressing urgency are the consequences of rapidly changing demographics and rising disposable incomes among urban communities. More than half the people of Asia and Latin America live in large towns and cities, expanding in size and populations all over the world. Though some food can be raised in city gardens and horticultural allotments, urban communities rely on food safely transported from rural farms, inland and maritime fisheries.

As people migrate from rural to urban communities and disposable incomes rise, eating habits change. Growing demand for processed convenience foods is illustrated by the replacement of cereals, pulses and cassava, hand ground and cooked into some form of porridge, with processed foods such as bread, biscuits, cakes and pasta. Of critical consequence for natural resource conservation is the growing demand for livestock products, which across SE Asia is rising by over 20 per cent a year.

Few of the world's cities were planned and laid out in expectation of the volume and density of vehicular traffic destined to grow progressively worse in all cities on all continents. To alleviate traffic congestion, the City of London Authority has imposed heavy tolls on private vehicles that enter the city on working days.

Too little investment is devoted to improving and maintaining rural infrastructures, to rural-to-urban and intra-urban transportation systems. The longer time taken to transport perishable food materials from rural producers to urban processors and markets, the greater is the probability of biological and economic loss.

Urban food security demands consistent access to a safe adequate supply of acceptable, affordable foods dependent on a. technologically efficient systems of preservation and processing, primary preservation being applied soon after harvest; b. logistically efficient and economic means of storage and transportation; c. reliable markets which retail foods that are safe, of acceptable quality, in unit quantities and prices that all segments of urban society can afford; d. national food and agricultural policies that provide and maintain the infrastructures, services, transportation facilities, social and economic conditions essential to efficient holistically integrated food systems.

## THE PHENOMENOLOGY OF FOOD SUSTAINABILITY

Sustainability is encountered with increasing frequency in a variety of arenas. As the global community of both developed and developing nations faces the challenges of finite natural resources, burgeoning public budget deficits, and growing interdependence and complexity, the need to do more with less has become the sine qua non of both government and private sector economic activity. Sustainability as an issue has both emerged from, and helped to shape, each of these challenges. For example, concern over the degradation and exhaustion of the environment has led to the explicit linking of economy and ecology, as necessary to sustaining growth while conserving the globe's natural endowments for future generations.

Tax-payer's "revolts" in the United States, combined with continued demand for public services, have forced government to reexamine the scope of its activities while seeking ever greater efficiencies. And in Eastern Europe, parallel but even deeper concerns have been expressed in city streets and squares, contributing to the dismantling of Communist dictatorships and their state-managed economies.

In the foreign assistance realm, the objective of making development investments more productive has taken on new urgency as developing country indebtedness reaches new heights, bilateral assistance declines, multilateral agencies try to divide their resources among ever more competing needs, and private capital and trade flows take on increased importance. Much of the task of developing in a sustainable fashion involves technical knowledge and skills, in the sense of specialized information and tools derived from the biological and physical sciences and applied to development and production problems.

In the agricultural sector, such things as biologically-based pest control, water-saving irrigation systems, crop diversification, or soils salinity management comes to mind. These often-termed "hard" technologies are indisputably important for growth, development, and sustainability in the sector. However, there is also a family of "soft" technologies, those deriving from the human and social sciences that play key roles. These tend to be overshadowed by their more visible brethren in the "hard" category.

The topic of this book is one of these "softer," less directly visible technologies, those relating to organizations and management. A key component of sustainable development is the institutional framework within which activities are conceived, planned, funded, implemented, and managed. While the technical quality and appropriateness of development activities are critical to success, sustainable institutions are equally so. To be able to grow and develop all economies need an infrastructure of institutions, both public and private, that operates efficiently and produces goods and services effectively. Institutions with these characteristics are particularly lacking in the Third World.

This book focuses on institutional sustainability and its role in agriculture and rural development. It concentrates on collaborations between international donor organizations and developing countries to design and implement projects aimed at introducing performance and capacity improvements, which in turn lead to sustainable institutions contributing to agricultural and rural development. Despite the drop in proportion of gross domestic product earned by agriculture relative to industry and services, many developing countries remain heavily dependent on agriculture. Especially for the bottom tier of developing nations, the vast majority of their populations pursue their livelihoods in rural areas, and their well-being depends on farming and allied occupations. Over the long run, maintaining and enhancing agricultural production demands a continuous process of acquisition, adaptation, and application of new technologies.

Technological change in agriculture has increased almost exponentially in complexity and speed, making the world marketplace for agricultural commodities increasingly volatile.

In some cases new technologies have placed previously unique or distinct commodities in direct competition with either natural or synthetic substitutes. For example, the use of biotechnology to produce natural vanilla flavour in U.S. laboratories threatens a $50 million export for Madagascar, where 70,000 small farmers produced three quarters of the world's vanilla beans. In other cases, the failure to adopt a new knowledge has placed large populations at risk of malnutrition and even starvation.

This is most vividly true in sub-Saharan Africa, where institutions have not been able to support a "green revolution" of increased food production based on new varieties of food plants and improved agricultural techniques. Dynamic, capable institutions that deal with this increased complexity and rate of change on a sustained basis are central to successful agricultural development.

Recent studies in the United States, notably that of Belasco, have drawn attention to the way in which changes in the food industry have provoked resistance from some sections of consumers, and the demand that government intervene more to protect the interests of the food consumer. The food industry, in turn, has counter-attacked in a number of ways to the barrage of criticism and public consciousness surrounding food issues. Belasco details these 'counter-revolutionary' (or perhaps 'counter-counter-revolutionary' would be more accurate!) strategies: food manufacturers have sought to dilute recommendations ('reduce' rather than 'avoid' foods that are bad for you); they have employed what marketing people call 'repositioning', altering the way products are described rather than the products themselves; and they have increasingly employed strategies both to differentiate products and to differentiate markets.

In the United Kingdom today we could scarcely fail to be aware of the importance of product differentiation: the food industry has employed advertising techniques to differentiate between products for many years. However, what is new, and very much a response to consumer resistance, is product differentiation in 'healthy' or 'ecologically-friendly' foods, an important aspect of what has been dubbed 'Green consumerism'. Similarly, the extent to which the market can be differentiated according to the tastes of different groups of consumers, has received widespread attention, notably in the food trade journals. We would argue, in fact, that some segments of the market in developed countries have entered a 'post-fordist' era, as far as the consumption of food is concerned.

That is, an era not so much of the mass consumption of homogeneous, industrially produced food as of the development of healthy foods for market 'niches', often reflecting ethnic variety and traditions, but utilizing the full armoury of the food processing industry, and targeted to consumers willing to pay for high value-added products. With the growing sophistication in manipulating the chemical constituents of food, highly processed food can be presented as 'healthy' food, manufactured to have low fat, low cholesterol and high fibre content, in line with current dietary recommendations.

The challenge facing the food industry, and this is linked to shifts in the food system more generally, is how to make healthy foods more marketable, and marketable foods appear more healthy. Both questions are capable of eliciting a response from food manufacturers, but to understand the background to this response we need to examine the patterns of resistance which have grown up to recent changes in the food industry, patterns which echo some of the forms of resistance to environmental changes.

The beginnings of what Belasco calls a 'countercuisine' are linked to a number of quite important social changes which, as we have already noted, shift the individual's attention from the sphere of production relations to those of consumption. Three aspects require our attention: the way in which we arrive at our impressions of what foods to avoid and what foods to consume (the quality of food as a commodity in the market); the way in which food 'signifies' and expresses other aspects of our lives (food as self-enhancement); and finally, the way in which our consumption of food is linked to broader questions of ownership and organization in the economy as a whole (food as part of a broader political economy).

Almost unnoticed, issues surrounding each of these aspects of the consumption of food have assumed enormous importance in recent years, but close examination reveals that what at first appear to be almost random evidence of social resistance to the modern food system have their roots in fundamental social changes. These social changes need to be outlined, and their implications examined. It is our contention that too much attention has been devoted to the 'signifying' aspects of food and diet, the semiology of food consumption, by sociologists and anthropologists, to the detriment of a wider understanding of the social transformations implied by the economic and technological changes in the food system.

As we have seen, women's roles have been transformed in a number of ways, some of which are clearly irreversible. Domestic work, including housework, has been opened up to important market forces, and the manufacture and purchase of 'white goods' for the home is now an important activity. At the same time the idea that housework is no longer onerous has served the interests of manufacturers and others. It is far from clear that technology in the home is labour-saving; this assumption, needs to be examined critically. Evidence exists that a human price is exacted for the benefits of speed and convenience which 'white goods' bring.

Housework standards change, and women expect (and are expected) to raise the standards of housework in turn. At the same time, it is likely that women's release from the worst forms of labour drudgery is associated with more time being spent by them on other activities in the home, particularly attention to children. This is not to say that many household tasks are not easier; they are. It is merely to point out that the definition of housework, and with it women's responsibilities in the home, is constantly shifting. It is not immutable. It is also clear that since the 1970s important changes have occurred in popular understanding of the relationship between food and health. Preventative medicine may only be in its infancy, and receive little official encouragement, but for some groups of people in the industrialized world, healthy eating is now considered essential. Healthy eating in the past depended critically on local custom and diet and, most importantly, income. Today this is still true, but local variations have less importance, and additional factors have made their appearance, which have engaged the attention of a battery of professionals, such as health educators, doctors, consumer groups and alternative therapists. The perceived need to diet to reduce obesity has given rise to a huge consumer market in low-calorie foods, including the controversial 'low-cal' liquid diets and innumerable diet 'systems'.

The publication of evidence about heart disease and cancer has led to some marked shifts in the public consumption of certain foods, especially in the United States, where the changes date back to the publication of the McGovern Report in 1977. Food has become one of the obsessions of our time, associated as it is with good health, longevity and the occurrence of stress. Physical fitness has also become an obsession in some quarters, perhaps also a 'fad'. Evidence from the United States suggests that, while in 1960 only a quarter of adults exercised regularly, by 1980 over half did so.

The point is not that everybody is exercising more, but that more people are, and that health is increasingly linked to diet in many people's minds. This is not a trend likely to be discouraged by the food industry, since it also represents a change with commercial possibilities. Indeed, the giant food firms have jumped on this bandwagon, adapting to each new nutritional recommendation—low sodium, low saturated fats, high fibre—to the point of confusing consumers grappling with labels and elusive media-speak, such as 'lite' and 'natural'.

Changes have also occurred in public perceptions of the two processes: appropriation and substitution. Following the scare over DDT between 1969 and 1972 in the United States, and subsequent publicity about the use of other pesticides, attention has been given to the effects of pesticide residues in food, especially by the London Food Commission in the United Kingdom. Few studies have been undertaken, and even fewer given publicity, about the relative nutritional quality of organically produced and chemically produced food. Pesticide use in the United States rose 500 per cent between 1950 and 1986, but in the latter year one-fifth of United States's crops were lost to pests, the *same percentage as in* 1950! The tactic employed by the food industry in meeting the criticism of environmentalists and whole food enthusiasts, has been that the industry can 'compensate' through industrial processes for the shortcomings of nature.

The industry argued that organic foods were more expensive (ignoring the hidden subsidies provided to chemically produced food), that organic foods could not meet market demand, that food additives increased the palatability of food, and that convenience removed the drudgery from food preparation. By the late 1960s in North America, and perhaps a decade later in the United Kingdom, food manufacturers began to 'reposition' themselves, as well as their food products.

Now they were on the side of emancipated women and environmentalists; they offered themselves as accomplices in women's drive for more independence and in the vanguard of responsible, sustainable resource management. Market researchers have credited much of the improvement in the food industry to their own responsiveness to consumer pressure. In the words of an industry spokesperson:

For example, ten years ago the only place people could find additive-free *natural* products were in the comparatively cramped and small premises of health food stores. Today such products, not only much improved and—dare we say it?—engineered to satisfy consumer preferences, are mainstream products in prime placing in major supermarket chains the length and breadth of Britain.

This represents one side of the story, but in practice healthier eating has also presented a challenge to the food industry which it has found difficult to grasp. The problem, in a nutshell, is how to leave out food additives and processing, and still add value to the final product.

The post-war period had seen additives 'substitute' for natural ingredients, while much that was natural had been removed from food. Food was given more value added through packaging, processing and ensuring it stayed 'fresh' longer. The challenge represented by making 'healthy' foods from 'health' foods was how to make profits by appearing to do less to the product. The industry responded to the challenge, as we have noted, by both market and product differentiation—identifying, and exploiting market opportunities for 'niche' products, such as low-calorie foods, ethnic health foods and fitness-related foods.

Finally, the food industry has been in the forefront of the promotion of food supplements; people can now supplement their inadequate diet from a range of commercially promoted food 'accessories'. In 1985 over US$3 billion was spent in the United States on vitamin and mineral supplements and over $4.5 billion in supplements to fortified breakfast cereals. This diet supplementation was the inevitable outcome of the way eating had changed in the United States. In 1909, 40 per cent of calories had been provided from fruit, vegetables and grains. By 1976 only 20 per cent of calories came from these sources, the rest from fats and refined sugars. As people ate more calories they ate fewer vitamins and minerals—supplements have helped to fill the vacuum left by changes in the 'affluent diet' of North America.

Another important social change that has accompanied the shifts in diet referred to above is that governments in the industrialized countries have been forced to make some accommodation to the pressures put upon them by food consumers, and interest groups representing consumers. In the United Kingdom this has come about largely as a result of successive food 'scares', such as those over salmonella, listeria and bovine spongiform encephalopathy ('mad cow disease') in the last few years. The extent to which governments will respond to consumer anxieties is still unclear, but the current debate about public nutrition policy and food legislation represents an excellent illustration of the kind of contradiction to emerge from the development of the modern food system.

The demand for more intervention in the food system presents difficulties for governments committed to the idea of choice in the marketplace. On the one hand it is difficult for them to resist, as a matter of principle, the demand for more information about food products. Issuing 'guidelines' about food and health is not inconsistent with conservative ideology, which places individual choice before government controls. The publicity given to the McGovern Report in the United States after 1977 served to divide the food lobby. Part of the food industry could take comfort from the encouragement being given to people to eat more cereals, vegetables and fruit. Another section of the industry tried to develop marketing strategies to overcome opposition to increased consumption of other items (particularly meat, dairy products and eggs).

The development of a 'fordist' diet in the 1950s and 1960s had meant that red meat consumption rose, in the United States from 121 Ibs per capita in 1930 to 160 Ibs per capita in 1970. By 1968 20 million tons of vegetable protein was being fed to livestock to produce 2 million tons of animal protein. Since 1980 there has been a steady reversal of this trend: beef consumption has fallen in the United States, and voluntary reductions in food consumption, like those recommended by the McGovern Commission for eggs, sugar and animal fats, have also begun to be registered. However, this, too, is only part of the total picture.

Changes in diet, encouraged by public debate, have not yet pushed or persuaded governments, in the United States or Western Europe, to take a more interventionist stand on other aspects of food consumption, notably the use of food additives, although recent legislation like that proposed in the United Kingdom in March 1990 would introduce more rigorous standards of hygiene in the food industry.

In the United States the Federal Food and Drug Administration (FDA) co-operates very closely with the food industry. In practice many of its recommendations are welcomed by the industry because they reinforce the idea that most food already on the supermarket shelves is fit for public consumption.

The FDA-initiated testing of food led to the conclusion that over a thousand substances used as food additives were 'generally recognized as safe' (GRAS) for use in food, whereas only two substances were banned as a result of FDA testing: a carcinogenic weed killer and, in 1969, cyclamates. The United States Government has proved reluctant to act as a watchdog on food additives. Meanwhile over 1 billion Ibs of additives are added to food products in the United States, equivalent to 5 Ibs of additives per capita. It is important to consider another aspect of food consumption: the meaning people attach to it, and the way in which food consumption practices help structure social relations more generally. Gofton has made a useful first attempt to come to grips with some aspects of the sociology of food consumption in the United Kingdom today. He notes several of the trends referred to above and in other chapters of this book: the growing concern for health; home-centred living; redefinitions of social roles within households; the trade-off between the time taken in food preparation and leisure activities; and the emphasis given in our society to individualism and hedonism.

Many of these changes are linked to the way society has become organized in the developed countries, such as the shift towards a more informational society where the production of information rather than goods is at a premium. Similarly, there has also been a shift towards relatively decentralized authority systems, particularly in the family, where individual members are more likely to make autonomous decisions about (among other things) what and when they eat. Finally, during the 1980s we witnessed in the United Kingdom what has been dubbed the beginnings of 'the enterprise culture', which placed importance, particularly in ideological terms, on individual entrepreneurship and initiative rather than bureaucratic surveillance and government responsibility. Gofton argues, convincingly we believe, that patterns of food consumption (and, we should add, patterns of resistance to highly processed, 'industrialized' foods) are closely related to changes in social behaviour and organization, which place private consumer choice and individualism before community-based or class-based patterns of behaviour.

The trends in consumption, implied by different market 'niches', together with underlying shifts in the way households and 'communities' are constituted around specific interests, are important components of post-industrial society.

Gofton also reviews various strands of what we might term the 'sociology of food' focusing on three major areas in which attention to food might be linked to 'post-industrial' and 'post-modernist' concerns: the semiotics of food (represented by Mary Douglas in particular); the debate initiated by Pahl and Wallace and Gershuny about changes in the way the household is constituted; and the work of Bourdieu on the relationship between upbringing, class and taste (including taste in food). Something of this approach is reflected, within British anthropology, in the work of Jack Goody.

The work of Pahl and Gershuny, important as it is, is principally concerned with work rather than food, but the other sociological currents certainly reflect serious attention to food consumption habits, and the role of these habits in our culture.

These approaches explore the phenomenology of food consumption, the way in which food tastes and habits operate not simply as indicators of lifestyle but also as ways of conveying meaning to experience. Other contributors to this debate include Charles and Kerr, whose recent work has addressed the relationship between eating habits, gender relations and the class structure, basing their analysis on empirical evidence drawn from interviews with over 200 women in the United Kingdom between 1982 and 1983. Charles and Kerr take as their point of departure the way in which food practices contribute to the reproduction of the social order, drawing on Bourdieu and Althusser in stressing the role of ideology in social reproduction. Their analysis places considerable emphasis on the meanings carried by food about the nature of the social occasion, and the way these meanings provide the ground rules for social structure, gender roles and class identities. This kind of research is phenomenological in outlook but essentially empirical, even occasionally empiricist, in design.

It is grounded less in what Giddens has termed the 'knowledge ability of [the] agents' themselves and more in the unconscious behaviour of these agents, whose cultural patterns help to define them within their society.

Research such as that undertaken by Charles and Kerr delineates some important aspects of social behaviour in Britain today, but we would argue that it fails to relate behaviour within the family to wider structural changes in the role of food within society, and to the expansion of the food system. Reading Charles and Kerr one could be excused for thinking that working-class people never ate 'fast foods' (there is no entry on fast foods in the index) while 'convenience foods' are relegated to just three pages of text. Apparently the women interviewed used convenience foods, but not in the main meal they prepared—convenience foods were not 'proper meals'.

Expending time and effort on the production of a meal in some way conferred goodness on it: perhaps a moral rather than a nutritional goodness but this distinction was not made by the women...A meal consisting of convenience foods...cannot constitute a proper meal, is by definition less healthy than a proper meal and involves much less preparation time...We may therefore see women's concern that the family should eat properly and healthily in terms of home cooked food provided at regular intervals as having been handed down through family tradition; it is a central part of family life.

This kind of analysis places evidence of continuity before evidence of change, and imbue the meanings people attach to their behaviour with more importance than the behaviour itself.

It is also instructive to note how the authors have renegotiated these meanings in the text.

It is not easy to establish from their work whether women are making more use of convenience foods, although the suggestion is that they probably are, because the analysis is largely concerned to demonstrate that any resort to convenience foods needs to be located within traditional family behaviour.

Emphasizing that people look upon food as 'natural' should not blind us to the fact that in practice it frequently is highly processed. What people *feel about food* may be important, but so is the evidence about *what they eat.* One suspects that if the same women were talking to researchers less concerned to establish its meaning for their argument about gender and class relationships, it would have been much more difficult to discuss food preferences in terms of the provision of a 'proper meal'. Instead of evidence for the reproduction of the existing social order, we would see evidence of change, in the social changes surrounding the way food is consumed as well as in the food itself. Phenomenological approaches to the meaning of food consumption would benefit from taking some cognizance of the processes through which food itself has become an industrially produced good.

This book has examined the effects of the modern food system in accelerating social changes, in both developed and developing societies. We have argued that the ideological aspects of the food system are not confined to those usually reported on by sociologists: the 'appropriateness' of food, and the meaning attached to food in everyday life, within the experience of working-class people. It is our contention that changes in the material basis of food production and consumption are linked to the transformation of 'nature', and that the establishment of new areas of commodity production influences the values attached to social relations.

Capitalism is an evolving system, whose values and practices do not lie embedded in the past, anymore than the behaviour of working-class people is lodged in static definitions of what is an appropriate, definition formed by their parents and grandparents within a quite different social milieu. Food has become fully commoditized; it is therefore to be expected that it's 'naturalness' would be emphasized by the food industry, in the process generating new symbolic meanings as a path to further accumulation.

As Massey has observed there needs to be a debate about the 'natural', which can draw on recent post-structuralist thinking. The 'denaturalization' of space, in the form of attention to 'location theory', was a preoccupation of some social scientists, particularly geographers in the 1960s. What is required now is similar attention to the way in which naturalization accompanies changes in technology and social relations. Nature has been refashioned in several ways, which this book has drawn attention to within an integrated framework of analysis.

1. Within the labour process the employment of women has, through routinization, become naturalized as women's labour has shifted into and out of the home.
2. Technological changes in agri-food production, now enhanced by biotechnology and genetic engineering, have manipulated biological processes, appropriating some and substituting others, redefining and refashioning nature as a source of profit and capital accumulation. As the food we consume has become more processed it has been presented as more 'natural' by the food industry.
3. Finally, the development of modern agriculture has forced a separation between the 'countryside' as an area of consumption (amenity, recreation, aesthetics) and the production of food and fibre from the land. The drive to protect the countryside, or more generally to seek greater protection for conservation and wilderness areas in other industrial societies, is defended and advanced on the basis of conserving what is 'natural', and a true embodiment or representation of 'nature'.

It is clear from this analysis that as the modern food system becomes more integrated, and the management of contradictions, such as those presented by the environment, become more urgent, the more the food system departs—in all three senses referred to above—from being 'natural'. Naturalization is the price society pays for seeking to transform its image of itself. Or, as Bourdieu has expressed it, each system produces the naturalization of its own arbitrariness. We have argued that many of the contradictions posed by the modern food system can be handled by policy interventions, such as those to contain environmental costs and to address public concern over the quality of industrially produced food. The modern food system developed out of a combination of factors. These included: state intervention in agricultural policy designed to stimulate the adoption of new technology; guaranteed markets; the food processing industries' access to female labour, partially released from full-time employment in the home by (initially) wartime restructuring; and changes in family farming which served to legitimate the demands of more 'efficient', small-scale but highly capitalized producers. The management of the contradictions of the modern food system can be handled in the industrialized countries of the North, at a price, for several reasons that require close attention.

As we have seen, productivity increases in agriculture have been subsidized through industrial accumulation in the countries of the North. In the post-war period of intensive accumulation, the significance of cheap food arises not simply, as initially understood from its role, as a wage good; but also from its contribution to a widening of the market for consumer goods in general, which has accompanied the growth of labour productivity within the advanced capitalist societies.

The costs of this policy, of continuing to support agricultural modernization, have been passed on to the consumer and taxpayer in the European Community, the United States and Japan. It is increasingly clear that this agricultural policy model, even when only partially understood, is being called into question, notably by conservative critics as well as those with 'Greener' credentials. At the level of ideological legitimation, which has remained important throughout the post-war period in helping to define the relationship between farmers and the state, the resistance of public opinion to the priority attached to this model, at great environmental and social cost, has become an increasingly important part of the new political agenda of the 1990s.

Furthermore, the rise to importance of what we have termed 'environmental managerialism', in the industrialized countries, represents a significant policy opening, which could not have been anticipated a decade ago. The improved management of 'externalities' associated with the food system can reduce the full impact of the transformation of the countryside, through negotiated accommodations to environmental concerns. In the United Kingdom we have been conditioned to accept a managed countryside for a least a century; in other countries of the European Community the emphasis on preserving the cultural association between family farmers and the environment is equally strong politically.

Indeed this nexus of interests recently gained prominence as the philosophical foundation of the EuropeanCommi-ssion's proposed rural development policy, as outlined in *The Future of Rural Society*. In North America, the issues are gather different, in that the separation of wild lands (to which public access is considered important) and agriculture, is more pronounced. Nevertheless, here too the armoury of interventionist policies designed to manage the contradictions of development is receiving more attention: low input farming, wilderness retention, the establishment of recreational priorities for an affluent, urban population.

Finally, as we have seen, in the industrialized countries of the North there has been considerable resistance to the complete industrialization of the diet. For a substantial minority of the population—in the United States usually considered to be about a third of the market—'healthy' eating has become an alternative to the excesses of the 'fordist' diet. The food industry has accommodated, indeed sought to exploit, many of these changes, whose origin we see in the wider educational opportunities of the post-war generation, as well as greater private affluence. As we have seen, it is possible to increase value added in food products without necessarily losing the nutritional value of food, although this poses real problems for the large food conglomerates in increasingly competitive, oligopolistic markets. Within some sectors of the durable consumer goods industries the development of 'healthy' convenience foods can also provide a stimulus to production, microwaves and toasted sandwich-makers replace or supplement other white goods, but without leading to the consumption of more unhealthy food. Changes in diet have also been prompted by wider changes in public attitudes: the increases in vegetarianism, the concern with animal welfare, the widespread interest in high-fibre, low-calorie foods as part of attempts to lose weight. These changes are significant, and are most unlikely to be reversed: they have helped to set in motion a series of effects on the supply side of the food system, which are reverberating and will continue to reverberate during the remaining years of this century and into the next.

Within the developed countries of the North, then, the modern food system poses problems for the economy and society which call for changes in policy, and the management of the environment, but which can be successfully addressed, albeit at a price in both financial and political terms. The implications of the food system for the South, we would contend, are altogether more radical. It is worth considering the differences carefully.

In the South the modern food system can only be partially adopted, because structural inequalities have prevented the industrial sector from acting as the 'motor' for the restructuring of agriculture around industrially produced food for mass consumption. In most developing countries the agricultural sector, and particularly staple production, has been appallingly neglected, not least in terms of the impact of agricultural intensification on the poor and the environment.

Where rising agricultural productivity is supported by state subsidies, or subsidies from the developed countries and their institutions, it has benefited some groups much more than others. The 'fordist' diet, exemplified by the penetration of the grains-livestock complex, has only reached a very narrow band of food consumers in even the so-called 'middle-income' countries of Latin America. In most of Africa and Asia, the fordist diet remains part of the mystique of Western cultural values, as distant from its audience as the movie star.

Environmental managerialism, too, does not represent a workable strategy for most governments in the South, where it has neither tradition nor institutional foundation.

In the North, the improved management of the environment, usually at the behest of relatively affluent, urban groups, is endorsed with relatively little political dissent; the modest interventions to ensure a better management of the countryside, or conservation of wilderness, have overwhelming public support in Europe and North America. In the South, on the other hand, land degradation is intimately linked to poverty in rural areas. A vast, largely rural population of poor people, many of them *very* poor, looks to the environment as the basis of its precarious livelihood.

Environmental problems in developing countries can only be realistically understood as the outcome of underdevelopment and poverty. The 'environment' lacks ideological resonance; it is to be 'tamed' or 'conquered', and made to yield economic revenues and livelihoods. Environmental managerialism, without its ideological underpinnings which explain its strong cultural appeal in the North, would need to be radically modified to make any impact on the causes of environmental degradation in the South. It can be argued, indeed, that attempts to manage the environment in developing countries, in as much as they are predicated on Northern experience, are not merely unworkable, they are also frequently prejudicial to the interests of the poor. In the Brazilian Amazon the disputed land and natural resources cannot be 'mediated' successfully by international agencies alone, whose principal concern is thought by many Brazilians (on both left and right of the political spectrum) to be the protection of the quality of life in the North, rather than the rights to livelihood of poor people in the South.

Many Brazilians say, and their views are at least partly convincing, that campaigns to protect the Amazon rain forest are the new face of 'neo-imperialism', prompted by fears of global warming (largely exaggerated in view of the much more serious effect of fossil fuel emissions) and the perceived need to preserve rare animal and plant species, rather than concern about poor frontier settlers or the pernicious social impacts of the Brazilian debt.

In many parts of the South, 'resistance' is to be understood primarily in terms of the right to livelihood, to citizenship and to the recognition of basic human rights. Struggles such as those surrounding land invasions, or the protection of indigenous people and rubber tappers in the forests, represent struggles for existence, rather than movements to secure improvements in the quality of life.

The development of the modern food system is linked to these struggles, albeit sometimes in tenuous ways, but the management of the environment cannot resolve the contradictions implied by the development process. Indeed, the effects of recent structural adjustment policy, and attempts to manage the enormity of the debt burden in Latin America and Africa in particular, have intensified environmental problems, and make any 'solution' that does not include major changes in these policies largely irrelevant. The implications of the partial adoption of elements of the modern food system in the South can only be understood, and the resulting problems successfully addressed, by changes in structural policies encompassing the global economy. They cannot be resolved, as to a large extent they can in the North, where they occur.

Finally, as far as changes in the diet are concerned, the partial development of the modern food system in the countries of the South has served to replace (and in some cases destroy) existing, indigenous food systems. This has occurred without effective resistance from a broadly based mass movement of consumers, educated as to their rights, and able to exert pressure on government to accede to their demands. It is virtually impossible to envisage public campaigns over salmonella or food additives in Mexico or Indonesia, or, what is altogether more telling, effective mass movements to introduce new standards of food hygiene in shops or on street corners. Meanwhile, food irradiation—increasingly contested by the radical food lobby in the North—opens up market opportunities in the South. It is clear, then, that what is at issue if we consider North-South relations, and examine the implications of the development of the modern food system within an international framework, is a set of concerns which stretch the parameters of our model, and our analysis.

To speak of resistance and struggle in the South, is to speak of the survival of alternative systems which link the production of food directly to its transformation and consumption, systems which embody quite different patterns of social reproduction, systems which—in the form of ubiquitous 'externalities'—carry many of the environmental and social costs of our 'successful' development model. Our ability to grasp the fact that the economic and political hegemony of our values, and our economic policies, have served to undermine the integrity of other food systems, remains the major challenge we in the North face today. For the spread of the modern food system marks the success of the North's cultural hegemony, as well as its economic supremacy. We need to address the sustainability of our own models, then, before we are in a position to hand them down to others.

## PUBLIC POLICY AND FOOD SECURITY

Estimates of 'Global food security', based on the quotient of total possible food production divided by world population, may be a diverting statistical exercise, but is of little practical value. Equitable access to the planet's resources, though highly desirable, never has been nor is ever likely to be a realisable objective. To state that over the next half-century world food production must exceed all that was produced since settled farming began 10,000 years ago is interesting but offers little practical guidance for long-term planning by national governments.

Food security can only be assessed and assured for discrete nations, communities and families within communities, a process that is the responsibility of national and local governments. International agencies can help weak and inexperienced governments by defining criteria to be considered and by providing long-term development assistance.

During the 1930s, the League of Nations Committee on Nutrition reported: "In the past, movement towards better nutrition has been largely the result of unconscious, instinctive groping for a better, more abundant life. Now needed is planning for better nutrition policies based on (a) consumption: bringing essential food within reach of all people; (b) adequate supply: production and equitable distribution of all essential food sources". The report urges (a) recognition of nutrition policy as of primary national importance; (b) better, widespread education on human nutrition; (c) more equitable distribution of income: "it is the poorest people who are most nutritionally deprived".

A committee of the US National Research Council appears to agree: "An important cause of malnutrition is absence of policies and programmes that foster the best use of available food supplies... Governments continually make decisions that affect nutritional status with little knowledge of nutritional consequences. Alleviation of hunger and malnutrition depend upon increasing the right kinds of food, reducing poverty and improving the stability of food supplies". Publications that discuss food security are many, vast and voluminous. They suggest primary causes, and propose various courses of remedial action. The League of Nations reports are among many that insist that food security be of highest priority in all governmental policies. Reutlinger [1987] states that food insecurity results from inappropriate macro-economic policies, from local economic and political structures that restrict the ability of households and individuals to have access to foods sufficient to satisfy their needs. Food insecurity may be transitory, lasting for relatively short periods, or chronic and of long duration, a consequence of poor planning to ensure resources adequate to produce or purchase sufficient food. Transitory hunger frequently results from unstable food production systems, sharp rises in food prices, or depression of disposable family incomes. If extreme and extended, transitory hunger can exacerbate into chronic hunger and eventually into famine. Famines have ravaged even when food stocks were plentiful: the 1943 famine in Bengal was precipitated by the price of a limited food supply rising to levels unaffordable by poor people.

Sen [1987] relates food security to entitlements and ownerships; families and individuals must have adequate access and purchasing power. Food security depends not on estimates of national aggregate demand but on fair exchange in international trade of goods and services. The poor must inevitably rely on food aid provided by social programmes. Chronic hunger and malnutrition are less influenced by a nation's total food supply than the degree of equity with which available resources are distributed and made accessible. Food and agricultural policies to ensure food security for all citizens should be a high priority for every government. Malnourished people, too weak to work effectively, eventually impose a financial burden on the nation's economy. Though some observers argue that food stocks of grain are of value only to alleviate temporary food insecurity, the prime purpose of strategic food stocks is to provide emergency reserves against regional, national, local and seasonal shortages, to stabilise food prices and counteract fluctuations in supply and availability. Reserve food stocks are customarily controlled by government agencies, authorised to maintain quantities sufficient for defined time periods. Reserve stocks must be replenished when they fall below a prescribed safe minimum. Reserve stocks, essential in regions susceptible to frequent drought, provide short-term relief but cannot be considered a panacea for chronic food insecurity.

Santorum and Gray [1993] list factors to be weighed in determining minimum reserve stocks. Stocks stored on farms are generally sufficient only to satisfy farmers' needs from one harvest to the next. Countries within a region that cannot individually afford to maintain national reserves can collectively contribute to and draw upon strategically dispersed food stocks. During the 1980s the Southern African Development Community (SADC) created and maintained a regional food security programme with grain stocks upon which member nations could draw in time of need. Where many are too poor to buy adequate food, where climatic change, civil strife and other adversities inflict serious disruptions on food production and distribution, food aid may be essential to survival and avoidance of famine.

The UN World Food Programme [WFP] is the most efficient distributor of food aid, designed to provide relief or to support development. Food aid for relief alleviates acute stress among people whose food supplies are disrupted by war, civil unrest, enforced migration, severe climatic catastrophes, and/or massive crop failure.

Food aid for development provides food as wages for economically productive work and to support basic social services. Food aid for development may support labour-intensive agricultural production, construction of roads, rural infrastructures, amenities and services essential to developing economies. Food aid helps to stabilise food prices, to provide for pregnant women, nursing mothers, school feeding and pre-school infants.

WFP administers food aid most efficiently. Misdirected, ill-conceived bilateral food aid can do more harm than good. One could cite a weary litany of bilateral food aid where indiscriminate dumping of donors' surplus crops and livestock products have depressed prices and discouraged agricultural production in recipient countries. Food aid administered by many bilateral agencies is motivated more by the donor's political and commercial interests than relieving acute or chronic distress among malnourished people.

WFP resources have been seriously overstretched, because of exceptional demands resulting from military, civil and inter-ethnic strife and conflict, mass migrations such as in Darfur, cataclysmic disruptions as produced by the

Tsunami. As extreme demands for food aid will inevitably persist, more generous and sustained support for the World Food Programme should be a high priority for all donor agencies. What constitutes nutritional adequacy has attracted scientific and unscientific interest for many centuries. Alchemists searched for but never discovered the *Elixir vitae*. In Britain during the mid-nineteenth century desirable dietary standards were described as: "the least costly foods to prevent starvation and disease during massive unemployment". The League of Nations standards were intended "to marry health and agriculture".

Our most primitive ancestors, by trial and error, identified certain foods as pleasant and digestible, others as obnoxious, insulting or injurious to health, foods acceptable and foods unacceptable. Our early antecedents chose their foods from plants and animals indigenous to their ecologies and climates resulting in widely different food preferences among nations and communities.

## CONCLUSION

As with 'sustainable development' there is no precise, universally accepted definition of 'food security'. In broad principle a state of food security exists where all individuals, families and communities enjoy consistent access to foods that in quantity, quality and biochemical composition provide hygienic, nutritional adequacy. The Brundtland Panel states: "Food security requires secure ownership of, or access to, food resources and income earning activities, including reserves and assets to offset risks, to ease shocks and meet all contingencies". This may be interpreted as all people having access to stocks and flows of food and cash sufficient to satisfy their basic nutritional needs. Everyone in the world need not be a subsistence farmer, but those who do not produce foods in quantities sufficient to satisfy their families' needs, must possess the means to acquire foods nutritionally adequate, readily accessible and affordable.

The report of the 1992 FAO/WHO international conference on nutrition states: "Food security is defined in its most basic form as access by all people at all times to the food needed for a healthy life. Food security has three dimensions: assurance of a safe, nutritionally adequate food supply at national and household levels; a reasonable degree of stability in the supply of food throughout each year and from one year to the next; every household having physical, social and economic access to food sufficient to meet its needs."

While there is agreement in broad principle on requirements for food security, concepts diverge significantly in semasiological and biological specifics, they change over time, and differ among specialists and agencies as to what constitutes a nutritionally adequate diet. Non-scientific and quasi-scientific publications frequently fail to make clear distinction among 'hunger', 'malnutrition', 'famine' and 'starvation'; between 'chronic' and 'transitory hunger'.

The noun 'security' derives from the Latin '*securus*' which means 'safe', 'free from worry and care'. People blessed with food security are safe from the risk of famine, starvation, chronic hunger and malnutrition. 'Famine' describes extreme food scarcity among large populations. 'Starvation' is derived from an Old English word meaning to die a slow lingering death from cold, disease, insufficient food and/or water. 'Malnutrition' defines a significant insufficiency or imbalance in essential nutrient intake, 'sub-nutrition' sometimes describes people who have too little food. 'Hunger' describes distressing discomfort caused by want of food.

'Transitory hunger' is experienced from time to time by active persons who enjoy healthy appetites. 'Chronic hunger' describes a painful and debilitating condition caused by long deprivation of food sufficient to sustain healthy growth and activity. The 1960s Freedom From Hunger Campaign, the 1974 World Congress' hope of eradicating hunger by 1984, and the FAO Millennium objective of reducing incidence of hunger by 50 per cent between 1990 and 2015, all relate to alleviation of chronic hunger and malnutrition. Roughly 18 per cent of the world's population (800 million, including 200m children), 25 per cent of South Asians (300 million people) and 35 per cent of sub-Saharan Africans (190 million) are classified by UN agencies as undernourished: their caloric intake is lower than is required for healthy activity. In 1980 30 per cent of all people in LICs were considered undernourished. By the year 2000 this proportion had fallen to 18 per cent.

In simplest terms, food security depends upon a dynamic balance among disposable income, demand, supply and distribution. Production of food crops, livestock and fisheries must progressively increase to satisfy expanding and diversifying needs and demands of growing populations. Efficient post-production systems, to ensure safe and effective protection, preservation, transformation and distribution must be economically integrated with production systems.

During the early 1960s, affluent OECD nations were home to 34 per cent of world population and controlled close to 90 per cent of global GNP. By 1990, the affluent minority had fallen to 16 per cent of the total but controlled more than 82 per cent of global GNP. Between 1960 and 1990 a new group of middle-income newly industrialised countries emerged, most in East Asia and Latin America, a change with considerable implications for the Planet's economy and future patterns of food demand. In 1990 Asians represented 52 per cent, in 2002 some 59 per cent of world population. Among Asian nations, middle-income communities are growing most rapidly, their diets diversifying with dilating demand for livestock products.

Food insecurity, chronic hunger and under-nutrition are both dismal consequences and clear indicators of extreme poverty. People with money, power and control over negotiable assets rarely suffer from chronic hunger. Government politicians and military generals who suffer from chronic hunger are not a common spectacle around the world. Alleviation of food insecurity requires greater opportunities for paid employment and more equitable access to critical resources and assets among and within nations.

A respected observer writes: "In the 1950s... it was assumed that adequate agricultural production would assure access to adequate food in the market and in the household. In the 1970s it became clear that production and availability alone do not lead to food security, since those who lack purchasing power (from permanent employment income) lack access to a balanced diet. Now it is evident that where availability and access are satisfactory, necessary biological absorption of food requires clean drinking water, environmental hygiene, primary health care and education".

Based on these considerations, the M. S. Swaminathan Research Foundation and the UN World Food Programme have published a *Food Insecurity Atlas for Rural India*. The atlas illustrates marked variability among Indian States in food availability, absorption of nutrients, vulnerability to chronic hunger and in sustainable agricultural production. The atlas describes such non-food factors as income earning opportunities, health care facilities, education, sanitation and environmental hygiene.

Due to climatic variability, years with too little or too much rain, damage and destruction by pests, parasites and pathogens, crop and livestock production inevitably change from year to year. To compensate for years of poor harvests governments and/or regional organisations should maintain reserve stocks to carry over surpluses from regions and seasons of abundance to those of scarcity. The cost of holding reserve stocks should be calculated as an insurance investment not an unwarranted expense.

Food security need not be synonymous with food self-sufficiency, a nation's ability to produce all food required by its population. For diverse reasons: climate, topography, soil and climatic conditions, many nations cannot be self-sufficient and must depend on food aid or imports.

Substantial reductions in food spoilage after harvest could be realised by establishing primary food preservation and protection facilities in rural areas where crops are cultivated and animals husbanded. Food saved from spoilage increases total food available and enhances food availability and security.

# 2

# Understanding the Nutrition

Nutrition is the provision, to cells and organisms, of the materials necessary to support life. Many common health problems can be prevented or alleviated with a healthy diet. The diet of an organism is what it eats, which is largely determined by the perceived palatability of foods. Dietitians are health professionals who specialize in human nutrition, meal planning, economics, and preparation.

They are trained to provide safe, evidence-based dietary advice and management to individuals (in health and disease), as well as to institutions. A poor diet can have an injurious impact on health, causing deficiency diseases such as scurvy, beriberi, and kwashiorkor; health-threatening conditions like obesity and metabolic syndrome; and such common chronic systemic diseases as cardiovascular disease, diabetes, and osteoporosis.

Nutrition science investigates the metabolic and physiological responses of the body to diet. With advances in the fields of molecular biology, biochemistry, and genetics, the study of nutrition is increasingly concerned with metabolism and metabolic pathways: the sequences of biochemical steps through which substances in living things change from one form to another. Nitrogen is needed by animals to build proteins. Carnivore and herbivore diets vary in their source of nitrogen, which is a limiting nutrient for both. Herbivores consume plants to get nitrogen and carnivores consume other animals to obtain nitrogen. Nitrogen is a common element in the atmosphere but exists in a state that is not usable by most living organisms, certain fungi and bacteria are able to convert atmospheric nitrogen into a form plants can adsorb and utilize.

The human body contains chemical compounds, such as water, carbohydrates (sugar, starch, and fibre), amino acids (in proteins), fatty acids (in lipids), and nucleic acids (DNA and RNA). These compounds in turn consist of elements such as carbon, hydrogen, oxygen, nitrogen, phosphorus, calcium, iron, zinc, magnesium, manganese, and so on. All of these chemical compounds and elements occur in various forms and combinations (e.g., hormones, vitamins, phospholipids, hydroxyapatite), both in the human body and in the plant and animal organisms that humans eat.

The human body consists of elements and compounds ingested, digested, absorbed, and circulated through the bloodstream to feed the cells of the body. Except in the unborn foetus, which receive processed nutrients from the mother, the digestive system is the first system involved in breaking down food prior to further digestion.

Digestive juices, excreted into the lumen of the gastrointestinal tract, break chemical bonds in ingested molecules, and modulate their conformations and energy states.

Though some molecules are absorbed into the bloodstream unchanged, digestive processes release them from the matrix of foods. Unabsorbed matter, along with some waste products of metabolism, is eliminated from the body in the feces. Studies of nutritional status must take into account the state of the body before and after experiments, as well as the chemical composition of the whole diet and of all material excreted and eliminated from the body (in urine and foeces).

Comparing the food to the waste can help determine the specific compounds and elements absorbed and metabolized in the body. The effects of nutrients may only be discernible over an extended period, during which all food and waste must be analysed.

The number of variables involved in such experiments is high, making nutritional studies time-consuming and expensive, which explains why the science of human nutrition is still slowly evolving. In general, eating a wide variety of fresh, whole (unprocessed), foods has proven favourable for one's health compared to monotonous diets based on processed foods. In particular, the consumption of whole-plant foods slows digestion and allows better absorption, and a more favourable balance of essential nutrients per Calorie, resulting in better management of cell growth, maintenance, and mitosis (cell division), as well as better regulation of appetite and blood sugar. Regularly scheduled meals (every few hours) have also proven more wholesome than infrequent or haphazard ones, although a recent study has also linked more frequent meals with a higher risk of colon cancer in men.

There are six major classes of nutrients: carbohydrates, fats, minerals, protein, vitamins, and water. These nutrient classes can be categorized as either macronutrients (needed in relatively large amounts) or micronutrients (needed in smaller quantities). The macronutrients include carbohydrates, fats, protein, and water. The micronutrients are minerals and vitamins. The macronutrients (excluding water) provide structural material (amino acids from which proteins are built, and lipids from which cell membranes and some signaling molecules are built), energy.

Some of the structural material can be used to generate energy internally, and in either case it is measured in Joules or kilocalories (often called "Calories" and written with a capital C to distinguish them from little 'c' calories). Carbohydrates and proteins provide 17 kJ approximately (4 kcal) of energy per gram, while fats provide 37 kJ (9 kcal) per gm., though the net energy from either depends on such factors as absorption and digestive effort, which vary substantially from instance to instance.

Vitamins, minerals, fibre, and water do not provide energy, but are required for other reasons. A third class of dietary material, fibre (*i.e.*, non-digestible material such as cellulose), is also required, for both mechanical and biochemical reasons, although the exact reasons remain unclear.

Molecules of carbohydrates and fats consist of carbon, hydrogen, and oxygen atoms. Carbohydrates range from simple monosaccharides (glucose, fructose, galactose) to complex polysaccharides (starch). Fats are triglycerides, made of assorted fatty acid monomers bound to glycerol backbone. Some fatty acids, but not all, are essential in the diet: they cannot be synthesized in the body. Protein molecules contain nitrogen atoms in addition to carbon, oxygen, and hydrogen.

The fundamental components of protein are nitrogen-containing amino acids, some of which are essential in the sense that humans cannot make them internally. Some of the amino acids are convertible (with the expenditure of energy) to glucose and can be used for energy production just as ordinary glucose in a process known as gluconeogenesis.

By breaking down existing protein, some glucose can be produced internally; the remaining amino acids are discarded, primarily as urea in urine. This occurs normally only during prolonged starvation. Other micronutrients include antioxidants and phytochemicals, which are said to influence (or protect) some body systems. Their necessity is not as well established as in the case of, for instance, vitamins.

Most foods contain a mix of some or all of the nutrient classes, together with other substances, such as toxins of various sorts. Some nutrients can be stored internally (e.g., the fat soluble vitamins), while others are required more or less continuously. Poor health can be caused by a lack of required nutrients or, in extreme cases, too much of a required nutrient. For example, both salt and water (both absolutely required) will cause illness or even death in excessive amounts.

## CARBOHYDRATES

Carbohydrates include sugars, starches and fibre. They constitute a large part of foods such as rice, noodles, bread, and other grain-based products. Carbohydrates may be classified chemically as monosaccharides, disaccharides, or polysaccharides depending on the number of monomer (saccharide or sugar) units they contain.

Monosaccharides, disaccharides, and polysaccharides contain one, two, and three or more sugar units, respectively. Polysaccharides are often referred to as complex carbohydrates because they consist of long, sometimes branched chains of single sugar units. Mono- and disaccharides are called simple carbohydrates. Dietary advice frequently but erroneously suggests that complex carbohydrates are superior to simple because they take longer to digest and absorb. Simple carbohydrates, on the other hand, are said to cause a spike in blood glucose levels rapidly after ingestion. These traditional claims are false. In fact, many digestible polysaccharides are processed as rapidly and simple sugars in the human body.

On the other hand, some simple carbohydrates (fructose, for example) are processed in a different way and do not spike blood sugar. Thus the distinction between "complex" and "simple" does not predict the nutritional value or impact of carbohydrates. A better way of determining what effect particular foods may have on blood sugar and ultimately on health in general is the glycemic index.

Carbohydrates are not essential nutrients (with the likely exception of fibre), but are typically an important part of the human diet. While it would not be accurate to categorize all carbohydrates as "bad" nutritionally, some carbohydrate sources may well have deleterious effects on health, especially when consumed in large quantities. Highly processed carbohydrates (sugars and starches) as well as fructose consumed in large quantities have been implicated in negative.

## FIBRE

Dietary fibre is a carbohydrate (or a polysaccharide) that is incompletely absorbed in humans and in some animals. Like all carbohydrates, when it is metabolized it can produce four Calories (kilocalories) of energy per gm. However, in most circumstances it accounts for less than that because of its limited absorption and digestibility. Dietary fibre consists mainly of cellulose, a large carbohydrate polymer that is indigestible because humans do not have the required enzymes to disassemble it.

There are two subcategories: soluble and insoluble fibre. Whole grains, fruits (especially plums, prunes, and figs), and vegetables are good sources of dietary fibre. There are many health benefits of a high-fibre diet. Dietary fibre helps reduce the chance of gastrointestinal problems such as constipation and diarrhoea by increasing the weight and size of stool and softening it. Insoluble fibre, found in whole-wheat flour, nuts and vegetables, especially stimulates peristalsis—the rhythmic muscular contractions of the intestines which move digesta along the digestive tract. Soluble fibre, found in oats, peas, beans, and many fruits, dissolves in water in the intestinal tract to produce a gel which slows the movement of food through the intestines.

This may help lower blood glucose levels because it can slow the absorption of sugar. Additionally, fibre, perhaps especially that from whole grains, is thought to possibly help lessen insulin spikes, and therefore reduce the risk of type 2 diabetes. The link between increased fibre consumption and a decreased risk of colorectal cancer is still uncertain.

## FAT

A molecule of dietary fat typically consists of several fatty acids (containing long chains of carbon and hydrogen atoms), bonded to a glycerol. They are typically found as triglycerides (three fatty acids attached to one glycerol backbone). Fats may be classified as saturated or unsaturated depending on the detailed structure of the fatty acids involved.

Saturated fats have all of the carbon atoms in their fatty acid chains bonded to hydrogen atoms, whereas unsaturated fats have some of these carbon atoms double-bonded, so their molecules have relatively fewer hydrogen atoms than a saturated fatty acid of the same length. Unsaturated fats may be further classified as monounsaturated (one double-bond) or polyunsaturated (many double-bonds).

Furthermore, depending on the location of the double-bond in the fatty acid chain, unsaturated fatty acids are classified as omega-3 or omega-6 fatty acids. Trans fats are a type of unsaturated fat with trans-isomer bonds; these are rare in nature and in foods from natural sources; they are typically created in an industrial process called (partial) hydrogenation. There are nine kilocalories in each gm. of fat. Saturated fats (typically from animal sources) have been a staple in many world cultures for millennia. Unsaturated fats (e. g., vegetable oil) are considered healthier while trans fats are to be avoided.

Saturated and some trans fats are typically solid at room temperature (such as butter or lard), while unsaturated fats are typically liquids (such as olive oil or flaxseed oil). Trans fats are very rare in nature, and have been shown to be highly detrimental to human health, but have properties useful in the food processing industry, such as rancidity resistance.

### ESSENTIAL FATTY ACIDS

Most fatty acids are non-essential, meaning the body can produce them as needed, generally from other fatty acids and always by expending energy to do so. However, in humans, at least two fatty acids are essential and must be included in the diet. An appropriate balance of essential fatty acids—omega-3 and omega-6 fatty acids—seems also important for health, although definitive experimental demonstration has been elusive.

Both of these "omega" long-chain polyunsaturated fatty acids are substrates for a class of eicosanoids known as prostaglandins, which have roles throughout the human body. They are hormones, in some respects.

The omega-3 eicosapentaenoic acid (EPA), which can be made in the human body from the omega-3 essential fatty acid alpha-linolenic acid (LNA), or taken in through marine food sources, serves as a building block for series 3 prostaglandins (e.g., weakly inflammatory PGE3). The omega-6 dihomo-gamma-linolenic acid (DGLA) serves as a building block for series 1 prostaglandins (*e.g.*, anti-inflammatory PGE1), whereas arachidonic acid (AA) serves as a building block for series 2 prostaglandins (e.g., pro-inflammatory PGE 2). Both DGLA and AA can be made from the omega-6 linoleic acid (LA) in the human body, or can be taken in directly through food.

An appropriately balanced intake of omega-3 and omega-6 partly determines the relative production of different prostaglandins, which is one reason why a balance between omega-3 and omega-6 is believed important for cardiovascular health.

In industrialized societies, people typically consume large amounts of processed vegetable oils, which have reduced amounts of the essential fatty acids along with too much of omega-6 fatty acids relative to omega-3 fatty acids. The conversion rate of omega-6 DGLA to AA largely determines the production of the prostaglandins PGE1 and PGE2.

Omega-3 EPA prevents AA from being released from membranes, thereby skewing prostaglandin balance away from pro-inflammatory PGE2 (made from AA) towards anti-inflammatory PGE1 (made from DGLA). Moreover, the conversion (desaturation) of DGLA to AA is controlled by the enzyme delta-5-desaturase, which in turn is controlled by hormones such as insulin (up-regulation) and glucagon (down-regulation).

The amount and type of carbohydrates consumed, along with some types of amino acid, can influence processes involving insulin, glucagon, and other hormones; therefore the ratio of omega-3 versus omega-6 has wide effects on general health, and specific effects on immune function and inflammation, and mitosis (*i.e.*, cell division).

## PROTEIN

Proteins are the basis of many animal body structures (e.g., muscles, skin, and hair). They also form the enzymes that control chemical reactions throughout the body. Each molecule is composed of amino acids, which are characterized by inclusion of nitrogen and sometimes sulphur (these components are responsible for the distinctive smell of burning protein, such as the keratin in hair). The body requires amino acids to produce new proteins (protein retention) and to replace damaged proteins (maintenance). As there is no protein or amino acid storage provision, amino acids must be present in the diet. Excess amino acids are discarded, typically in the urine. For all animals, some amino acids are essential (an animal cannot produce them internally) and some are non-essential (the animal can produce them from other nitrogen-containing compounds). Twenty-one proteinogenic amino acids are found in the human body, along with non-proteinogenic amino acids (e.g., gamma-aminobutyric acid).

Ten of the proteinogenic amino acids are essential and, therefore, must be included in the diet. A diet that contains adequate amounts of amino acids (especially those that are essential) is particularly important in some situations: during early development and maturation, pregnancy, lactation, or injury (a burn, for instance). A complete protein source contains all the essential amino acids; an incomplete protein source lacks one or more of the essential amino acids.

It is possible to combine two incomplete protein sources (e.g., rice and beans) to make a complete protein source, and characteristic combinations are the basis of distinct cultural cooking traditions. Sources of dietary protein include meats, tofu and other soy-products, eggs, legumes, and dairy products such as milk and cheese.

Excess amino acids from protein can be converted into glucose and used for fuel through a process called gluconeogenesis. The amino acids remaining after such conversion are discarded.

## MINERALS

Dietary minerals are the chemical elements required by living organisms, other than the four elements carbon, hydrogen, nitrogen, and oxygen that are present in nearly all organic molecules. The term "mineral" is archaic, since the intent is to describe simply the less common elements in the diet. Some are heavier than the four just mentioned, including several metals, which often occur as ions in the body.

Some dietitians recommend that these be supplied from foods in which they occur naturally, or at least as complex compounds, or sometimes even from natural inorganic sources (such as calcium carbonate from ground oyster shells). Some minerals are absorbed much more readily in the ionic forms found in such sources. On the other hand, minerals are often artificially added to the diet as supplements; the most famous is likely iodine in iodized salt which prevents goiter.

### MACROMINERALS

Many elements are essential in relative quantity; they are usually called "bulk minerals". Some are structural, but many play a role as electrolytes.

Elements with recommended dietary allowance (RDA) greater than 200 mg/day are, in alphabetical order (with informal or folk-medicine perspectives in parentheses):

- Calcium, a common electrolyte, but also needed structurally (for muscle and digestive system health, bone strength, some forms neutralize acidity, may help clear toxins, provides signaling ions for nerve and membrane functions).
- Chlorine as chloride ions; very common electrolyte;
- Magnesium, required for processing ATP and related reactions (builds bone, causes strong peristalsis, increases flexibility, increases alkalinity).
- Phosphorus, required component of bones; essential for energy processing.
- Potassium, a very common electrolyte (heart and nerve health).
- Sodium, a very common electrolyte; not generally found in dietary supplements, despite being needed in large quantities, because the ion is very common in food: typically as sodium chloride, or common salt. Excessive sodium consumption can deplete calcium and magnesium, leading to high blood pressure and osteoporosis (Note: Some sources suggest high blood pressure is due to high water retention per osmosis).
- Sulfur, for three essential amino acids and therefore many proteins (skin, hair, nails, liver, and pancreas). Sulfur is not consumed alone, but in the form of sulfur-containing amino acids.

## TRACE MINERALS

Many elements are required in trace amounts, usually because they play a catalytic role in enzymes.

*Some trace mineral elements (RDA < 200 mg/day) are, in alphabetical order*:

- Cobalt required for biosynthesis of vitamin $B_{12}$ family of coenzymes. Animals cannot biosynthesize $B_{12}$, and must obtain this cobalt-containing vitamin in the diet.
- Copper required component of many redox enzymes, including cytochrome c oxidase.
- Chromium required for sugar metabolism.
- Iodine required not only for the biosynthesis of thyroxine, but probably, for other important organs as breast, stomach, salivary glands, thymus, etc.; for this reason iodine is needed in larger quantities than others in this list, and sometimes classified with the macrominerals.

- Iron required for many enzymes, and for haemoglobin and some other proteins.
- Manganese (processing of oxygen).
- Molybdenum required for xanthine oxidase and related oxidases.
- Nickel present in urease.
- Selenium required for peroxidase (antioxidant proteins).
- *Vanadium (Speculative*: there is no established RDA for vanadium. No specific biochemical function has been identified for it in humans, although vanadium is required for some lower organisms.)
- Zinc required for several enzymes such as carboxypeptidase, liver alcohol dehydrogenase, and carbonic anhydrase.

## VITAMINS

Some vitamins are recognized as essential nutrients, necessary in the diet for good health. (Vitamin D is the exception: it can be synthesized in the skin, in the presence of UVB radiation.) Certain vitamin-like compounds that are recommended in the diet, such as carnitine, are thought useful for survival and health, but these are not "essential" dietary nutrients because the human body has some capacity to produce them from other compounds.

Moreover, thousands of different phytochemicals have recently been discovered in food (particularly in fresh vegetables), which may have desirable properties including antioxidant activity, however, experimental demonstration has been suggestive but inconclusive.

Other essential nutrients that are not classified as vitamins include essential amino acids, choline, essential fatty acids, and the minerals discussed in the preceding part.

Vitamin deficiencies may result in disease conditions, including goitre, scurvy, osteoporosis, impaired immune system, disorders of cell metabolism, certain forms of cancer, symptoms of premature aging, and poor psychological health (including eating disorders), among many others. Excess levels of some vitamins are also dangerous to health (notably vitamin A), and for at least one vitamin, B6, toxicity begins at levels not far the required amount. Deficient or excess levels of minerals can also have serious health consequences.

## WATER

It is not fully clear how much water intake is needed by healthy people, although some assert that 6–8 glasses of water daily is the minimum to maintain proper hydration. The notion that a person should consume eight glasses of water per day cannot be traced to a credible scientific source. The effect of, greater or lesser, water intake on weight loss and on constipation is also still unclear. The original water intake recommendation in 1945 by the Food and Nutrition Board of the National Research Council read: "An ordinary standard for diverse persons is 1 milliliter for each calorie of food.

Most of this quantity is contained in prepared foods." The latest dietary reference intake report by the United States National Research Council recommended, generally, (including food sources): 2.7 litres of water total for women and 3.7 litres for men.

Specifically, pregnant and breastfeeding women need additional fluids to stay hydrated. According to the Institute of Medicine—who recommend that, on average, women consume 2.2 litres and men 3.0 litres—this is recommended to be 2.4 litres (approx. 9 cups) for pregnant women and 3 litres (approx. 12.5 cups) for breastfeeding women because an especially large amount of fluid is lost during nursing.

For those who have healthy kidneys, it is somewhat difficult to drink too much water, but (especially in warm humid weather and while exercising) it is dangerous to drink too little. People can drink far more water than necessary while exercising, however, putting them at risk of water intoxication, which can be fatal.

In particular, large amounts of de-ionized water are dangerous. Normally, about 20 per cent of water intake comes in food, while the rest comes from drinking water and assorted beverages (caffeinated included). Water is excreted from the body in multiple forms; including urine and faeces, sweating, and by water vapour in the exhaled breath.

## ANTIOXIDANTS

As cellular metabolism/energy production requires oxygen, potentially damaging (e.g., mutation causing) compounds known as free radicals can form. Most of these are oxidizers (*i.e.*, acceptors of electrons) and some react very strongly. For the continued normal cellular maintenance, growth, and division, these free radicals must be sufficiently neutralized by antioxidant compounds.

Some are produced by the human body with adequate precursors (glutathione, Vitamin C), and those the body cannot produce may only be obtained in the diet via direct sources (Vitamin C in humans, Vitamin A, Vitamin K) or produced by the body from other compounds (Beta-carotene converted to Vitamin A by the body, Vitamin D synthesized from cholesterol by sunlight).

Phytochemicals and their subgroup, polyphenols, make up the majority of antioxidants; about 4,000 are known. Different antioxidants are now known to function in a cooperative network. For example, Vitamin C can reactivate free radical-containing glutathione or Vitamin E by accepting the free radical itself. Some antioxidants are more effective than others at neutralizing different free radicals. Some cannot neutralize certain free radicals. Some cannot be present in certain areas of free radical development (Vitamin A is fat-soluble and protects fat areas, Vitamin C is water soluble and protects those areas). When interacting with a free radical, some antioxidants produce a different free radical compound that is less dangerous or more dangerous than the previous compound.

Having a variety of antioxidants allows any byproducts to be safely dealt with by more efficient antioxidants in neutralizing a free radical's butterfly effect. Although initial studies suggested that antioxidant supplements might promote health, later large clinical trials did not detect any benefit and suggested instead that excess supplementation may be harmful.

## PHYTOCHEMICALS

A growing area of interest is the effect upon human health of trace chemicals, collectively called phytochemicals. These nutrients are typically found in edible plants, especially colourful fruits and vegetables, but also other organisms including seafood, algae, and fungi. The effects of phytochemicals increasingly survive rigorous testing by prominent health organizations. One of the principal classes of phytochemicals are polyphenol antioxidants, chemicals that are known to provide certain health benefits to the cardiovascular system and immune system.

These chemicals are known to down-regulate the formation of reactive oxygen species, key chemicals in cardiovascular disease. Perhaps the most rigorously tested phytochemical is zeaxanthin, a yellow-pigmented carotenoid present in many yellow and orange fruits and vegetables. Repeated studies have shown a strong correlation between ingestion of zeaxanthin and the prevention and treatment of age-related macular degeneration (AMD).

Less rigorous studies have proposed a correlation between zeaxanthin intake and cataracts. A second carotenoid, lutein, has also been shown to lower the risk of contracting AMD. Both compounds have been observed to collect in the retina when ingested orally, and they serve to protect the rods and cones against the destructive effects of light. Another carotenoid, beta-cryptoxanthin, appears to protect against chronic joint inflammatory diseases, such as arthritis.

While the association between serum blood levels of beta-cryptoxanthin and substantially decreased joint disease has been established, neither a convincing mechanism for such protection nor a cause-and-effect have been rigorously studied. Similarly, a red phytochemical, lycopene, has substantial credible evidence of negative association with development of prostate cancer.

Some of the correlations between the ingestion of certain phytochemicals and the prevention of disease are, in some cases, enormous in magnitude. Yet, even when the evidence is obtained, translating it to practical dietary advice can be difficult and counter-intuitive. Lutein, for example, occurs in many yellow and orange fruits and vegetables and protects the eyes against various diseases.

However, it does not protect the eye nearly as well as zeaxanthin, and the presence of lutein in the retina will prevent zeaxanthin uptake. Additionally, evidence has shown that the lutein present in egg yolk is more readily absorbed than the lutein from vegetable sources, possibly because of fat solubility. At the most basic level, the question "should you eat eggs?" is complex to the point of dismay, including misperceptions about the health effects of cholesterol in egg yolk, and its saturated fat content.

As another example, lycopene is prevalent in tomatoes (and actually is the chemical that gives tomatoes their red colour). It is more highly concentrated, however, in processed tomato products such as commercial pasta sauce, or tomato soup, than in fresh "healthy" tomatoes. Yet, such sauces tend to have high amounts of salt, sugar, other substances a person may wish or even need to avoid.

*The following table presents phytochemical groups and common sources, arranged by family*:

| Family | Sources | Possible Benefits |
|---|---|---|
| Flavonoids | Berries, herbs, vegetables, wine, grapes, tea | General antioxidant, oxidation of LDLs, prevention of arteriosclerosis and heart disease |
| Isoflavones (phytoestrogens) | Soy, red clover, kudzu root | General antioxidant, prevention of arteriosclerosis and heart disease, easing symptoms of menopause, cancer prevention |
| Isothiocyanates | Cruciferous vegetables | cancer prevention |
| monoterpenes | Citrus peels, essential oils, herbs, spices, green plants, atmosphere | Cancer prevention, treating gallstones |
| Organosulfur compounds | Chives, garlic, onions | Cancer prevention, lowered LDLs, assistance to the immune system |
| Saponins | Beans, cereals, herbs | Hypercholesterolemia, Hyperglycemia, Antioxidant, cancer prevention, Anti-inflammatory |
| Capsaicinoids | All capiscum (chile) peppers | Topical pain relief, cancer prevention, cancer cell apoptosis |

## INTESTINAL BACTERIAL FLORA

It is now also known that animal intestines contain a large population of gut flora. In humans, these include species such as Bacteroides, *L. acidophilus*, and *E. coli*, among many others. They are essential to digestion, and are also affected by the food we eat. Bacteria in the gut perform many important functions for humans, including breaking down and aiding in the absorption of otherwise indigestible food; stimulating cell growth; repressing the growth of harmful bacteria, training the immune system to respond only to pathogens; producing vitamin $B_{12}$, and defending against some infectious diseases.

# 3

# Kitchen Operation

The operation of a dining room and kitchen presents the best opportunity for the make a profit and, at the same time, presents the best possibility for losing large sums of money. Generally speaking, large amounts of money are involved in the kitchen operation.

More important, however, is the food business. It is of particular importance to your health and well-being of your Brothers who eat in the dining room are naturally affected by the food served them.

A kitchen operation should not be undertaken with less than thirty people who will be eating and paying 'board' costs. Because of fixed expenses that are independent of the number of people eating , operating a kitchen with less than thirty 'men' is financially not feasible.

Every topic that is operating a kitchen should either elect or appoint a kitchen steward. The proper supervision of the kitchen is sufficiently demanding in time that it justifies having a member responsible for its management. The steward should sign all bills and/or receipts when turning them over to the Treasurer for payment or record keeping purposes. The Treasurer then has the authority to make the necessary disbursements.

The responsibility of the steward is strategic when considering that he is the one person who will either make the income for the kitchen 'cover' expenses or have the kitchen realize a deficit. The Treasurer must formulate and discuss the kitchen budget with the steward. It must be determined exactly what amount may be spent for food on a weekly basis.

The Treasurer must, from time to time, check up on the status of kitchen costs with the steward to make sure he is remaining within his allotted budget. Only by using measures designed to impose strict controls on the operation of the kitchen can the unit be kept from incurring a large deficit.

## MENUS

The most frequent source of complaint in houses is the food. The reason for this is usually not in its preparation, but rather in the choice of menus. A good steward will plan well balanced, varied menus, and will garnish his main meals with relishes, appetizers, soups and salads; all of which are inexpensive and have often proved to be excellent investments in good will and nutrition. Avoid a set menu for each day of the week. Nothing hurts morale more than "Thursday is macaroni and cheese day."

## HOW TO LOSE MONEY IN THE KITCHEN?

There are several well established ways in which a kitchen operation can lose money. The first is by the patronage of dishonest vendors who will bill you for a certain weight or quantity of merchandise, and then won't deliver the correct amount. The steward should arrange delivery times with the vendors so that he may personally inspect each delivery. If the delivery is insufficient according to the delivery slip, the slip should be changed before the steward signs it, acknowledging receipt of the merchandise. When buying in less than full case quantities, a count should be made carefully at the time of delivery to ascertain that the amount or quantity is as stated on the delivery receipt or invoice.

A second area of loss is when the kitchen 'help' frequently takes home considerable quantities of food when they leave the house at the end of the day. It is taken for granted that kitchen 'help' eat their meals while on the premises. It is, however, known that some people who work in kitchens take home enough food to supply their entire families. This can constitute a considerable drain on finances.

To prevent a third area of loss, arrangements should be made to keep the kitchen and food storage area locked at all times when the cook is not on duty. It is a sad fact, but true, that disappearance of food and supplies costs every unit of money out of their kitchen budget.

A fourth loss is the practice of permitting members to eat at odd hours or between meals. Definite serving hours must be established for each meal and the kitchen declared "off limits" at all other times.

## GUEST MEALS

Each topic should define and regulate guest meals in their bylaws. Such meals are equally the evening or Sunday meal, which normally constitute 60 percent of the daily meal cost per "boarder", and any charge for such meals should be based on that percentage, as a minimum. Any member who abuses a guest privilege is costing each 'boarder'; thus, he is being unfair to the its members.

There are cases where a member not living in the house wishes to eat certain meals on a regular basis at the house. Such rates may be established by using the daily meal cost per boarder, and using 60 percent of that amount to be charged for evening or Sunday meals, 25 percent of that amount for the noon meal and 15 percent of that amount for breakfast. Even then, a member is not paying his full share and it is reasonable to add 10 percent to these rates.

The practice of refunding for missed meals can become very involved and should not be done unless there is an unusual situation or it is for an extended period of time.

Since most Treasurers have had little or no training in food management, consideration of the following six topics would be helpful in obtaining a more efficient and less costly dining facility in your kitchen.

- *Labor*:
  - Hire reliable cooks, follow up on job application references.
  - Pay liveable wages.
  - Work out acceptable working hours (no more than 48 hours a week).
  - Laws are very strict with regard to payment of overtime. Know the laws!
  - Don't make unusual demands.
  - Have some incentive plans.
  - Give pay raises, when appropriate.
  - Provide good physical working conditions.
  - Listen to employee's problems—don't ignore their suggestions.
  - Place yourself in their position.
  - Set ground rules and be sure both sides understand them.
  - Let employees know about vacations, wages, days off, etc.
  - Let employees know to whom they are to report (chain of command).
  - Compliment them when they have done a good job.
  - Cost of labor should never exceed 30 percent of your total board income.
- *Purchasing*:
  - Don't buy from everyone—be selective.
  - Know what you are getting.
  - Designate one person to do the buying.
  - Get price lists from vendors.
  - It is not always necessary to buy Premium, Prime, Grade A, etc., in food items.
  - Don't buy more than needed.
  - Take advantage of good buys.
  - Know delivery times.

- Don't accept poor merchandise.
- Try to set up food purchasing on competitive bids—shop around.
- Food cost should not exceed 50 percent of your board income.
- Utilize or create a food purchasing cooperative.

• *Equipment*:
- Take care of equipment.
- Do 'preventable' maintenance when possible.
- Replace worn out equipment as soon as possible.
- Follow company instructions on equipment as to cleaning, safety, etc.
- Watch for warranty on equipment.
- Purchase labor saving devices.
- Purchase commercial grade equipment, not home grade equipment.

• *Sanitation*:
- Don't ever let this aspect of the kitchen operation deteriorate.
- Be strict in this area (you'll never be sorry).
- Give the cook assistance in this area.
- If bothered by rats, mice or insects, call in a qualified exterminator.
- Discard or replace equipment that is unsanitary.
- Have plenty of hot water.

• *Charges and Collections:*
- Collect from all who are not paying for 'board' but eating occasional meals.
- For extra functions, the kitchen account should be reimbursed by the account sponsoring the event (i.e., social, rush, homecoming).
- Don't put anyone on a free meal basis.

• *Administration*:
- Take a monthly inventory of kitchen supplies and food.
- Are you having excessive leftovers?
- Strictly enforce rules on notifying cook when people won't be eating a particular meal.
- Your total board cost per man should not exceed that charged by the dormitories.
- Set up kitchen policy similar to dormitories.

- Consider increasing board prices following increases in food and prices or cut down on meals, quantity or service.
- Have your cook sign a year long contract.

*Caution*: In many college towns, unscrupulous fraternity cooks, to whom the inefficient steward leaves the buying, receive personal rebates, either in money or merchandise. Too much emphasis cannot be put on the importance of checking up regularly on the kitchen ?help?, of switching dealers occasionally and of checking regularly on deliveries as they come in.

## EMPLOYING KITCHEN EMPLOYEES

The employment of a knowledgeable, reliable and likeable cook should not be a hasty, poorly planned process. Your topic is entering into a strictly business relationship and you should approach the hiring of your cook in that manner.

*The following are tips when hiring kitchen employees*:

- Have the applicant fill out a simple job application. The job application serves as a source of information, both during the interview and following employment (if that should happen).
- Check out job and personal references listed on the application. Don't take anything for granted. Find out what kind of employee your applicant was, job attendance record and general attitude.
- The applicant should be personally interviewed by the President and Treasurer. If they are in agreement that the applicant is qualified, the advisor should personally interview the applicant.
- If all are in agreement that hiring the applicant is in the best interest, employ the applicant.
- Before employing an applicant, make sure there is agreement on wages, time off (including vacations), insurance, working hours, job expectations and sick days.
- In attempting to establish a fair wage, check with the other fraternities and sororities on campus, and the dormitory food service, to determine what they are paying their employees—that will be the fair wage.
- The dormitory food service is a good source of potential employees. Don't be afraid to advertise in the local newspaper.
- Refer to Internal Revenue Service guidelines in order to comply with federal and state employment laws.

### EMPLOYMENT CONTRACT

There are 'pros' and 'cons' to using an employment contract that should be obvious.

*'Pros' to utilizing a contract when employing kitchen personnel*:

- The employee has a legal responsibility to fulfill commitments stated in the contract.
- The contract specifies job expectations and wages so as to avoid future disputes.
- It lets the employee know you mean 'business'.

*'Cons' to utilizing a contract when employing kitchen personnel*:

- The topic has a legal responsibility to employ the person in accordance with the conditions of the contract and limits the 'grounds for discharging' an employee.
- Regardless of the status of the kitchen account, the topic must pay the employee in accordance with the conditions of the contract.

## FOOD PURCHASING COOPERATIVES

Many campuses and/or Greek Systems operate a food purchasing 'coop'. These coops are mostly referred to as a Fraternity Management Association *(which may offer additional services)* or simply, the Fraternity CoOp, and can save thousands of dollars every year by buying in quantity.

Because of the wide array of these coops, both in operation and quality, it is recommended that you investigate it, if it exists on your campus. If one doesn't exist, have you thought about starting one?

The operation of a kitchen facility is no small task. However, if done properly. Additionally, it can produce substantial profits for the properly managed. Most certainly, it provides an opportunity for members to develop their management, decision making and leadership skills.

## EIGHT STEPS TO EFFECTIVE PURCHASING OF FOOD AND SUPPLIES

### Step 1: Determine Desired Image of Food Quality and Service

An image is the memory or an imagined picture of service, food quality, atmosphere, comparative prices and other characteristics of the operation which you want your customers to have. A poor image reflects poor service, food quality, etc.

Ask people what they like. Comments can help determine your image. Do you want to serve high quality food and create that type of image? Or, do you want to serve only low quality food or something between high and low?

### STEP 2: KNOW CUSTOMERS' FOOD PREFERENCES

Knowing food preferences specifically is part of Step 1, but deserves special attention. The 'customer' is always 'right' is not the answer, but if you want to improve your menu, customer information is certainly necessary. Would your customers like one or several changes in your operation? How do you know? Asking customers for their suggestions and comments is one way. Try to chat with a customer once in awhile, and after a few discussions, a pattern may develop which can be quite revealing.

### STEP 3: ESTABLISH ONE PERSON. FOOD PURCHASING CONTROL AND AUTHORITY WITH RESPONSIBILITY

One person control of purchasing will help maintain consistency of product and profitability through more effective cost control. This means one person can concentrate on food grades and prices, quality specifications, market conditions, vendor evaluations and other necessary purchasing activities. If one person is given the authority to purchase, make sure there is a second in command who can take over in the temporary or permanent absence of the buyer.

One person control will promote fast decision making, faster competitive decisions and reduce frustrations normally associated with committee decisions.

### STEP 4: MAINTAIN INVENTORY CONTROL

Accurate inventory control is required to determine accurate food cost figures. It should and can be maintained by perpetual records or by physical stocktaking at regular intervals. Inventory records should be maintained for permanent reference in a stock book with space provided for each item. This will help cut losses, control food costs and reduce write offs due to damaged or outdated merchandise.

When food costs get out of line, inventory control may indicate pilferage or significant differences between book inventory levels and actual physical product counts.

### STEP 5: UNDERSTAND AND KNOW FOOD COST CONTROL PROCEDURES AND FOOD COSTS

A knowledge of food cost is absolutely necessary in order to determine the total cost of operating, total profits, possible kitchen shrink, economical minimum order size and, more importantly, menu price.

A recent survey of 60 firms found that 16 of the 60 (27%) did not know what the ingredients of their menu were costing them, and, consequently, had no sound basis on which to price out their menus. Competition was probably setting menu prices.

Change in food cost as a percentage of sales is a possible indicator of shrinking and improper kitchen control. Changes in food cost must be studied for menu pricing and portion control.

## STEP 6: COMMUNICATE WITH SUPPLIER: KNOW PRODUCTS AND AVAILABILITY IN YOUR AREA

Smart purchasing is done when you know what is available. Smart selling by distributors is accomplished when they know what ingredients and products you need.

## STEP 7: CHECK ALL DELIVERIES

A purchasing system includes buying, receiving and checking the merchandise upon delivery. While the kitchen follows up on product quality, another check by a third person is advisable as an anticollusion, antipilferage, control device.

*Checking and receiving systems include*:

- Trained and competent personnel—more than one person if possible.
- Adequate space for proper checking.
- Equipment designed to provide efficient product movement.
- Specifications to be used as standards of quality.
- Scheduled hours, if possible, in order to insure the availability of a checker when delivery is made.

When merchandise is delivered, it should be placed in a safe, quality control location immediately upon off-loading by the driver. Count all unit sale items and weigh all high value items sold by weight; randomly weigh all other items.

Visually check quality of produce and packaged items where quality is essential for compliance with invoice description and/or specifications. Move all items immediately to storage areas and lock if immediate access is not necessary.

Compare invoice prices against purchase order. Verify and mark (stamp or signature) all receiving invoices. Send all documents to buyers for further verification and book inventory update.

## STEP 8: EVALUATE AND IMPROVE

Menu prices result in part from a supplier?s ingredient cost and a foodservice operator?s labor cost. This cost can be reduced by increasing the number of units handled per dollar of supplier labor cost and of foodservice operator cost. This increased productivity should lower the per serving cost to the consumer, provided hourly or fixed labor costs can be used in several alternative functions or can be transferred to other productive activities.

*In order to reduce the per unit cost of handling food both by the supplier and the foodservice operator, there are several questions which an operator should answer*:

- Can order size be increased?
- Can more cases be handled per man hour and per dollar of labor cost?
- Can there be fewer but larger deliveries?
- Can job performance be improved?
- Can costly labor functions be performed by competent but lower wage employees?

*Labor Transfer*: Research revealed that in 58% of deliveries, the driver stored the merchandise. This means that a supplier would certainly realize a substantial savings if the driver unloaded only and the foodservice personnel stored. The foodservice operator would realize an increase in cost. Due to wage differences between the truck driver and the foodservice personnel, an obvious cost savings would accrue to the delivery system. It was projected that this annual savings would amount to $592.

*Decrease Deliveries*: Handling efficiency and labor productivity can be improved by reducing the number of deliveries by onehalf, and reducing the number of suppliers by onehalf. This assumes an average weekly number of cases of 283. Or the same number of suppliers could be used, but alternate weekly deliveries be scheduled from each supplier, or at least half the normal weekly deliveries would be scheduled. This would result in a net gain of 8.25 man-hours per 1,000, or an annual savings of $709.

*Single Delivery*: The onestop concept of delivery means simply that a supplier provides all the necessary products to a foodservice operation. All products for a given week, for example, would be on one invoice, representing one delivery.

There is a potential savings of 12.02 man-hours per 1,000 cases, or an annual savings of $1,184. The supplier would realize savings of 9.14 man-hours per 1,000 cases, and an annual dollar savings per establishment of $1,074. The operator would realize savings of 3.49 man-hours per 1,000 cases, and an annual dollar savings of $110.

No additional storage space would be required. The space utilization factor for the 60 foodservice operators surveyed was approximately 6070%. One stop is a feasible alternative.

## ESSENTIAL DUTIES/RESPONSIBILITIES

- Gathers all dirty dishware from tubs brought to the dishroom, rinses and stacks in dishracks, always clearing dishes of leftovers and trash in order to prepare for automated washing.
- Loads full dishracks on belt and ensures correct placement in accordance to the instructions for the operation of the machine.

Operates automatic dish washing machine by using controls as instructed.

- Loads dishwashing solutions into automatic dispensers and regulates the output of detergents and chemicals to the dishwashing machine by monitoring and adjusting controls.
- Unloads clean dishes from racks after being processed through dish machine, inspects for cleanliness and carefully stacks in specified carts and shelves for the easy use by restaurant and kitchen staff.
- Manually scrubs pots, pans and other kitchen equipment that cannot be washed automatically, using detergents, scourers, and special solutions as required. Inspects for cleanliness, manually dries with hand towels, and puts away in correct places.
- Manually polishes all silver, stainless steel and pewter used in food service, using standard polishing cloth and products, in order to present clean and attractive equipment to diners.
- Maintains the automatic dishwashing equipment in good condition and working order in accordance with manufacturers' instructions in order to prolong the life of the equipment, prevent breakdowns and to meet mandated health compliance regulations.
- Keeps the dishroom in clean and orderly condition at all times by sweeping, mopping, emptying trash, wiping counters and equipment and organizing shelves in order to maintain a sanitary work station and to meet mandated health compliance requirements.
- Mops kitchen floors as requested and at end of each shift, cleans all kitchen work surfaces as regularly scheduled by manager including walls, ceilings, hoods, vents and ovens.
- Gathers all trash cans from kitchen work areas at end of each shift and empties into outside trash compactor.
- Sweeps loading dock and kitchen entrance areas, clearing litter and debris to trash bins, for the safety of employees and purveyors.
- Performs other duties as assigned, requested or deemed necessary by management.

**OTHER DUTIES/RESPONSIBILITIES**

- Contacts purveyors and contractors, in writing or by phone, when in need of product or service.
- Unloads deliveries as they arrive, and accounts for ordered items by comparing packing lists to actual items received. Transports deliveries to stock room by carrying boxes or using a dolly. Assists the stock room personnel with sorting and storing of delivered goods.

- Maintains clean employee breakroom and restrooms by sweeping, mopping, cleaning counters and refilling supplies on a daily basis.
- Provides assistance to other employees and departments to contribute to the best overall performance of the department and hotel.

## TRAINING

### STEWARDING TO THE TOP

Kitchen stewarding is growing to be one of the most sought after jobs, with qualified youngsters taking on the industry with an extremely professional approach and redefining the role of a kitchen steward.

### CHANGING TRENDS

Earlier it was the onus of the chef to plan the menu, keep the kitchen clean, manage costs and budget, look into aspects of hygiene and, of course, cook. But with the increasing thrust on different cuisines, the role of chefs became more specific leading to a growing need to hire cleaners to do the job. Supervisors were later required to oversee the work of cleaners. Slowly, they evolved to become stewards, taking care of every aspect of the kitchen from maintenance, cleaning, tracking inventory, keeping an eye on the temperature in which utensils, pots and crockery are washed, refrigeration of food and monitoring the work of the cleaners.

Today, a kitchen steward complements the role of a chef and the F&B manager. He helps the chef purchase the necessary ingredients and stocks the food the right way and at the right temperature, while helping the F&B manager control the inventory and checking breakages. The kitchen steward has lent professionalism, dignity and technicality to what was previously considered a menial chore.

Prakash Vishwanathan, kitchen stewarding executive, Courtyard Marriott "A few years ago, we didn't need sound knowledge to be in the industry. Today, it is not just about doing dishes and mopping the floors; there are host of technical things one needs to be informed about to handle the job - from choosing the right kind of kitchen equipment including the cooking equipment to cleaning the dishes, and the pots. We also require a certain amount of accounting information to help buy cutlery and hire labour." A steward is the only person in touch with the entire operations of a kitchen. Maintenance and cleanliness aside, he also understands the know-how of food presentation while serving the guests.

### THE CAREER PATH

There are no specific qualifications required to be a kitchen steward. Hotels like Le Royal Meridien insist that it is the attitude they look for while recruiting management trainees in their hotel. Explains Paul Dhas, HR, director, Le Meridien, "The trainee should have the right attitude towards the kitchen, the hotel and even the guests, as we also let them handle guests. The first year, we focus on kitchen training, then cross training in the second year, where they handle the responsibilities of a chef and the kitchen. The final year, they don the chef's hat." Different hotels have different hierarchical policies. After two years of experience, a kitchen steward could go on to become a supervisor and then a chief steward, who is in charge of all the kitchens in the hotel. There are hotels which dispense elaborate hierarchies and have only supervisors and executive stewards. Because of their exposure to cooking, some stewards also go on to become executive chefs of hotels. A working knowledge of the kitchen and cooking also gives stewards an edge to become the restaurant manager, as they are also involved in planning of the menu. The more enterprising ones make a successful career as a general manager.

## PAY SCALES

A kitchen steward starts on a salary of Rs 3,000 and a kitchen supervisor earns about Rs 7,000, while an executive steward can draw anywhere between Rs 10,000 and Rs 12,000 per month. A chief steward is in similar rank as an F&B manager and is indispensable to a hotel. His remuneration is anywhere between Rs 30,000 and Rs 40,000 per month.

So, if you are thinking of specialising in kitchen stewarding, do not dismiss the option as something monotonous and mundane. The opportunities are plenty and the horizons can be explored. There are success stories in the industry to testify this fact. Go ahead and give it your best shot.

*Some of the broad roles of a kitchen steward*:

- Cleaning and organising dishes including buffet
- Controling inventory.
- Monitoring the use of machines for different kinds of utensils like pots and crockery.
- Maintaining hygiene and quality in the kitchen and different equipment used there.
- Keeping a tab on breakage and missing cutlery.

# FEMALE AND MALE SERVANTS

## FEMALE SERVANTS

### Upper Servants

*Housekeeper*: In households where domestics employed number over twenty-five, the housekeeper's sole duty is to engage, manage and dismiss the female servants, with the exception of lady's maid, nurse and cook, whom the mistress engages. In smaller households, the housekeeper manages the stores, both ordering and dispersing them. She tends to the house linen, both repairing it and replacing it as necessary. She supervises the china-closet, the stillroom department, and superintends the arrangement of bedrooms for visitors and their servants.

Her daily routine includes: overlooks the stillroom, sees what china and linen is given out for breakfast, presides over the housekeeper's room breakfast, gives out the stores for the day, assist in washing china, makes rounds of the bedrooms and replaces supplies such as candles, writing paper and soap, makes sure the rooms are clean and in order, presides over the servant's hall dinner, arranges dessert for dinner, makes tea in the afternoon, and makes the coffee for dinner. She also makes preserves and bottles fruit. She keeps the household accounts, and does most of the needlework. In smaller households, the cook often assumes the duties of the housekeeper.

*Lady's Maid*: A lady's maid attends to her mistress's appearance. She arranges her hair and assists in dressing her. She packs and unpacks the mistress when traveling. She may also make her mistress's dresses. Depending on the size of the household, she may assume some of the housekeeper's duties. In a typical day, she: brings up hot water as necessary, brings up tea before breakfast, prepares clothes for dressing, assists the mistress in dressing, puts the room in order, puts out necessities for walking, riding or driving, assists in taking off her outdoor attire, puts evening dress in order, assists in dressing her for dinner, sits up for her, assists in undressing her, puts away her jewels, keeps her wardrobe in repair and washes the lace and fine linens. She also attends to any pets the mistress may have.

**Senior Servants**

*Governess*: A governess taught the children of middle and upper class households until they were old enough to go away to school, college, or to a private tutor.

She was generally a well-educated middle-class girl who needed to earn her own living. But although she was expected to have the bearing and education of a 'lady' she was treated as a servant. This often left her in limbo—neither an insider or an outsider, as the other servants resented her as too educated and too good for their ranks.

*Nurse*: The nurse is in charge of caring for the household's children from the time they are born, until they are turned over to the care of the governess. She washes and dresses the children, feeds them, takes them on outings, and puts them to bed. She makes the children's ordinary under-clothing, and repairs their general clothing. Most nurses have dinner brought to them in the nursery, but some dined with the other servants.

### Under Servants

*Cook*: In large households, only the cooking proper is the duty of the cook. All ingredients are prepared for her use by the kitchen maids. A first-class cook attends to the family breakfast after having her own. She makes out the menu for luncheon and dinner, which is sometimes reviewed and altered by the mistress. In town, she orders from the tradespeople who serve the house. She prepares the soup for the following day, prepares the pastry, jellies, creams and entrees for the day, all in the morning. The afternoon is usually her free time, unless there is a dinner party or guests. She then prepares dinner, and once dinner is served, her duties are over for the day. It is also her duty to lock the doors and windows of the basement, to let the kitchen fire burn low, and to turn off the gas in the kitchen and passages before retiring. In smaller households, the cook assumes the duties of the head kitchen-maid and even scullery maid.

*Kitchen Maid*: In large households, the head kitchen maid is an under-cook and assumes many of the plain-cooking responsibilities. In small households, the kitchen maid prepares vegetables, game and poultry, does the dairy-work, and bakes the bread. If there is no stillroom maid, she makes the cakes for luncheon, tea and dessert and the rolls for breakfast. She keeps the kitchen clean and keeps things in order.

*Housemaid*: In large households, the upper housemaid undertook lighter jobs such as making beds and tidying bedrooms. She made sure rooms were supplied with the necessary linens, and that they were kept in repair. She dusted the china ornaments, and tended to the flower arrangements. She kept an eye on the lower housemaids, who would light the fires, clean the living rooms, polish the brass, carry water upstairs for washing, and empty the chamberpots. Some maids were assigned to specific rooms, such as the still-room, laundry, dairy or nursery.

*Scullery Maid*: Her chief duty is to clean and scour the pots and pans, as well as the cooking utensils. She cleans the scullery, servant's hall, larders, and kitchen passages. She usually dines in the kitchen with the kitchen maid.

## MALE SERVANTS

### Upper Servants

*House Steward*: A House Steward is employed only in larger households where the accounts are too extensive for the Housekeeper to manage. The House Steward has a sitting-room for his duties of household accounting. He may also performance as a Land Steward. Those households having Land Stewards give them their own separate dwelling. The House Steward engages men and women servants, with the exception of the family, ladies' maids, nurses and valet. He pays their wages and dismisses them. He orders household goods, pays the household bills and keeps the household books. He usually submits the household books to his master once a month for review. He does not wear livery.

*Valet*: Valets are generally kept by single gentlemen and elderly gentlemen. A butler may performance as a valet for a single man. A valet brushes his master's clothes, cleans his boots, carries up the water for his bath, puts out his clothes for dressing, shaves him if necessary, assists him in dressing, packs and unpacks his clothes when traveling. He also loads his rifle when shooting, stands behind his master's chair at dinner, waits at his breakfast and luncheon, attends to the master's wardrobe and sees that everything is in repair and order. A valet to an elderly gentleman attends to his health needs also, and may sleep in the room with his master. He does not wear livery.

*Butler*: The butler is the head of his department and responsible for the performance of those under him (the footmen). He has usually served his apprenticeship in domestic service, slowly working his way up the hierarchy. His responsibilities increase with the size of his establishment. He is in charge of the plate chest and makes sure it is properly cleaned before use. He keeps accounts of the wine handed out and consumed by the household. He decants the wine for luncheon and dinner, and puts away decanters after each meal. He also bottles wine, and country butlers brew beer. A butler takes over the valet's duty when there isn't one in the household. A butler announces visitors during the afternoon hours. He readies rooms for use every day, as well as tidies them. In households with only one footman, the butler assumes some of the pantry work.

### Senior Servants

*Coachman*: His duties vary depending on the number of footmen employed, and whether or not there is a second-coachman on staff. In families with more than one coachman, the head coachman drives a pair of horses and the second coachman drives one horse. Nightwork is the duty of the second coachman. The head coachman supervises those under him (second coachman and grooms), and sees that the horses are properly fed and taken care of. He also has charge of the the stables and is responsible for ordering supplies. He assists the groom in cleaning the carriages and harness. In some families, coachmen have their meals with the servants. In others, they have their own rooms in the stables.

*Head Gardener*: The head gardener is in charge of the hot-houses, green-houses and conservatories on the estate. He supervises the rest of the gardeners, their number depending on the size of the gardens.

### Under Servants

*Footman*: A typical day for a footman is the following routine: He takes coals to the sitting-room, cleans the boots, trims the lamp wicks, cleans the plate, lays the breakfast table, carries in breakfast, waits at breakfast, removes breakfast, answers the door in the morning after 12 o'clock, delivers notes, lays the luncheon table, takes in and waits luncheon, clears the table and cleans the silver, lays the dinner table, goes out with the carriage in the afternoon, attends to fires throughout the day and evening, prepares table for tea, cleans up after tea, waits at dinner, clears the dinner table, helps clean the plate, washes the glass and silver used at dinner, takes in coffee and dessert after dinner, waits in attendance in front hall when dinner guests are leaving, attends to the gentlemen in the smoking room, attends to lighting in the house at dusk, goes out with the carriage in the evening and valets the young gentlemen in the family. Footmen dress in livery. When one footman is employed, the butler assists in his duties. When two footmen are kept in lieu of a butler and footman, the head footman assumes the duties of the butler. When two or three footmen are kept with a butler, the head footman is called an under-butler, although he remains in livery.

*Groom*: He attends to the horses and exercises them. He cleans the carriages and harness, and feeds the horses. He also readies the stables for the master's inspection each morning.

# 4

# What, When and How to Eat?

## WHAT TO EAT?

It is very important to eat the right kind of food, but it is even more important to be balanced and use common sense. Those who are moderate in their habits and cheerful can eat almost anything with good results. Of course, people who live almost entirely on such denatured foods as polished rice, finely bolted wheat flour products, sterilized milk and meat spoiled in the cooking, refined sugar and potatoes deprived of most of their salts through being soaked and cooked will suffer.

There are many different diet systems, and some of them are very good. If their advocates say that their way is the only way, they are wrong. Many try to force their ideas upon others. They find their happiness in making others miserable. They are afflicted with the proselyting zeal that makes fools of people. This is the wrong way to solve the food problem. Let each individual choose his own way and allow those who differ to continue in the old way.

Many have changed their dietary habits to their own great benefit. After this they become so enthused and anxious for others to do likewise that they wear themselves and others out exhorting them to share in the new discovery. This does no good, but it often does harm, for it leads the zealot to think too much of and about himself, and it annoys others. Many are like my friend who lunched daily on zwieback and raw carrots. "I think everybody ought to eat some raw carrots every day; don't you?" she said. We cannot mold everybody to our liking, and we should not try.

If we conquer ourselves, we have about all we can do. If we succeed in this great work, as suggested, evolve enough tolerance to be willing to allow others to shape their own ends. To volunteer undesired information does no good, for it creates opposition in the mind of the hearers. If the information is sought, the chances are that it may in time do good. It is well enough to indicate how and where better knowledge may be obtained. We should at all times attempt to conserve our energy and use it only when and where it is helpful.

Such conduct leads to peace of mind, effectiveness, happiness and health. The tendency to become too enthusiastic about a dietary regime that has brought personal benefit is to be avoided, for it brings unnecessary odium upon the important subject of food reform. People do not like to change old habits, even if the change would be for the better, and when an enthusiast tries to force the change his actions are resented. He makes no real converts, but as pay for his efforts he gains the reputation of being a crank.

Those who wish to be helpful in an educational way should be patient. The race has been in the making for ages. Its good habits, as well as its bad ones, have been acquired gradually. If we ever get rid of our bad habits it will be through gradual evolution, not through a hasty revolution. We need a change in dietary habits, but those who become food cranks, insisting that others be as they, retard this movement. Only a few will change physical and mental habits suddenly.

If those who know are content to show the benefits more in results than in words, their influence for good will be great. What shall we eat? How are we to know the truth among so many conflicting ideas? We can know the truth because it leads to health. Error leads to suffering, degeneration and premature death. As the homely saying goes, "The proof of the pudding is in the eating." Let us look into some of the diet theories before the public and give them thoughtful consideration.

The late Dr. J.H. Salisbury advocated the use of water to drink and meat to eat, and nothing else. The water was to be taken warm and in copious quantities, but not at or near meal time. The meat, preferably beef, was to be scraped or minced, made into cakes and cooked in a very warm skillet until the cakes turned grey within. These meat cakes were to be eaten three times a day, seasoned with salt and a little pepper.

The doctor had a very successful practice, which is attested by many who were benefited when ordinary medical skill failed. His diet was not well balanced. In meats there is a lack of the cell salts and force food. Especially are the cell salts lacking when the flesh is drained of its blood. The animals of prey drink the blood and crunch many of the bones of their victims, thus getting nearly all the salts. But in spite of his giving such an unbalanced diet, the doctor had a satisfactory practice and good success. Why? Because his patients had to quit using narcotics and stimulants and they were compelled to consume such simple food that they ceased overeating. It is a well known fact that a mono-diet forces moderation, for there is no desire to overeat, as there is when living on a very varied diet.

Another fact that the Salisbury plan brings to mind is that starch and sugar are not necessary for the feeding of adults, although they are convenient and cheap foods and ordinarily consumed in large quantities. The fat in the meat takes the place of the starch and sugar. Atomically, starch, sugar and fat are almost identical, and they can be substituted one for the other. Nature makes broad provisions.

Dr. Salisbury's career also serves to remind us that a mixed diet is not necessary for the physical welfare of those who eat to live. Vegetarians dwell upon the toxicity of meat. But Dr. Salisbury fed his patients on nothing but meat and water, and the percentage of recoveries in chronic diseases was considered remarkable. Meat is very easy to digest and when prepared in the simple manner prescribed by the doctor and eaten by itself it will agree with nearly everybody. But when eaten with soup, bread, potatoes, vegetables, cooked and raw, fish, pudding, fruit, coffee, crackers and cheese, there will be overeating followed by indigestion and its consequent train of ills. However, it is not fair to blame the meat entirely, for the whole mixture goes into decomposition and poisons the body.

The cures resulting from Dr. Salisbury's plan also help to disprove the much heralded theory of Dr. Haig, that uric acid from meat eating is the cause of rheumatism. Overeating of meat is often a contributory cause. We are told that the rheumatics who followed Dr. Salisbury's plan got well. They regained physical tone. They lost their gout and rheumatism. They parted company with their pimples and blotches. All of which would indicate that the blood became clean.

The chief part derived from Dr. Salisbury's plan and experience is the helpfulness of simple living and moderation. An exclusive diet of meat is not well balanced. Energy produced from flesh food is too expensive. The good results came from substituting habits of simplicity and moderation for the habit of overeating of too great variety of food. The same results may be obtained by putting a patient on bread and milk.

Dr. Salisbury's patients had unsatisfied longings, doubtless for various tissue salts. The addition of fresh raw fruits or vegetables would improve his diet, for apples, peaches, pears, lettuce, celery and cabbage are rich in the salts in which meats are deficient. .

Dr. Emmet Densmore recommended omitting the starches entirely, that is, to avoid such foods as cereals, tubers and legumes. He believed that it is best to live on fruits and nuts. He recommended the sweet fruits—figs, dates, raisins, prunes—instead of the starchy foods. The doctor did much good, as everyone does who gets his patients to simplify. He also had good results before discovering that starch is a harmful food, when he fed his patients bread and milk. Starch must be converted into sugar before it can be used by the body. The sugar is what is known as dextrose, not the refined sugar of commerce. The sweet fruits contain this sugar in the form of fruit sugar, which needs but little preparation to be absorbed by the blood. Dr. Densmore reasons thus: Only birds are furnished with mills; hence the grains are fit food for them only. Other starches should be avoided because they are difficult to digest, the doctor wrote.

Raw starches are difficult to digest, but when they are properly cooked they are digested in a reasonable time without overburdening the system, provided they are well masticated and the amount eaten is not too great and the combining is correct. Rice, which contains much starch, digests in a short time. We can do very nicely without starch. We can also thrive on it if we do not abuse it. The two chief starch-bearing staples, rice and wheat, contain considerable protein and salts in their natural state.

In fact, the natural wheat will sustain life for a long time. Man has improved on nature by polishing the rice and making finely bolted, bleached wheat flour, deprived of nearly all the salts in the wheat berry. The result is that both of them have become very poor foods.

The more we eat of these refined products the worse off we are, unless we partake freely of other foods rich in mineral salts. Not long ago a lady died in England who was a prominent advocate of a "brainy diet". Her brainy diet consisted largely of excessive quantities of meat, pork being a favourite. She died comparatively young, her friends say from overwork. Such a diet doubtless had a large part in wearing her out. To overeat of meat is dangerous. A gentleman is now advocating a diet of nothing but cocoanuts. This is a fad, for they are not a balanced food. He has published a book on the subject. Perhaps his advocacy is influenced by his interest in the sale of cocoanuts.

The vegetarians condemn the use of meat. Some of them are called fruitarians. It is very difficult to decide who are the most representative of them. Some advocate the use of nothing but fruit and nuts. Others add cereals to this. Others use vegetables in addition. Some even allow the use of dairy products and eggs, that is, all foods except flesh. They say that meat is an unnatural food for man and condemn its use on moral grounds. It is difficult to decide what is natural, for we find that man is very adaptable, being able to live on fruits in the tropics and almost exclusively on flesh food, largely fat, in the arctic regions.

In nature the strong live on the weak and the intelligent on the dull. There is no sentiment in nature. In her domain might, physical or mental, makes right. Sentiments of right and justice are not highly developed except among human beings, and even there they are so weakly implanted that it takes but little provocation for civilized man to bare his teeth in a wolfish snarl. With some vegetarianism is largely a matter of aesthetics, ethics and morality.

Morality is based on expediency, so it really is a question whether meat is an advantageous food or not. Another vegetarian argument is that man's anatomy proves that he was not intended by nature to eat meat. Good arguments have been used on both sides, but they are not very convincing nor are they conclusive. It is hard to draw any lines fairly. Another objection to meat is that it is unclean and full of poisons, that these poisons produce various diseases, such as cancer.

We are also informed that refined sugar causes cancer, and the belief in tomatoes as a causative factor is not dead. Cancer is without doubt caused principally by dietary indiscretions but it is impossible to single out any one food. No matter what foods we eat, we are compelled to be careful or they will be unclean. Those who wish clean meat can obtain it. The amount of poison or waste in a proper portion of meat is so small that we need give it no thought.

Those who eat in moderation can take meat once a day during cold weather and enjoy splendid health. During warm weather it should be eaten more seldom. On the other hand, meat is not necessary. We need a certain amount of protein, which we can obtain from nuts, eggs, milk, cheese, peanuts, peas, beans, lentils, cereals and from other food in smaller amounts. The amount of protein needed is small—about one-fifth of what the physiologists used to recommend. Those who think meat eating is wrong should not partake of it. They can get along very well without it.

The organism can stand it if the life is active in the fresh air, but it will not do for people who are housed. Much meat eating causes physical degeneration. The body loses tone. Experiments have shown that vegetarians have more resistance and endurance than the meat eaters, but the meat eaters get so much stimulation from their food that they can speed up in spurts. The excretions of meat eaters are more poisonous than those of vegetarians.

Eggs produced by hens fed largely on meat scraps do not keep as well as those laid by hens feeding more on grains. In short, meat eating leads to instability or degeneration, if carried to excess. Young children should have none of it and it would be a very easy matter for the rising generation to develop without using meat, and we believe this would be better than our present plan of eating.

However, let us give flesh food the credit due it. When meat eaters are debilitated no other food seems to act as kindly as meat, given with fruits or vegetables. When properly prepared and taken in moderation meat digests easily and is quite completely assimilated. Many make the mistake of living too exclusively on starch and taking it in excess. The result is fermentation and an acid state of the alimentary tract. Dr. Daniel S. Sager says that, "About all that we have to fear in eating is excessive use of proteids."

Experience and observation do not bear out this statement, for it is as easy to find people injured by starch as by protein. One form of poisoning is as bad as the other. The doctor also warns against nearly all the succulent vegetables, saying that on account of the indigestible fibre, most of them are unfit for human consumption. Dr. E.H. Dewey condemned the apple as a disease-producer, and inferentially, other fruits. Dr. Charles E. Page objects to the use of milk by adults, on the ground that it is fit food only for the calves for whom nature intended it. Many writers have repeated this opinion. Most of the regular physicians have a very vague idea of dietetics and proper feeding. When asked what to eat they commonly say, "Eat plenty nourishing food of the kinds that agree with you." They do not point out the fundamentals to their patients. Sometimes they advise avoiding combinations of milk and fruits. Sometimes they say that all starches should be avoided and in the next breath prescribe toast, one of the starchiest of foods. At times they proscribe pork and pickles but they are seldom able to give a good diet prescription. What people need is a fair knowledge of what to do and the don'ts will take care of themselves. All foods have been condemned as unfit for human consumption by people who should know.

However, those who look at these matters with open eyes and open minds will come to the cease that man is a very adaptable animal; that if necessary he can get along without almost all foods, being able to subsist on a very small variety; that he can live for a long period on animal food entirely; that he can live all his life without tasting flesh; that he can live on a mixed diet; that he can adopt a great many plans of eating and live in health and comfort on nearly all of them, provided he does not deprive himself of the natural salts and gets some protein; and finally and most important, that moderation is the chief factor in keeping well, for the best foods produce disease in time if taken in excess.

Those who object to flesh, dairy products, cereals, tubers, legumes, refined sugars, fruits or vegetables, should do without the class which they find objectionable, for it is easy to substitute from other classes. Eggs, milk or legumes may be taken in place of flesh foods. The salts contained in fruits may be obtained from vegetables. The starch, which is the chief ingredient of cereals, is easily obtained from tubers and legumes; fats and sugars will take its place. Commercial sugar is not a necessity. The force and heat derived from it can be obtained from starches and fats.

Outside of milk in infancy, there is not a single indispensable food. Some people have peculiarities which prevent them from eating certain foods, such as pork, eggs, milk and strawberries, but with these exceptions a healthy person can eat any food he pleases, provided he is moderate. We eat too much flesh, sugar and starch and we suffer for it.

This does not prove that these foods are harmful, but that overeating is. Sometimes the food question becomes a very trying one in the home. One individual has learned the fact that good results are obtained by using good sense and judgement in combining and consuming food, and he tries to force others to do as he does. This is unfortunate, for most people object to such actions, and though the intention is good, it accomplishes nothing, but prejudices others against sensible living.

The best way is to do right yourself and let others sin against themselves and suffer until they are weary. Then, seeing how you got out of your trouble, perhaps they will come to you and accept what you have to offer. The attempt to force people to be good or to be healthy is merely wasted effort.

## WHEN TO EAT?

Three meals a day is the common plan. This is a matter of habit. Three meals a day are sufficient and should not be exceeded by man, woman or child. Lunching or "piecing" should never be indulged in. Children who are fed on plain, nutritious foods that contain the necessary food elements do not need lunches. Lunching is also a matter of habit, and we can safely say that it is a bad habit. If three meals a day are taken, two should be light. He who wishes to work efficiently can not eat three hearty meals a day. If it is brain work, the digestive organs will take so much of the blood supply that an insufficient amount of blood will be left to nourish the brain. The worker feels the lack of energy. He is not inclined to do thorough work, that is, to go to the root of matters, and he therefore does indifferent work.

One rule to which there is no exception is that the brain can not do its best when the digestive organs are working hard. If there is a piece of work to be done or a problem to be solved that requires all of one's powers it is best to tackle it with an empty stomach, or after a very light meal. If the work is physical, it is not necessary to draw the line so fine. But it is well to remember that hard physical work prevents digestion.

All experiments prove this. So if the labour is very trying, the eating should be light. Those who eat much because they work hard will soon wear themselves out, for hard work retards digestion, and with weakened digestion the more that is eaten, the less nourishment is extracted from it. Those who labour hard should take a light breakfast and the same kind of a noon meal. After the day's work is done, take a hearty meal. Those who perform hard physical labour, as well as those who work chiefly with their brains, should relax a while after the noon meal. A nap lasting ten to twenty minutes is very beneficial, but not necessary if relaxation is taken.

During sleep the activities of the body slow down. Most people who take a heavy meal and retire immediately thereafter feel uncomfortable when they wake in the morning. The reason is that the food did not digest well. It is always well to remain up at least two hours after eating a hearty meal. Most people would be better off if they took but two meals a day. Those who have sedentary occupations need less fuel than manual labourers, and could get along very well on two meals a day. However, if moderation is practiced, no harm will come from eating three times a day.

In olden times many people lived on one meal a day. Some do so today and get along very well. It is easy to get plenty of nourishment from one meal, and it has the advantage of not taking so much time. Most of us spend too much time preparing for meals and eating. Once when it was rather inconvenient to get more meals, we lived for ten months on one meal a day. We enjoyed our food very much and was well nourished. For twelve years we have lived on two meals a day, one of them often consisting of nothing but some juicy fruit. Many others do likewise, not because they are prejudiced against three meals per day, but they find the two meal plan more convenient and very satisfactory. Meat, potatoes and bread, with other foods, three times a day is a common combination. No ordinary mortal can live in health on such a diet. Such feeding results in discomfort and disease, and unless it is changed, in premature aging and death. The body needs only a certain amount of material. Sufficient can be taken in two meals. If three meals is the custom less food at a meal should be eaten. However, the general rule is that those who eat three meals per day eat fully as large ones as those who take only two.

As a rule, the meal times should be regular. We need a certain amount of nourishment, and it is well to take it regularly. This reduces friction, and is conducive to health, for the body is easily taught to fall into habits of regularity and works best when these are observed. There should be a period of at least four and one-half to five hours between meals. It takes that long for the body to get a meal out of the way. Stomach digestion is but the beginning of the process, and this alone requires from two to five hours.

On the two-meal plan it makes very little difference whether the breakfast or the lunch is omitted. After going without breakfast for a week or two, one does not miss it. Miss the meal that it is the most troublesome to get. Dr. Dewey revived interest in the no-breakfast plan. He considered it very beneficial.

The doctor did not give credit where credit is due, for he insisted on going without breakfast. Omitting lunch or dinner accomplishes the same thing. He got his beneficial results from reducing the number of meals, and consequently the amount of food taken, but it is immaterial which meal is omitted.

Heavy breakfasts are very common in England and in our country. On the European continent they do not eat so much for breakfast, a cup of coffee and one roll being a favourite morning meal there. To eat nothing in the morning is better than to take coffee and rolls. To eat enough to steal one's brain away is a poor way to begin the day. Much better work could be done on some fruit or a glass of milk, or some cereal and butter than on eggs, steak potatoes, hot bread and coffee, which is not an uncommon breakfast.

When we consider the best time to eat, we come back to our old friend, moderation, and find that it is the best solution of the question, for if the meals are moderate we may with benefit take three meals a day, but no more, for there is not time enough during the day to digest more than three meals. However, it is not necessary to eat three times a day.

## HOW TO EAT?

It seems that all of us ought to know how to eat, for we have much practice; yet the individuals who know the true principles of nourishing the body are comparatively few. Very few healers are able to give full and explicit directions on this important subject. Some can give partial instructions, but we need a full working knowledge.

In one period of our racial history there were times when it was difficult to obtain food, as it is now among some savage people. Then it was without doubt customary to gorge, as it is among some savages now when they get a plenteous supply of food, especially of flesh food. Even among so-called civilized people, the distribution of food is so uneven that some are in want somewhere, nearly all the time.

In parts of Russia, we are informed, the peasants go into a state of semi-hibernation during part of the winter, living on very small quantities of inferior food. With rapid transportation and the extensive use of power-propelled machinery, famine should be unheard of in civilized countries. In our land there is a sufficient quantity of food and people seldom suffer because they have not enough, but considerable suffering is due to excessive intake and to poor quality of food.

Weight for weight, white bread is not as valuable as whole-wheat bread, though it contains as much starch. Measure for measure, boiled milk is inferior as a food to untreated milk, either fresh or clabbered. Such facts make it necessary for us to know how to eat.

The correct principles of taking nourishment to the best advantage have been fairly well known for a long time, and perhaps they have been fully discussed years ago by some authors, but so far as we know Dr. E.H. Dewey is the first one who grouped them and gave them the prominence they deserve.

*He employed many pages in explaining clearly and forcibly these principles, which can be briefly stated as follows*:

- First, be guided by the appetite in eating. Eat only when there is hunger.
- Second, during acute illness fast, that is, live on water.
- Third, be moderate in eating.
- Fourth, masticate your food thoroughly.

*Dr. J.H. Tilden teaches his patients the same in these words*:

- "Never eat when you feel badly.
- "Never eat when you have no desire.
- "Do not overeat.

- "Thoroughly masticate and insalivate all your food."

Because these true dietetic principles are so important let us give them enough consideration to fix them in the mind. They should be a part of every child's education. They should be so thoroughly learned that they become second nature, for if they are observed disease is practically impossible. Accidents may happen, but no serious disease can develop and certainly none of a chronic nature if these rules are observed, provided the individual gives himself half a chance in other ways. When the eating is correct, it is difficult to fall into bad habits mentally. Correct eating is a powerful aid to health. Health tends to produce proper thinking, which in turn leads the individual to proper acting.

## EAT ONLY WHEN THERE IS HUNGER

Hunger is of two kinds, normal and abnormal. The real or normal hunger was given us by nature to make us active enough to get food. If it were not for hunger, there would be no special incentive for the young to partake of nourishment and consequently many would die comfortably of starvation, perhaps enough to endanger the life of the race. Normal hunger asks for food, but no special kind of food. It is satisfied with anything that is clean and nourishing. It is strong enough to make a decided demand for food, but if there is no food to be had it will be satisfied for the time being with a glass of water and will cause no great inconvenience. Abnormal hunger is entirely different. It is a very insistent craving and if it is not satisfied it produces bodily discomfort, perhaps headache. The gnawing remains and gives the victim no rest. Very often it must be pampered. It calls for beefsteak, or toast and tea, or sweets, or some other special food. If not satisfied the results may be nervousness, weakness or headache or some other disagreeable symptom.

When missing a meal or two brings discomfort, it is always a sign of a degenerating or degenerated body. A healthy person can go a day without food without any inconvenience. He feels a keen desire for food at meal times, but as soon as he has made up his mind that he is unable to get it or that he is not going to take any the hunger leaves. Normal hunger is a servant. Abnormal hunger is a hard master.

A person in good condition does not get weak from missing a few meals. One in poor physical condition does, although this is more apparent than real. In the abnormal person a part of the food is used as nourishment, but on account of the poor working of the digestive organs, a part decomposes and this acts as an irritant or a stimulant. The greater the irritation the more food is demanded. The temporary stimulation is followed by depression and then the sufferer is wretched. This depression is relieved by more food. Please note that it is relieved, not cured. The relief is only temporary.

All food stimulates, but only slightly. It is when the food decomposes that it becomes stimulating enough to cause trouble. It is well to remember that considerable alcoholic fermentation can take place in an abused alimentary tract. The stimulation obtained from too much food is very much like the stimulation derived from alcohol, tobacco or morphine. At first there is a feeling of well-being, which is followed by a miserable feeling of depression that demands food, alcohol, tobacco or morphine for relief, as the case may be, and no matter which habit is obtaining mastery, to indulge it is courting disaster. When a habit begins to assert itself strongly, break it, for later on it will be very difficult, so difficult that most people lack the will power to overcome it.

If there is abnormal hunger, reduce the food intake. Instead of eating five or six times a day, reduce the meals to two or three. It is quite common for such people to take lunches, which may consist of candies, ice cream, cakes, milk or buttermilk and various other things which most people do not look upon as real food. Take two or three meals a day, and let a large part of them be fresh vegetables and fresh fruits. Eat in moderation and the troublesome abnormal hunger will soon leave. By indulging it you increase it.

Many people get into trouble because they believe that they have to have protein, starch and fat at every meal. This is not necessary, for the blood takes up enough nourishment to last for quite a while. A supply of the various food elements once a day is sufficient, which means that protein needs be taken but once a day, starch once a day and fat once a day. Starch and fat serve the same purpose and one can be replaced by the other.

Cultivate a normal hunger, then fix two or three periods in which to take nourishment, and partake of nothing but water outside of these periods. If there is no desire for food when meal time comes, eat nothing, but drink all the water desired and wait until next meal time.

## DURING ACUTE ILLNESS FAST

This is so obviously correct that we should expect every normal individual to be guided by it. Even the lower animals know this and act accordingly. This rule we should go without food when ill, but to do so is contrary to the teachings of medical men. They teach that when people are ill there is much waste, which is true, and that for this reason it is necessary to partake of a generous amount of nourishing food, so they give milk, broth, meat, toast and other foods, together with stimulants. Feeding during illness would be all right if the body could take care of the food, which it cannot. In all severe diseases digestion is almost or quite at a standstill and the food given under the circumstances decomposes in the alimentary tract and furnishes additional poison for the system to excrete.

Food under the circumstances is a detriment and a burden to the body. In fevers, the temperature goes up after feeding. This shows that more poison has entered the blood. In fevers little or none of the digestive fluids is secreted, but the alimentary tract is so warm that the food decomposes quickly. Feeding during acute attacks of disease is one of the most serious and fatal of errors. There is an aversion to food, which is nature's request that none be taken.

When an animal becomes seriously ill, it wants to fast, and does so unless man interferes. Here we could with advantage do as the animals do. Nature made no mistake when she took hunger away in acute diseases, and if we disregard her desires, we invariably suffer for it. We should make it a rule to take no food, either liquid or solid, during acute disease.

Those who have had no opportunity to watch the rapidity with which people recover from serious illness may take the ground that sick people would starve to death if they were to be treated thus, for some of these acute diseases last a long time. Typhoid fever, for instance, occasionally lasts two or three months. It never lasts that long when treated by natural means, and it is very mild, as a rule. The fever will be gone in from seven to fourteen days in the vast majority of cases, and then feeding can be resumed.

Chronic disease is often due to neglected acute disease, at other times to the building of abnormality through errors of life which have not resulted in acute troubles. While acquiring chronic disease, the individual may be fairly comfortable, but he is never up to par. Most chronic diseases can be cured quickly by taking a fast, but usually it is not necessary to take a complete fast. The desire for food is not generally absent and there is usually fair power to digest.

One of the most satisfactory methods, if not the most satisfactory one, of treating chronic disease is to reduce the food intake, and instead of giving so much of the concentrated staples, feed more of the succulent vegetables and the fresh fruits, cooked and raw, using but small quantities of flesh, bread, potatoes and sugar. This gives the body a chance to throw off impurities. There are always many impurities in a deranged body.

## BE MODERATE IN YOUR EATING

This is often very difficult, for most people do not know what moderation is. In infancy the too frequent feeding and the overfeeding begin. The common belief that infants must be fed every two hours, or oftener, is acted upon. The result is that the child soon loses its normal hunger, which is replaced by abnormal hunger. When food is long withheld it begins to fret.

The mother again feeds and there is peace for an hour or so. When mothers learn to feed their children three times a day and no more there will be a great decrease in infant ills and a falling off in the infant mortality. The healthiest children we have seen are fed but three times a day. They become used to it and expect no more. Another thing that makes it difficult to be moderate is impoverishing the food through refinement and poor cooking. These processes take away a great part of the mineral salts which are present in foods in organic form. These salts can not be replaced by table salt, for sodium chloride is but one of many salts that the body needs and an excess of table salt does not make up for a deficiency in the others. Children fed on refined, impoverished foods are not satisfied with a reasonable amount. There is something lacking and this makes itself known in cravings, which demand more food than is needed to nourish. We have noticed many times that children are satisfied with less of whole wheat bread than of white bread, and that the brown unpolished rice satisfies them more quickly and completely than the polished rice. In other words, depriving the foods of their salts is one of the factors that leads to overeating. Simplicity is a great aid to moderation.

It is also necessary to exercise the conservative measure, self-control. Some writers suggest to eat all that is desired and then fast at various intervals to overcome the effects of overeating. In other words, they advise to eat enough to become diseased and then fast to cure the trouble. This is better than to continue the eating when the evil results of an excessive food intake make themselves known, but it does not bring the best results. Such people have their spells of sickness, which are unnecessary.

If they stop eating as soon as the disease makes itself known, it does not last long. By exercising self-control sickness will be warded off. By using will power daily it grows stronger and those who force themselves to be moderate at first, are in time rewarded by having moderation become second nature. People should always stop eating before they are full. Those who eat until they are uncomfortable are gluttons. They should be classed with drunkards and drug addicts.

## THOROUGHLY MASTICATE ALL FOOD

Horace Fletcher has written a very enthusiastic book on this subject. Enthusiasm is apt to lead one astray, and even if thorough mastication will not do all that Mr. Fletcher believed, it is very important, and we owe Mr. Fletcher thanks for calling our attention to the subject forcibly. Thorough mastication partially checks overeating. Our foods have to be finely divided and subdivided or they cannot be thoroughly acted upon by the digestive juices. The stomach is well muscled and churns the food about, helping to comminute it, but it can not take the place of the teeth. All foods should be thoroughly masticated. While the mastication is going on the saliva becomes mixed with the food. In the saliva is the ptyalin, which begins to digest the starch. Starch that is well masticated is not so liable to ferment as that which gets scant attention in the mouth. Starches and nuts need the most thorough mastication. If thorough mastication were the rule, meat gluttons would be fewer, for when flesh is well chewed large quantities cause nausea.

Milk digests best when it is rolled around in the mouth long enough to be mixed with saliva. To treat milk as a drink is a mistake, for it is a very nourishing food. All kinds of nuts must be well masticated. If they are not they cannot be well digested, for the digestive organs are unable to break down big pieces of the hard nut meats.

The succulent vegetables contain considerable starch. If mastication is slighted they often ferment enough to produce considerable gas. Fruits are generally eaten too rapidly, and therefore often produce bad results. Even green fruits can be eaten with impunity if they are very thoroughly masticated. Those who are fond enough of liquors to take an excess should sip their alcoholic beverages very slowly, tasting every drop before swallowing. This would decrease their consumption of liquor greatly. Even water should not be gulped down. It should be taken rather slowly, especially on hot days. During hot weather many drink too much water. This tendency can usually be overcome by avoiding iced water and by drinking slowly.

*These four rules should be a part of your vital knowledge. Remember them and try to put them into practice*:

1. "Eat only when hungry.
2. During acute illness fast.
3. Be moderate in your eating.
4. Thoroughly masticate all food."

# 5

# Cookery and Public Sector Catering

## INTRODUCTION

We examine the contract, travel and public sector catering. In many occasions the public sector and travel catering operations, are often serviced by contract caterers. However, there are still occasions where organizations provide their own in-house catering and by dividing the sector into three subdivisions, it allows us to discuss the distinct differences between the various operations. The three subsectors have shown a dramatic increase in the past few years with some sectors such as the cruise ships showing a growth in business looking to continue in the next ten years or more. The stage aims to give an overview of the sectors to enable the reader to get an understanding of the type of technology often used as well as the marketing and financial implications for each sector.

## CONTRACT CATERING

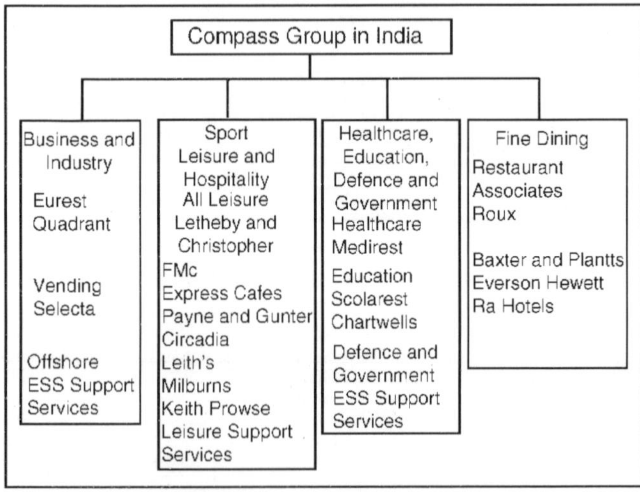


**Fig.** Structure of Compass Group the Largest Catering Company in the India.

Contract catering has evolved greatly in the past ten years and it is not uncommon to find contract catering companies investing in any of the sectors that are covered in this stage. Traditionally, contract catering has been associated with non-profit or institutional catering, including workplace canteens, hospitals and schools however, today contract catering firms such as Compass or Sodexho have branched outside the remits of traditional contract catering and today it is not uncommon for contract catering firms to develop brands under which they operate restaurants.

Compass Group employs 90,000 employees and has 8,500 sites in the India alone. Worldwide the compass group employees 400,000 employees and annual revenue of approximately ₹11 billion. The BHA in 2006 in the India alone contract catering reached revenues of just under ₹4 billion, showing a 0.8% drop in turnover from the previous year. Worth noting is the decline of contract catering in Healthcare, MOD, Local authority and private education.

**Table. Contract Catering Market Segments by Number or Means served**

| | 2001 | | 2003 | | 2005 | | % change 2001-2005 |
|---|---|---|---|---|---|---|---|
| | m | % | m | % | m | % | |
| Business and industry | 588 | 38 | 613 | 36.9 | 645 | 41.2 | 9.7 |
| State education | 227 | 14.7 | 281 | 16.9 | 265 | 16.9 | 16.7 |
| Public catering | 177 | 11.4 | 185 | 11.1 | 210 | 13.4 | 18.6 |
| Healthcare | 238 | 15.4 | 232 | 14 | 204 | 13 | –14.3 |
| MOD | 135 | 8.7 | 161 | 9.7 | 105 | 6.7 | –22.2 |
| Private education | 125 | 8.1 | 135 | 8.1 | 100 | 6.4 | –20 |
| Local authority | 42 | 2.7 | 37 | 2.2 | 22 | 1.4 | –47.6 |
| Oil rigs, training centers, construction sites | 15 | 1 | 14 | 1 | 16 | 1 | 6.7 |
| **Total** | **1,547** | **100** | **1,661** | **100** | **1,567** | **100** | **1.3** |

For the purposes of this text we shall define contract caterers as: individuals or firms who undertake the responsibility of operating and controlling a company' s catering facilities within that company' s guidelines for a specified contract arrangement. Contract caterers are usually engaged for a specific period of time, after which the contract may be renewed or dissolved as both parties wish. Catering contracts can be classified mainly in five types:

- *Cost plus/management fee*: These are contracts where the client is billed for the cost of the operation plus a management fee.
- *Fixed price/performance guarantee*: Contracts where the clients agree a total subsidy and the costs may not rise above the agreed figure.
- *Profit and loss concession*: The client and the caterer agree to share the profits or loss of the operation.
- *Total risk*: Total investment covered by the caterer who earns all profits.

- *Purchasing*: A contract for purchasing only.

Contract caterers are involved in all types of industrial catering situations, ranging from the small independent concerns to the large multinational organizations and may become involved for different reasons: for example, the organization' s dissatisfaction with the existing services; complaints about the standard of catering have been made at staff meetings and repeated attempts to improve the facilities have failed, or the company does not wish to become involved in operating the catering facilities itself as it may not be its core business or recognizes that it does not have the expertise and so engages the services of contract caterers.

## INDUSTRIAL CATERING

Industrial catering can be defined as catering taking place in businesses. For example, major retail operators will offer catering to their employees and whilst sometimes they may have an in-house catering division, most often they will hire a contract caterer.

Another example of industrial catering is the catering supplied to employees of organizations that provide financial services. Other businesses that may be included would be catering in oil rigs, construction sites, and training or conference centres. Indeed the subsector is so large that it exceeds an annual turnover of ₹660 million. Typical contracts agreed between organizations and caterers tend to be fixed price and profit/loss concession and total risk.

### Financial Implications

Product pricing is a major issue for industrial catering. The market can be characterized as semi-captive as it would be convenient for employees to use the caterer but they also have the choice to use other food and beverage providers or bring in their own lunch. Of course there are exceptions to this such as catering provided in oil rigs where employees have no alternative but to consume what is provided by the caterer. Supermarkets tend to offer good quality luncheons not only in the form of sandwiches but also in hot and freshly prepared food at very competitive prices. Caterers have to ensure good quality of food is provided with food items that are around the range of ₹3–₹5.

### Marketing

Ensuring that the caterer is the prime choice for the employees of the business can be affected by the marketing efforts of the caterer. Day specials and promotional packages will often be advertised on a company' s intranet or message board. Traditional methods such as flyers may also be used but the speed and cost effectiveness of an e-mail makes it a prime method of communicating with potential clients.

**Product and Service Styles**

Counter service and take-away service styles tend to be the preferred service style for such operations, however buffet style and self-service may be used. The main products are snacks and take-away food, so product packaging can be important as some caterers may have limited seating space and employees may also chose to buy the product and consume it later.

**Staffing**

These operations tend to be staffed by regular members of staff. Caterers will often have other operations in nearby sites so staff mobility between operations can be an option. This flexibility can become important especially when there is need to cover staff leave or sickness periods from one outlet to another.

**Technology**

Food holding technology is very important. An off-site central kitchen may be used that supplies a number of operations. Ensuring that the quality of food is maintained through the transportation and delivery is paramount. Electronic point of sale technology can help with forecasting of sales thus reducing wastage. Communication technologies such as access to host company electronic boards or intranets and group mailing lists can be a great advantage to the caterer for marketing purposes.

**EVENT MANAGEMENT**

An increasingly important area in Hospitality Management is that of Event Management. Although event management involves all those aspects that are required to organize a successful event, the provision of food and beverage is often of paramount importance to guarantee the success of the event. Policy decisions relating to function catering are largely determined by a number of characteristics inherent in this type of catering.

The first is the season. The second is the concentration of events during these months, which are mainly at weekends, particularly Friday and Saturday events, during which time an operation must seek to maximize its sales potential. Third, a considerable amount of information is available to the caterer in advance of the organized functions; this includes the number of guests to be catered for and for which meal periods, for example lunch or dinner; their time of arrival and departure; the menu they are to be given and the price being paid per guest.

The basic policies relating to function catering are usually quite specific to this form of catering. If function trade is an establishment' s only source of business then the policies laid down will only relate to this type of trade. In other establishments, however, such as hotels, the function facilities may be one of a number of catering outlets, although even in these organizations the banqueting department will often have policy decisions relating specifically to this department.

**Banqueting and Functions and Large-scale Events**

Function and event catering may be described as the service of food and beverages at a specific time and place, for a given number of people, to an agreed menu and price. Examples of function catering include social functions, such as weddings and dinner dances; business functions such as conferences, meetings and working lunches; and those functions that are organized for both social and business reasons such as outdoor catering at a sports event, show or exhibition. Function catering is found in both the commercial and non-commercial sectors of the catering industry. The term 'banqueting' can often be used within hotels to describe the department that deals with function catering. The typical hotel function or banqueting 'season' runs between the months of October and May with the busiest months being December and January. For the rest of the year some of the facilities may be used for providing separate restaurant facilities for tour groups who normally have limited time available for meals and whom the hotel may wish to keep apart from the normal day-to-day restaurant business. The function facilities may also frequently be let on a day or half-day basis for such occasions as antique shows, trade exhibitions, fashion shows, etc. where the requirement of food and beverages may be very limited.

This function season is more noticeable in certain types of establishments, particularly those organizations whose sole purpose is function catering, and those that offer purpose-built facilities such as hotels. In other establishments such as public houses, department store restaurants, industrial cafeterias, etc. the function season is not so evident, as existing dining facilities are usually adapted for function events rather than specific facilities being available; however, even these types of operations are still likely to experience peak periods during the year when the function facilities are in greater demand than at other times. This characteristic fluctuating of demand associated with function catering has implications for such establishments' basic policy decisions.

**Financial Implications**

The logistics required for such events can be extremely complicated. Often the event might take place in a location that there is no production capabilities and the food and beverage will have to be produced at another site and then transported and served on-site. For the company taking on such a project there are the additional costs of transportation to take into account. When negotiating the contract the caterer will have a number of ready-made and coasted menus but often in events such as weddings the customer might require a very specific product that the caterer will have to customise. Using the wedding as event example, beverages will often be included in the cost per head or cover. Meaning, cost per customer. Because the margins per head are normally very small the caterer makes the money on the volume of the event. The pricing structure for an establishment' s function catering facilities will be largely determined by its cost structure, with particular reference to its fixed and variable costs. This is most in evidence in the non-commercial sector where functions may not be fully costed, that is not taking into account the fixed costs of the operation.

Where the costing of function menus is based mainly on covering food and labour costs, it is important to remember that both of these increase with the size and quality of function offered. However, due to the volume of sales the food and labour costs as a percentage of actual sales will slightly decrease; it is necessary therefore to not only consider the food costs per function but also the potential benefits to be gained from a reduction in labour costs. There are a variety of pricing structures that may be used for costing functions, the adoption of any one being determined by such factors as the type of organization, the standards of food and beverage service to be offered, and the cost structure of the establishment.

**Marketing**

There is such a varied type of events that a catering company or a hotel banqueting department may use any of the traditional marketing such as Leaflets, radio, TV, magazine and newspaper adverts. Brewin Dolphin, a financial research company, the market for weddings is worth ₹4.2 billion each year with the average wedding to about ₹16,000 no wonder hotel banqueting departments and contract catering operators are competing for this lucrative segment. Sample function menus produced by an establishment need to be of a good quality and appearance as the customer will often wish to take them away to study before deciding on the function menu.

These sales tools should also be of a standard consistent with the level of operation and the type of image it is trying to project. Function 'folders' containing details of all the different facilities offered by an establishment are often produced by organizations which may be distributed to prospective clients advertising the establishment' s function facilities.

*A function 'folder' often colour-coded for easy reference by the client, would most likely be composed of the following*:

- An envelope type folder with the company' s logo, title and address clearly displayed.
- A personal letter from the function/banqueting manager to the client.

- A list of function rooms together with details of the numbers that could be accommodated for different types of functions, for example a formal lunch or dinner, a dinner dance, a buffet type reception, a theatre-style conference/meeting, etc.
- Plans of the room with basic dimensions, position of power points, telephone points, ceiling heights, etc.
- Sample menus for lunch, dinner, buffets, meetings, etc.
- Details of audio-visual equipment available for meetings, for example lecterns, microphones, overhead projectors, screens, etc.
- Details of accommodation facilities available, often at special rates for guests attending a function/meeting.
- Coloured postcards of the hotel/function rooms.
- Relevant simple maps and parking arrangements where necessary.

### Product and Service Styles

The product may vary depending on the type of the event and it may be anything from buffet style service to full table ser vice depending on the customer request. Silver service and family service styles are quite common when table service has been requested. Functions may include a reception stage where canapés and appetisers are served by "satellite waiters". This is often known as the Butler style of service.

### Staffing

Caterers as well as banqueting departments will normally have a core of staff and will then use agency staff to cope with larger events. Because of this the quality of service may suffer as the operator cannot guarantee the skill level of the agency staff. Some contract catering companies train their own casual staff and they then have a 'Bank' of casual staff that they may call upon when needed.

### Technology

Food holding technology is very important to contract caterers. Because the business is more predictable as the numbers of customers are known hotel kitchens may use their staff to prepare the food for a large function before hand and load it to already plated to specially designed racks that can fit into combination ovens. Food can then be either completely cooked at the time needed and served straight from the racks or pre-cooked/chilled and then re-constituted.

## SPORT VENUE CATERING

Sport venue catering includes catering offered in stadia, football, cricket, rugby, horse racing venues, private health and fitness clubs, golf and other sports. The sector is hard to quantify as each country has a large number of venues and catering operations are largely fragmented. In 2004, Mintel was estimating the sector in the India to worth ₹354 million. With the introduction of new venues since 2004 including the Wembley and Arsenal Stadia in London in 2007 and 2006, respectively, the India sector is estimated to exceed the ₹400 million mark in revenue today.

In the India there are 365 stadia whilst the USA currently has 1,726. With 9,379 stadia around the world the revenues generated through the sale of food and drinks alone must be well over the ₹10 billion mark today.

**Table. Number of Satdia Around the World**

| | **Number of Menu** |
|---|---|
| Africa | 525 |
| Asia | 884 |
| Central America | 260 |
| Europe | 3,780 |
| Middle East | 424 |
| North America | 2,125 |
| Oceanla | 260 |
| South America | 1,121 |
| **Total** | **9,379** |

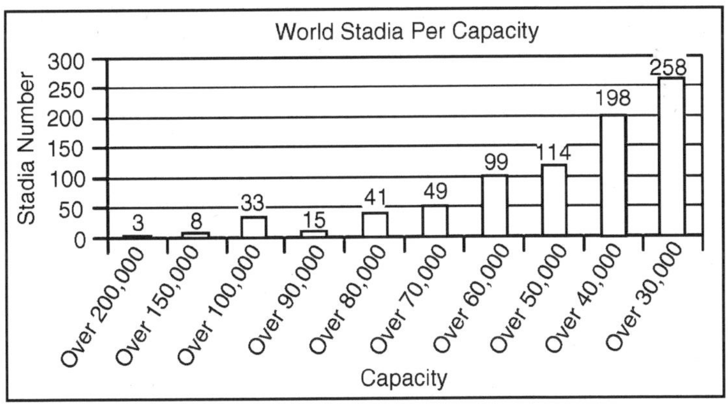


**Fig.** Number of World Stadia Per Capacity

There are three common types of contracts often found between caterers and venue operators. The first is where the venue takes a percentage of the revenue generated by the contract caterer. The second is where the venue simply leases their facilities therefore enjoying a fixed stream of income. The third is a relatively newer type of arrangement where both caterer and venue work in partnership setting a joint venture and splitting the profits generated equally.

### Financial Implications

With approximately 9% of the world' s stadia having a capacity of over 30,000 the logistics required for the catering of such large operations can be extremely complex. If we consider the newly finished Wembley stadium in London, India, the catering logistics required are phenomenal. The stadium has a capacity of 90,000. With 60 bars and 41 food and beverage outlets the stadium hospitality facilities include conference rooms of up to 1,000 cap acity and reception rooms for up to 3,000 capacity. With 803 points of sale and a total of 3,000 hospitality employees, Wembley is one of the biggest catering sites in Europe. It includes a 950 cover Atrium restaurant, serving buffet food, the great hall and banquet space for up to 1,500 people, as well as four signature restaurants of 650 covers each, including two à la carte eateries and two brasseries. It also features two Champagne and seafood bars as well as two large free-flow public catering areas, 162 private boxes, two super boxes and a royal suite for up to 400 people Kühn.

### Marketing

Many of the venues will try to entice the consumer earlier than the starting time of the event to maximize sales. Often leaflets might be handed at to the public featuring 'early bird' offers as well as the type of food and drinks on offer at the venue. Meal deals often seen in fast-food operations are also a popular promotional tool to increase multiple item purchasing. For example, a consumer may be offered to buy a pint of specific lager and a pie and gets a bag of crisps for free. The major contract caterers such as Delaware North, Compass and Sodexho use the Internet extensively as a marketing and promotional tool.

### Product and Service Styles

Soft and hot drinks and sandwich markets appear to be the most popular items just as to Mintel. However, it is not uncommon for exclusive restaurants to be featured in many of the worlds stadia. However, it is worth mentioning something specific to stadia in terms of service styles; often catering staff may be seen moving around the stadium selling food and beverages whilst a game is taking place. They can be on foot carrying trays or in some cases in specially converted bicycles that allow the sale of cold bottled beverages or even warm food.

### Staffing

Staffing can be a major 'headache' for the human resources management of such an operation. Because of the fluctuation of the events that could range from the corporate entertainment of a handful of people to that of a few thousands the organizations involved tend to have a core of permanent staff whilst they manage an often enormous database of casual staff that can be called upon to cover a certain event. Two major problems emanate from such a setup. The first is that of consistency, so organizations will have to ensure that all staff are trained to ensure standards of production and service are maintained at all times. The second is ensuring that the casual staff in the database get enough work every week to keep them interested in coming back for more work in the future.

**Technology**

Two key considerations in such environments are paramount: health and safety, and speed of service. Advancements in technology enable operators to have better control of their food production ensuring health and safety standards are maintained throughout the production and service delivery. With large stadia that often have an excess of 500 selling points, EPOS systems and networking technology has to be extremely robust. Technology can also ensure that food production and food holding can be achieved with larger numbers than ever before.

The new Wembley stadium in the India features a beer dispensing system that has the pumping capability of four pints per sixteen seconds with the stadium number of sales points that means at optimum production their 803 points of sale can produce 45,169 pints in fifteen minutes. That is half the total possible capacity of the stadium and in theory it would mean the end of customer queuing for a pint.

## LEISURE VENUE CATERING

Leisure venue catering is catering offered in venues such as museums, theatres, cinemas, historic buildings, zoos, wildlife parks, art galleries.

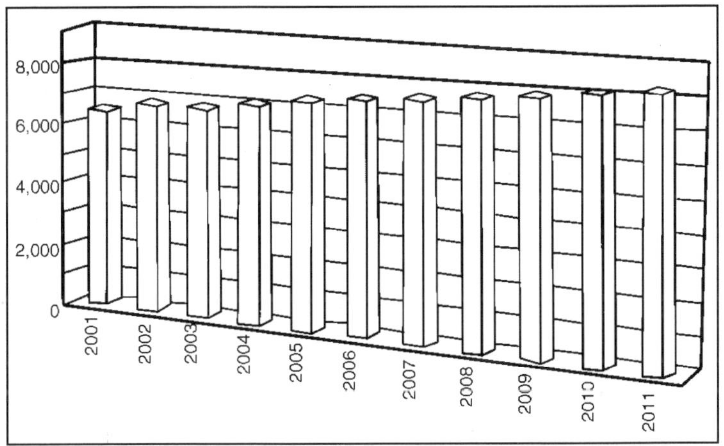


**Fig.** Trends in the Leisure Venue Catering Market, 2001-2002 (in million Pounds)

Perhaps, because of the captive nature of the market the key management issues that appear to be prevalent are that of pricing and quality. In the India, the market has exceeded the ₹2 billion mark since 2006. However, the growth of the sector compared to that of free-standing restaurants is quite slow suggesting that improvements could be made.

Although the majority or leisure venues outsource their catering a significant number chooses to keep their catering in house. This is more prevalent in cinema and theatre catering.

**Financial Implications**

Although catering in museums has shown the largest growth in the leisure venue catering in recent years Museums and art galleries in the India have lost a major competitive advantage. With the introduction of free admission consumers have the option to go to a high street restaurant and re-enter the museum or gallery later. What was once a captive market has now become at best a semi-captive one.

This meant that catering in such establishments has to offer a better value for money than it has done in the past, ensuring that costs remain low whilst quality of product and price remains competitive enough to entice visit ors to buy from their outlets.

In order to ensure higher profit margins whilst remaining competitive leisure caterers will have to ensure that they maximize their sales per available customer within the venue. That means that vendors must ensure that the long queues that often put off consumers must be minimized.

**Marketing**

Apart from the common promotional techniques used such as meal deals and discounted offers, catering in leisure venues over the past years had a reputation of bad value for money.

Caterers today must not only ensure that customers are enticed to buy their in-house products but also that they develop a brand that communicates quality and efficiency to the consumer.

This one of the main reasons leisure venue operators will often chose to outsource their food and beverage provision to well-established contract catering companies.

The main operators in the India are Compass, Sodexho and Elior although there are other operators such as DO&CO, Searcy and Caterleisure.

**Product and Service Styles**

The majority of visitors purchase snacks or take-away food such as burgers, hot dogs, crisps and chocolate. Therefore the majority of the food provision can take often the form of retail. Counter, buffet and take-away service styles tend to be amongst the more popular for leisure catering.

**Table. Types of Food Bought at Leisure Venues, 2007**

| | Percentage of a sample of 809 visitors |
|---|---|
| Cold snacks (e.g. crisps, chocolate, nut) | 47 |
| Hot take-away food (e.g. hotdog, burger, hot pie/pastry | 45 |
| Cold take-away food (e.g. sandwiches, ice cream) | 45 |
| Hot snacks (e.g. chips, nachos) | 30 |
| Hot sit-down meal (e.g. pizza) pasta , shepherds pie,curry) | 27 |
| Cold sit-down meal (e.g. salad, sandwiches) | 19 |
| Healthy snacks (e.g. fruit, energy/ cereal bars) | 19 |
| Others | 1 |
| Did not buy food | 15 |

### Staffing

In recent years, the minimum wage in the India has been increased much faster than inflation rates. This has caused an added challenge to operators and for a sector that was traditionally perceived as an expensive one compared to high street vendors transferring the added cost to the consumer farther expanded the gap between consumer expectations and value for money delivered. When catering is kept in house, operators have a separate staff division that focuses on hospitality. Casual staff are also used as there is a fluctuation of visitors depending on day of the week, weather and time of the year. During weekends and school breaks, for example, leisure parks tend to be at their busiest. This in turn does affect the quality of service especially with the larger operators.

### Technology

One of the key allies in recovering product and service quality lies in the investment of information technology. The latest EPOS technology can help managers keep track of customer preferences as well as employee productivity, this can be a great tool in allowing the manager to identify a member of staff that may be in need of further training or even award that excellent member of staff that could otherwise go unnoticed.

## TRAVEL CATERING

Travel catering has a number of characteristics not commonly associated with other food and beverage outlets. It frequently involves the feeding of a large number of customers arriving together at a catering facility, and who need to be catered for in a specific time, for example, on board a plane. The plane only carries sufficient food and beverage supplies for a specific number of meal periods. If for any reason this food cannot be served to customers, alternative supplies may not be readily available.

The service of the food and beverages may be particularly difficult due to the physical conditions within the service area, for example, turbulence on board a plane. The types of restaurants described previously are usually catering for a specific and identifiable socio-economic market. Travel catering often has to cater for 'mixed markets'.

Finally, there are the problems of staffing these food and beverage facilities: the extra costs involved in the transportation and service of the food and beverages; space restrictions and the problem of security while the operation is in transit. Four main types of travel catering may be identified: Airline catering, Cruise ship and Ferry boat catering, Train catering and Motorway catering.

## AIRLINES

The major new trend of the past ten years in the Airline industry in Europe has been the introduction and substantial growth of the budget or 'no frills' airline phenomenon. Companies such as Easyjet and Rynair have shown amazing growth.

The total airline growth from the year 2000 to 2006 has been an amazing 30% but mainly due to the increase in budget airlines the in-flight catering expenditure had a downward trend in recent years.

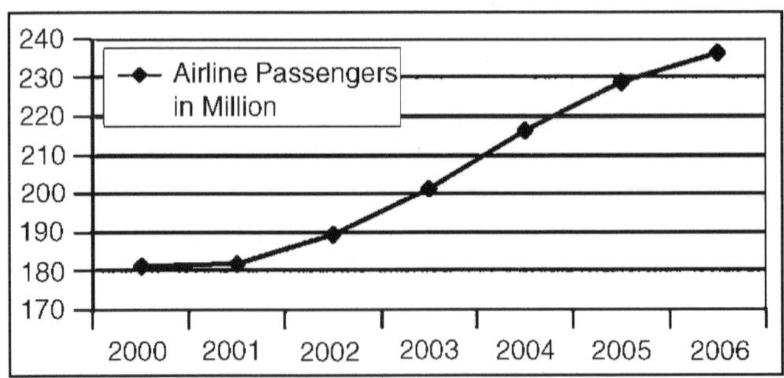


**Fig.** Airline Passengers, 2000-2008

Airline catering has increased and developed considerably over the past twenty-five years. Originally consisting of sandwiches and flasks of tea, coffee and alcoholic beverages, the progress to today' s full and varied service has paralleled that of aircraft development itself. In budget airlines, however, the product has gone back to the basic trolley with sandwiches, snacks chocolate and limited selection of beverages on offer. Airline catering falls into two main areas: terminal catering, and 'in-transit' or 'in-flight' catering.

**Table. Onboard Catering Market, by Sector**

| | 2002 | | 2005 | | 2007 | | % change 2002-2007 |
|---|---|---|---|---|---|---|---|
| | ₹m | % | ₹m | % | ₹m | % | |
| In-flight | 613 | 72 | 590 | 72 | 577 | 72 | –6.0 |
| Ferry | 170 | 20 | 155 | 19 | 152 | 19 | –10.6 |
| Rail | 69 | 8 | 75 | 9 | 73 | 9 | +4.2 |
| **Total** | **852** | **100** | **820** | **100** | **802** | **100** | **–5.9** |

## Financial Implications

The cost of a hot meal and beverage to the airline is about ₹6.50 but the biggest cost to the airline is the waiting to restock the aircraft and time at an airport can mean a big loss of income to the carrier. If, for example, a carrier flies from London, India to Athens, Greece, it may cost the airline less to stock up for the return trip as well, limiting the waiting time at the Greek airport. This is especially true for budget airlines as they are well known for their strategy of limiting their turnaround time.

## Marketing

Airlines have tried to different experiments to alleviate the widely held customer perception that airline food is bland. Some airlines have tried introducing high street brands in their food packaging. Quite often the quality of the food is used in their marketing campaigns as a unique selling point, and airlines will employ a well-known chef to design their menu as part of their marketing efforts

## Product and Service Styles

The in-flight catering service varies considerably with the class of travel, type and duration of flight. For the economy travellers, the food and beverage portions are highly standardized with the meals portioned into plastic trays that are presented to the passengers and from which they eat their meals. Disposable cutlery, napkins, etc. may be used to increase the standard of hygiene and reduce the weight carried and storage space required.

Gourmet food in the airlines is another recent trend. Stephan Pyles, of the Dallas restaurant, working with American Airlines whilst Charlie Trotter, the Chicago chef, introduces dishes created for premier United Airlines passengers. The lower than normal air pressure can affect customer perception of taste as well as digestion and executive chefs designing a menu will often taste it mid-air to ensure they have compensated for this. Added to that is the fact food is not cooked on board, it is just warmed. Meals are prepared twelve to sixteen hours in advance chilled and then held at low temperatures. Service is from a gueridon trolley, where food is portioned in front of the customers and any garnishes, sauces, etc. are added just as to their immediate requirements. The crockery used may be bone china and this combines with fine glassware and cutlery to create an atmosphere of high-class dining. Some airlines offer full silver service menu for their first class and business travellers.

A characteristic of airline catering is that this service is often contracted out to a specialist catering firm, which will supply a similar service to many airlines. The meal is usually included in the price of the fare with the exception of budget airlines. The growth in air travel has made competition fierce, and the area of food service is now a particularly competitive aspect of the total service offered by an airline. An interesting concept currently in the USA is that of gourmet meals delivered to the airport by the SkyMeals company.

### Staffing

Food and beverage outlets at air terminals usually consist of selfservice and waiter service restaurants, supplemented by vending machines and licensed bars. The major restaurant brands often seen in high streets can also be seen in airport terminals. In flight catering service is delivered by the flight attendants, who often see the service of food and drinks as secondary to their responsibility of ensuring the health and safety of passengers, this can be especially true if customers are flying in the economy class. Although health and safety should always remain flight attendants primary responsibility airlines that wish to claim a competitive advantage ought to train and offer incentives to individuals that offer exceptional service.

### Technology

The main issues with aircraft are that of space and weight. Ensuring that on-board ovens are lighter, take less space and consume less energy are of primary importance. Advancements in technology may mean that airlines may be able to offer a menu fully cooked on board one day.

## CRUISE SHIPS/FERRY BOATS

The cruise ship sector is one of the fastest moving sectors in the hospitality industry. The number of passengers has grown to more than 12 million in 2006 from approximately 500,000 in 1970.

Forecasts suggest that by 2012 the global industry will reach 20 million passengers with the USA and India leading in terms of cruise ship passengers.

Budget or 'no frills' cruise liners are making an appearance with new companies such as Caspi Cruises, Easy Cruise, whilst older budget companies such as Thomson or Louis Cruise Line increase their fleet capacity.

On the other hand, Ferry boat catering has slumped as the numbers of Ferry travellers has dramatically decreased due to the increase of low-cost airlines. In India, the onboard catering market was valued at ₹155 million for 2005, a 19% decrease since 2000, and the trend is still going today.

**Financial Implications**

Whilst cruise ship catering promises growth Ferry boat catering is extremely competitive. Mintel is forecasting a downward trend continuing well into 2010. Traditional cruise liners are looking to be more innovative continuing with all inclusive packages but offering optional extras. Wedding and honeymoon packages are another two products often offered by cruise liners.

**Marketing**

Cruise liners are expanding their marketing strategies to target non-traditional market segments. Increasing competition in the budget sector forces them to think innovatively in finding ways to sell their product without conflicting the more traditional brands.

Special promotions, discounts during low season, special occasions, anniversary gifts to customers are some of the promotional tools used by most liners.

**Product and Service Styles**

Sea or marine catering varies from the provision of food and beverages on the short sea route ferries to the large cruise or passenger liners where the catering facilities are an important part of the service offered by the shipping line and are usually included in the price of the fare.

On the cruise liners the standard of catering facilities is high because they are an important sales feature in a competitive activity.

On the short sea routes, however, price is usually a more important factor and because of the necessity to feed large numbers of people in a short time the catering service provided is usually of the popular and fast-food type.

In the cruise liners companies appear to be more innovative than ever with companies such as Princess Cruises serving dinner in customer cabins or suite balconies ensuring extra food and beverage income.

The Gourmet 'bug' is also appearing in the cruise sector with celebrity chefs such as Todd English on Queen Mary 2; Nobu Matsuhisa and Wolfgang Puck on Crystal; Marco Pierre White on the new P&O Ventura and Gary Rhodes on two P&O' s ships, Oriana and Arcadia. Service styles can range depending on cruise liner from full silver service to self-service and buffet. With Ferry boats the service style often is cafeteria or take away due to the short journeys involved.

**Staffing**

After casino sales one of the largest revenue generators in cruise liners is beverage sales. Staff are trained extensively in up- selling techniques and with traditional cruise liners the recruitment process ensures that some of the best staff are hired. With the added incentive of tax-free incomes many hospitality professionals consider a few months on a cruise liner.

The organization on cruise ships can be extremely hierarchical. Most front line employees tend to stay for only a few trips as the nature of the ship means that there is not much to do but work whilst on a cruise ship.

**Technology**

Advanced EPOS technology and bar dispensing equipment mean better control of sales, stock control and wastage ensuring better profit margins as well as the facilitation of special discounts. Advancement in waste disposal technology ensures waste is better compacted shredded and incinerated.

**TRAINS**

Mintel Reports, unlike Ferry and in flight catering, rail catering is showing an upward trend in revenues generated. Rail catering may be conveniently divided into two areas: terminal catering and in-transit catering.

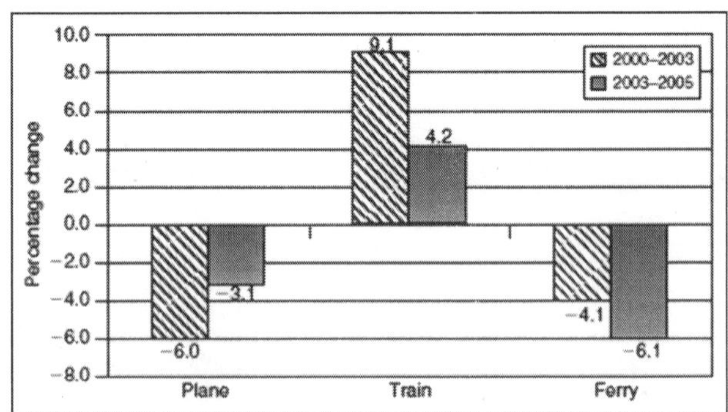


**Fig.** Percentage Change in Value of the UK Onboard Catering

**Table. Rail F&B Gross Profit, 2005**

| | |
|---|---|
| F&B sales | ₹78,929,599 |
| Food | ₹30,237,417 |
| On train food condemnage | ₹222,920 |
| Liquor and tobacco | ₹3,395,625 |
| Total cost of goods sold | ₹33,855,963 |
| Gross profit | ₹45,073,636 |
| %Gross profit | 57% |

There are 2,500 rail stations across the India. The main rival to rail is the low-cost airlines but the introduction of Eurostar in 2003 raised the rail market share in the India. The improvements of the West Coast Mainline and the introduction of the Pendolinos train by Virgin Trains passenger numbers increased by a 20%. In the US sales reached $79 million in 2005.

**Financial Implications**

With a 4.2% increase in rail catering revenue the sector appears a positive one. The main products purchased are hot beverages and snacks so the focus is in the reduction of costs to ensure higher profit margins. Spend per passenger increases as the length of journey increases, however some companies offer all inclusive ticket prices which help raise the food and beverage revenue generated.

**Marketing**

The provision of food and beverage in rails is often used as promotional tool. Ticket inclusive packages are often advertised in an effort to entice customers away from low-cost airlines. The sector is not as aggressive as it could be with its promotional efforts on food and beverage sales. The majority of train companies advertise their services in their in-house magazine whilst some have an e-marketing campaign and also use local and international media advertising.

**Product and Service Styles**

Catering at railway terminals usually comprises licensed bars, self-service and waiter service restaurants, fast food and takeaway units, supplemented by vending machines dispensing hot and cold foods and beverages. In-transit catering can feature three kinds of service.

The first is the traditional restaurant car service where breakfast, lunch and dinner are organized in sittings and passengers go to the restaurant car for service where appropriate seating accommodation is provided, and then return to their seats on the train after their meal. In a Pullman service, these meals are delivered direct to the seat of first-class passengers only.

The second type of service is the buffet car, which is a self-service operation in which passengers go to the car and buy light refreshments over the counter. The third is a trolley service where snacks and drinks are delivered to customers at their seats.

Innovative approaches to catering on trains are also in evidence such as the operation of 'Cuisine 2000' using cook-chilled foods prepared centrally, buffet cars turned into bistros on the London to Birmingham route, and on the east coast Anglo- Scottish route 'A taste of Scotland' restaurant service.

### Staffing

In the India, the Network rail is undertaking a project that looks to rejuvenate the provision of skills in the rail catering and other rail staff. In partnership with local colleges the programme aims to bring all staff to a National Vocational Qualification standard. For example, in 2004 the country' s first Rail Academy–run by York College in partnership with the National Railway Museum the academy was funded with ₹1.25 million. Other similar initiatives have been introduced all over the India ensuring that rail employees are well trained.

### Technology

There have been a number of advancements in railway kitchen design and technology enabling operators to serve more complicated menus than ever before. Also the same benefits enjoyed by the other sectors with the advancement of EPOS and beverage dispensing technologies are also enjoyed by the rail sector.

## ROADS/MOTOR SIDE

Road catering has progressed from the inns and taverns of earlier days used by those travelling on foot and horseback to the present-day motorway service areas and other roadside catering outlets. High street fast-food operations are also now appearing both on MSAs and as free-standing drive-through.

As an example, in the India, there are 86 MSAs. Moto is the biggest MSA operator with 42 sites followed by Welcome Break and Roadchef. These three operators control 89% of the market whilst McDonalds are slowly emerging as a significant MSA operator.

### Financial Implications

The numbers of cars on the road are on the increase. In India from 1999 to 2004 there was an increase of almost 3 million cars.

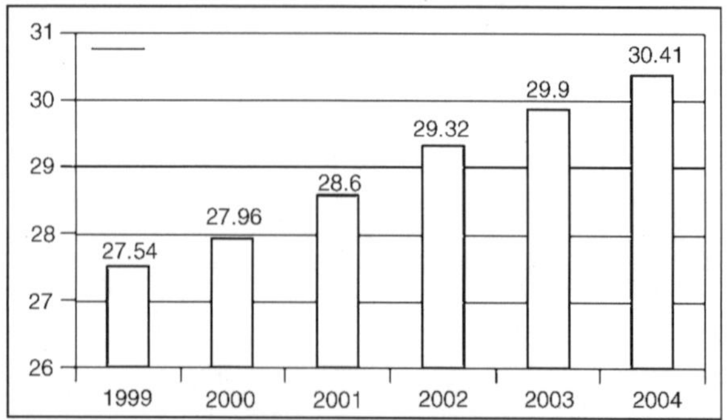


**Fig.** Cars, 1999-2004

There is a constant decrease of households without cars whilst the percentage of females holding driving licences has risen from 49% in 1989/1991 to 61% in 2002/2003.

This does have implications as demographics change so do trends in consumer expenditure. Public transport in the India only accounts for 12% of traffic, this would suggest a steady growth of motorway catering revenue well into 2010.

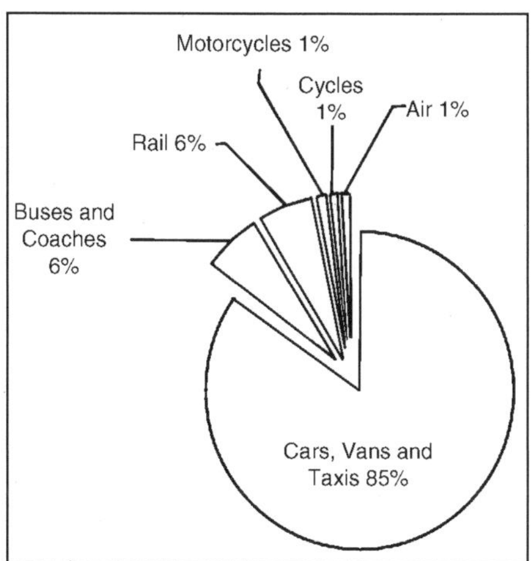


**Fig.** Transpor by Mode 1999-2003

## Marketing

MSAs main marketing tool are the road signs. The main motive for consumers stopping at such a facility is that of convenience. Advertising is heavily regulated and often operators may not be allowed to use their own brand in motorway signage.

## Product and Service Styles

MSAs provide a valuable catering service to the travelling public and their food and beverage facilities usually include self-service and waiter service restaurants, vending machines, and take-away foods and beverages.

## Staffing

These service areas are often open twenty-four hours a day and have a particular problem of staffing as some employees have to be brought to and from work over a distance of 20–30 miles.

Also, because of their isolated locations, the hours they are open and the sheer volume of numbers involved at peak periods, these service areas are also particularly prone to vandalism and littering.

### Technology

In the USA, public wireless Local Area Network is widely available. In the India, talks for public wireless LAN in MSA' s first started in 2003 with the first hotspots installations around 2004. This added service may have an effect on the average food and beverage expenditure of customers in MSAs. The longer a business person spends online whilst at an MSA the more likely they will need to purchase food or drinks.

## VENDING MACHINES

Vending today has become synonymous with selling from a machine. It is also known as 'automatic retailing' or selling from an 'electronic cafeteria' and involves a machine providing the customer with a product in exchange for some form of payment, coins, credit cards, etc.

Although vending was in evidence in the India prior to the Second World War, mainly in the form of chocolate and cigarette machines, it was not until the 1950s that the vending of drinks and snack items really became established in this country.

The markets for vended products have grown steadily over the last forty years. In beverage vending, canned drinks, cartons and bottles have shown the greatest increase in growth whilst snack foods have increased the greatest.

**Table. Forecast of Expenditure on Vended Products by Sector**

| Drinks | Confectionery/snacks/meals | | | | Total | |
|---|---|---|---|---|---|---|
| | ₹m | Index | ₹m | Index | ₹m | Index |
| 2004 | 815 | 100 | 640 | 100 | 1,455 | 100 |
| 2005 | 877 | 108 | 682 | 107 | 1,559 | 107 |
| 2006 | 917 | 113 | 726 | 113 | 1,643 | 113 |
| 2007 | 974 | 120 | 767 | 120 | 1,741 | 120 |
| 2008 | 1,007 | 124 | 798 | 125 | 1,805 | 124 |
| 2009 | 1,045 | 128 | 826 | 129 | 1,871 | 129 |

Mintel, the value of the vending market grew by 15% between 1999 and 2004 to reach ₹2.2 billion.

However, the market has actually declined by 3% in real terms, although their forecasts show a steady growth both in revenue and numbers of vending machines showing a 5% steady increase.

The number of machines increased by 13% over the same period, indicating that the growth in the market can be attributed mainly to the expansion in the number of machines, rather than a rise in the unit value of products.

*Factors to consider when outsourcing vending operations to a contractor*:

- No capital outlay for machine–it is supplied by contractor.
- Some installation costs paid by client, for example water and electricity.
- Operating costs such as ingredients, commodities, cups, maintenance, cleaning and servicing done by contractor.
- Selling prices set between client and contractor. Reimbursement costs, direct and indirect to contractor.

*The range of vending machine equipment or hardware is divisible into two major groups*:

- *Beverage venders*: Beverage vending machines have accounted for the largest share of vending sales over the last thirty years and consequently their design has been developed further than the food vending machines.
- *Food vending machines or merchandisers*: Food vending machines may vend a variety of food products - confectionery, snacks, plated meals, etc. and are usually vended in one of three types of machine:
  - *Snack machines*: Confectionery, crisps, biscuits, etc. are usually vended from an ambient temperature machine as these items have a relatively long shelf life and do not have any special temperature requirements. Because of these factors, servicing of the machines except for re-stocking purposes, can be kept to a minimum thereby also reducing operating costs.
  - *Refrigerated machines*: Snack items such as sandwiches and rolls have a limited shelf life and need to be date-stamped and vended through a refrigerated machine. Plated foods such as salads, cold meats, etc. must be vended from refrigerated machines where the holding temperature is between 2°C and 5°C. At this temperature the food may be kept for 2-4 days, although some operations work on a twenty-four hour cycle only.
  - *Hot meal machines*: Food for a hot vending service may be vended in a number of ways. The first is the heated food vendor which will hold the temperature of the plated food at about 69°C for up to six hours. The second is the hot can vendor which usually offers a choice of items. The selection of hot canned meals, for example soups, baked beans, pasta dishes, casseroles, etc. are held at a temperature of 68°C in the machine without deterioration in the quality of the food. Money is placed into the appropriate slot and the hot can is vended together with a disposable bowl and suitable cutlery to eat the food with; the can is easily opened by the use of a ring pull top. The third involves

the use of a microwave oven adjacent to a refrigerated merchandiser. Cooked food is plated by kitchen staff, rapidly cooled and placed into a refrigerated merchandiser; if limited kitchen facilities are available, ready plated or semi-prepared foods may be bought in from a supplier, plated and put in the vending machine. The food is heated when placed in the microwave, which has an automatic timing device for the different foods which begins when a token or code is put into the microwave. The time taken for a meal to be heated thoroughly depends on whether it is a snack item or a full meal. Snack items being heated from a refrigerated state takes between ten and thirty seconds, and a main meal between forty and sixty seconds, depending on the quantity and depth of the food, and the power supply feeding the microwave. The range of products available for hot meal vending is now quite considerable although snacks and sandwiches still account for the largest percentage.

Within each of these groups the type of vending machine used will depend largely on the type of product being vended. For confectionery and pre-packed goods a simple mechanical unit with a drawer at the base of the column is all that is required; it can be free-standing, wall-mounted or be positioned on a fixed surface and does not require any electricity or water supply.

Snack and sandwich vending machines require a power supply only and because their products are easily consumed, the machines can be situated outside wards, in the corridors of hotels, etc. close to the customer market.

Machines vending plated meals need to be situated close to the kitchen facilities and adjacent to the dining area; some banks of vending machines are sited such that the kitchen is behind the machines for ease of stocking and the dining area is in front of them.

These types of machines may be a rotating drum or revolving shelf design whereby a button is pushed rotating or revolving shelves until the required item is reached and then removed through a flap door.

The basic question of whether to use vending machines or not should be taken after careful consideration of the organization' s catering and financial policies and an assessment of what vending has to offer.

*The main advantages associated with vending include the following*:

- *Flexibility*: Vending can provide a twenty-four hour food and beverage service, either alone or in conjunction with other catering services. Customers can use a vending machine when they want to, rather than only when a cafeteria is open.
- *Situation*: Vending machines can be sited close to the customer market,

for example in office corridors, thus reducing workers ' time away from the workplace queuing for a snack or drink; customers are also more likely to take a vended drink back to their workplace and consume it there, rather than spend time away from their work, for example in a cafeteria. Satellite vending machines can also be used to serve areas that would not normally benefit from a catering facility; for example, in a large industrial complex, machines can be sited some distance from the main kitchen and dining area.

- *Quality control*: In terms of quality, vending machines can sell a consistent product, particularly beverages, pre-packed snacks and bought in meals from a supplier. Meals prepared in the kitchen can also be plated under tighter quality and portion control.
- *Hygiene control*: Reduced handling of vended foods also reduces the possibilities of food contamination. Many beverage machines now also have built-in, self-clean mechanisms.
- *Operating control*: Labour savings can be made as once cleaned and stocked vending machines should require the minimum of maintenance, thus reducing labour costs. Wastage, pilferage and cash losses should also be negligible.
- *Speed*: Vending machines can 'sell' products quickly and efficiently, for example a hot chips machine which can vend portions of freshly prepared chips, always giving a standard product, at a standard price.
- *Sales promotion*: Products for sale in a vending machine can look attractive and stimulate 'impulse purchases', particularly glass-fronted merchandisers displaying fresh fruits, sweets, etc.

*The disadvantages associated with using vending include the following*:

- *Impersonality:* Vending machines lack the 'personal touch' and some customers will always prefer to be served food and beverages in the traditional manner rather than from a machine.
- *Inflexibility of the product*: Initially the range of products available for vending was quite limited; today, however, vending machines offer a much wider selection, and beverages in particular can be highly customised.
- *Reliability:* One of the major causes of dissatisfaction with vending machines in the past has been that the coin mechanism could become jammed and the machine would give no service. This in turn left the machines open to abuse and vandalism. Since their introduction the vending machines' coin mechanism has been a mechanical device which could be regularly jammed with foreign coins, washers, etc. Today, however, the electronic coin mechanism can detect even the

most accurately produced fake coins, which even when fed into the machine, do not jam it. Electronic mechanisms are constantly being improved and are incorporated into the majority of new machines. These electronic mechanisms are also capable of accepting different valued coins, displaying a running total as they are added and of giving change.

- *Limiting:* For large-scale food and beverage service, vending machines have limitations. In some situations they are best suited as a backup to the main catering services although a bank of vending alleviates queuing and waiting time. They are also of less use in up-market situations, except in the form of mini-bars, for example in hotels.

## Financial Implications

The vending market is a retail-based operation and profits rely on high volume turnover, however the sector is highly competitive and pricing wars by different vendors may eat into profits.

The vending market grew by 15% between 1999 and 2004, the market has actually declined by 3% in real terms, as the slump in the cigarette segment and inflationary pressures slowed year-on-year growth.

The number of machines increased by 13% over the same period, indicating that the growth in the market can be attributed mainly to the expansion in the number of machines, rather than a rise in the unit value of products.

**Table. Forecast of the Number of Vending Machines, 2004-2009**

| Machines (in Thousand Units)* | Index | | Machines (in Thousand Units)* | Index | |
|---|---|---|---|---|---|
| 2004 | 770 | 100 | 2005 | 785 | 102 |
| 2006 | 805 | 104 | 2007 | 820 | 106 |
| 2008 | 842 | 109 | 2009 | 866 | 112 |

* Number of machines in circulation

However, it is expected that sales of the vending industry will fall from ₹14 billion to ₹12.5 billion by 2010.

## Marketing

*The markets available for vended products are varied and numerous and may be grouped into three main areas*:

- The general market vending machines and their products may be situated in areas to which the general public largely has access; for example, shopping courts, MSAs, garage forecourts, airports, seaports, ferries, rail and bus terminals, libraries, swimming and leisure centres, stadiums, exhibition centres, cinemas and theatres.

- The industrial market includes those establishments where vending machines are provided for employers and employees in office blocks and shops, factories and sites, etc. Eighty per cent of companies in the India having installed vending machines at some or all of their premises.
- The institutional market includes establishments such as hospitals and schools, prisons, sports complexes, universities and colleges and more recently hotels, replacing to some extent floor service.

**Product and Service Styles**

*Vending operates in a very competitive market and a number of developments and market trends may be identified in the vending sector*:

- *Cashless systems:* The development of card operated vending has probably been the most important technological development in vending. The leading supplier of this type of system is Girovend, the main component being a credit card type of pass or card which can record the user' s own data; it can be used for personnel control such as security, identity passes, attendance recording, leisure facilities, etc. For catering purposes, customers can buy any food and beverage items from a vending machine by placing their card into the machine instead of cash; their card is then debited with the amount for the items purchased.
  - The card first has to be loaded with credit and this can be done in a number of ways. First, supervised loading whereby a supervisor collects customers' cash amounts and loads the cards via a vending machine; the disadvantage to this method is that the handling of cash is still involved and at least one person has to be employed to do this job. Second, customers self-load their own cards with a cash value before making their purchases. By inserting the card into the loader a customer can check its balance and increase the amount by feeding the appropriate money into the machine; this method' s disadvantage is that special loaders are required and cash is still handled. Third, is the direct-debit loader linked to the wages department so that a card holder may direct debit different values from his/her salary; in this way cash hand ling is eliminated completely.
  - The advantages to the customer of card vending are that it is a convenient method of payment; loose change does not have to be carried, it is not 'lost' in the machine and, overall, a faster service can be given.

- The card holders can be divided into user type groups and these categories may then be separated into different price bands. Vending machines payments can be broken into cashless, free-vend and coin operated systems. This enables different charges to be made for the same product, for example for regular employees, temporary staff, free vend for visitors, etc. Cash refunds can be given to users giving up their cards, or money can be paid back into an employee account; machines can also be programmed to stop accepting stolen cards. Finally, the sales information stored in these machines can be printed out by item, price list or type of user, and a comparison between actual and cash loaded on to the cards can be given; such upto- date information greatly aids financial control and cost accounting.

- *Mixed product vending*: Where the design of the machine allows, different products may be vended together and complement each other, for example, pre-packed snacks with carton juices together form a substitute for a main meal at certain times of the day. Smaller units, for example vending confectionery, can also be attached to the side of the larger machines and utilize their coin or card mechanism.
- *Fresh brew vending*: Machines using fresh brew systems for tea and coffee ensure that a better quality end product is dispensed to the customer. In-cup drink machines where the ingredients are already in the cup also offer better hygiene, operation and servicing, control and range of products. Some beverage machines are now capable of offering 100 different selections for both hot and cold drinks and have capacities of up to 1,000 cups.
- *Space economization*: The efficient utilization of business space in offices, factories, hospitals, industrial units, etc. is of great importance today. This has led many operations to critically review their catering facilities and the space allocated to them, particularly where a twenty-four hour service is needed. In many situations vending is being used as a space and cost saving alternative to installing traditional catering services. Furthermore, the vending manufacturers themselves are aware of the amount of space vending machines need, and are researching ways of reducing their overall size yet at the same time trying to increase the range and quality of products they can offer.
- *Compatibility with cook-chill*: The cook-chill method of food preparation serves the vending industry well by allowing plated meals to be prepared in advance and vended for later consumption either in a chilled state, for example salads, cold meats, pâtés, etc. or for use in conjunction with some type of heating system, for example microwaves.

Vending has now established itself as a method of food service that may be considered for many types of operations and situations. In some sectors of the catering industry it is employed as a total feeding system, for example staff cafeterias and restrooms, hospital canteens, etc. in others it is an economic alternative to other types of catering service at different times of the day, for example, night shifts in hospitals, twenty-four hour factories, offices, etc.

**Staffing**

The reduced labour costs is one of the biggest advantages of the vending machines along with the availability of the product. Operators can stock a large number of machines with a very small number of staff and with very little training. However, often, there are hidden costs such as maintenance costs.

**Technology**

Without advancements in technology vending machines would not exists and similarly if technology did not evolve the consumer would prefer alternative means of purchasing the goods. Today technological advancements in stock control and maintenance have enabled vending machines to become more reliable. Telemetry and on-site hand-held systems have helped to reduce the number of out-of-stock situations, or quickly identify malfunctioning machines. With advancements in Internet technology vending machines can be easily monitored for conditions and levels of stock. Vending machine technology has improved the storage conditions for perishable goods, and has enabled hot food vending.

# 6

# Carbohydrates: Structure and Forms

A carbohydrate is an organic compound with the empirical formula $C_m(H_2O)_n$, that is, consists only of carbon, hydrogen and oxygen, with the last two in the 2:1 atom ratio. Carbohydrates can be viewed as hydrates of carbon, hence their name. Structurally however, it is more accurate to view them as polyhydroxy aldehydes and ketones. The term is most common in biochemistry, where it is a synonym of saccharide. The carbohydrates (saccharides) are divided into four chemical groupings: monosaccharides, disaccharides, oligosaccharides, and polysaccharides.

In general, the monosaccharides and disaccharides, which are smaller (lower molecular weight) carbohydrates, are commonly referred to as sugars. The word saccharide comes from the Greek word sakkharon meaning "sugar". While the scientific nomenclature of carbohydrates is complex, the names of the monosaccharides and disaccharides very often end in the suffix -ose. For example, blood sugar is the monosaccharide glucose, table sugar is the disaccharide sucrose, and milk sugar is the disaccharide lactose.

Carbohydrates perform numerous roles in living things. Polysaccharides serve for the storage of energy and as structural components. The 5-carbon monosaccharide ribose is an important component of coenzymes and the backbone of the genetic molecule known as RNA. The related deoxyribose is a component of DNA. Saccharides and their derivatives include many other important biomolecules that play key roles in the immune system, fertilization, preventing pathogenesis, blood clotting, and development. In food science and in many informal contexts, the term carbohydrate often means any food that is particularly rich in starch (such as cereals, bread and pasta) or sugar (such as candy, jams and desserts).

Formerly the name "carbohydrate" was used in chemistry for any compound with the formula $C_m(H_2O)_n$. Following this definition, some chemists considered formaldehyde $CH_2O$ to be the simplest carbohydrate, while others claimed that title for glycolaldehyde. Today the term is generally understood in the biochemistry sense, which excludes compounds with only one or two carbons. Natural saccharides are generally built of simple carbohydrates called monosaccharides with general formula $(CH_2O)_n$ where n is three or more. A typical monosaccharide has the structure H-$(CHOH)_x$(C=O)-$(CHOH)_y$-H, that is, an aldehyde or ketone with many hydroxyl groups added, usually one on each carbon atom that is not part of the aldehyde or ketone functional group. Examples of monosaccharides are glucose, fructose, and glyceraldehyde.

However, some biological substances commonly called "monosaccharides" do not conform to this formula (e.g., uronic acids and deoxy-sugars such as fucose), and there are many chemicals that do conform to this formula but are not considered to be monosaccharides (e.g., formaldehyde $CH_2O$ and inositol $(CH_2O)_6$).

The open-chain form of a monosaccharide often coexists with a closed ring form where the aldehyde/ketone carbonyl group carbon (C=O) and hydroxyl group (-OH) react forming a hemiacetal with a new C-O-C bridge. Monosaccharides can be linked together into what are called polysaccharides (or oligosaccharides) in a large variety of ways. Many carbohydrates contain one or more modified monosaccharide units that have had one or more groups replaced or removed. For example, deoxyribose, a component of DNA, is a modified version of ribose; chitin is composed of repeating units of N-acetylglucosamine, a nitrogen-containing form of glucose.

## MONOSACCHARIDES

Monosaccharides are the simplest carbohydrates in that they cannot be hydrolyzed to smaller carbohydrates. They are aldehydes or ketones with two or more hydroxyl groups. The general chemical formula of an unmodified monosaccharide is $(CH_2O)_n$, literally a "carbon hydrate". Monosaccharides are important fuel molecules as well as building blocks for nucleic acids. The smallest monosaccharides, for which n = 3, are dihydroxyacetone and D- and L-glyceraldehyde.

### Classification of Monosaccharides

*Monosaccharides are classified according to three different characteristics*: the placement of its carbonyl group, the number of carbon atoms it contains, and its chiral handedness. If the carbonyl group is an aldehyde, the monosaccharide is an aldose; if the carbonyl group is a ketone, the monosaccharide is a ketose. Monosaccharides with three carbon atoms are called trioses, those with four are called tetroses, five are called pentoses, six are hexoses, and so on. These two systems of classification are often combined. For example, glucose is an aldohexose (a six-carbon aldehyde), ribose is an aldopentose (a five-carbon aldehyde), and fructose is a ketohexose (a six-carbon ketone).

Each carbon atom bearing a hydroxyl group (-OH), with the exception of the first and last carbons, are asymmetric, making them stereocentres with two possible configurations each (R or S). Because of this asymmetry, a number of isomers may exist for any given monosaccharide formula. The aldohexose D-glucose, for example, has the formula $(CH_2O)_6$, of which all but two of its six carbons atoms are stereogenic, making D-glucose one of $2^4 = 16$ possible stereoisomers. In the case of glyceraldehyde, an aldotriose, there is one pair of possible stereoisomers, which are enantiomers and epimers. 1,3-dihydroxyacetone, the ketose corresponding to the aldose glyceraldehyde, is a symmetric molecule with no stereocentres.

The assignment of D or L is made according to the orientation of the asymmetric carbon furthest from the carbonyl group: in a standard Fischer projection if the hydroxyl group is on the right the molecule is a D sugar, otherwise it is an L sugar. The "D-" and "L-" prefixes should not be confused with "d-" or "l-", which indicate the direction that the sugar rotates plane polarized light. This usage of "d-" and "l-" is no longer followed in carbohydrate chemistry.

**Ring-straight Chain Isomerism**

The aldehyde or ketone group of a straight-chain monosaccharide will react reversibly with a hydroxyl group on a different carbon atom to form a hemiacetal or hemiketal, forming a heterocyclic ring with an oxygen bridge between two carbon atoms.

Rings with five and six atoms are called furanose and pyranose forms, respectively, and exist in equilibrium with the straight-chain form. During the conversion from straight-chain form to cyclic form, the carbon atom containing the carbonyl oxygen, called the anomeric carbon, becomes a stereogenic centre with two possible configurations: The oxygen atom may take a position either above or below the plane of the ring.

The resulting possible pair of stereoisomers are called anomers. In the $\alpha$ anomer, the -OH substituent on the anomeric carbon rests on the opposite side (trans) of the ring from the $CH_2OH$ side branch. The alternative form, in which the $CH_2OH$ substituent and the anomeric hydroxyl are on the same side (cis) of the plane of the ring, is called the $\beta$ anomer. You can remember that the $\beta$ anomer is cis by the mnemonic, "It's always better to $\beta$e up."

Because the ring and straight-chain forms readily interconvert, both anomers exist in equilibrium. In a Fischer Projection, the $\alpha$ anomer is represented with the anomeric hydroxyl group trans to the $CH_2OH$ and cis in the $\beta$ anomer.

**Use in Living Organisms**

Monosaccharides are the major source of fuel for metabolism, being used both as an energy source (glucose being the most important in nature) and in biosynthesis. When monosaccharides are not immediately needed by many cells they are often converted to more space efficient forms, often polysaccharides. In many animals, including humans, this storage form is glycogen, especially in liver and muscle cells. In plants, starch is used for the same purpose.

## DISACCHARIDES

Two joined monosaccharides are called a disaccharide and these are the simplest polysaccharides. Examples include sucrose and lactose. They are composed of two monosaccharide units bound together by a covalent bond known as a glycosidic linkage formed via a dehydration reaction, resulting in the loss of a hydrogen atom from one monosaccharide and a hydroxyl group from the other. The formula of unmodified disaccharides is $C_{12}H_{22}O_{11}$.

Although there are numerous kinds of disaccharides, a handful of disaccharides are particularly notable. Sucrose, pictured to the right, is the most abundant disaccharide, and the main form in which carbohydrates are transported in plants. It is composed of one D-glucose molecule and one D-fructose molecule.

*The systematic name for sucrose, O-α-D-glucopyranosyl-(1 → 2)-D-fructofuranoside, indicates four things:*

- *Its monosaccharides*: Glucose and fructose.
- *Their ring types*: Glucose is a pyranose, and fructose is a furanose.
- How they are linked together: The oxygen on carbon number 1 (C1) of α-D-glucose is linked to the C2 of D-fructose.
- The -oside suffix indicates that the anomeric carbon of both monosaccharides participates in the glycosidic bond.

Lactose, a disaccharide composed of one D-galactose molecule and one D-glucose molecule, occurs naturally in mammalian milk. The systematic name for lactose is O-β-D-galactopyranosyl-(1 → 4)-D-glucopyranose. Other notable disaccharides include maltose (two D-glucoses linked α-1,4) and cellulobiose (two D-glucoses linked β-1,4).

## OLIGOSACCHARIDES AND POLYSACCHARIDES

Oligosaccharides and polysaccharides are composed of longer chains of monosaccharide units bound together by glycosidic bonds. The distinction between the two is based upon the number of monosaccharide units present in the chain. Oligosaccharides typically contain between three and ten monosaccharide units, and polysaccharides contain greater than ten monosaccharide units. Definitions of how large a carbohydrate must be to fall into each category vary according to personal opinion.

Oligosaccharides are found as a common form of protein post-translational modification. Such post-translational modifications include the Lewis and ABO oligosaccharides responsible for blood group classifications and so of tissue incompatibilities, the alpha-Gal epitope responsible for hyperacute rejection in xenotransplantation, and O-GlcNAc modifications. Polysaccharides represent an important class of biological polymers. Their function in living organisms is usually either structure- or storage-related. Starch (a polymer of glucose) is used as a storage polysaccharide in plants, being found in the form of both amylose and the branched amylopectin. In animals, the structurally similar glucose polymer is the more densely branched glycogen, sometimes called "animal starch". Glycogen's properties allow it to be metabolized more quickly, which suits the active lives of moving animals.

Cellulose and chitin are examples of structural polysaccharides. Cellulose is used in the cell walls of plants and other organisms, and is claimed to be the most abundant organic molecule on earth. It has many uses such as a significant role in the paper and textile industries, and is used as a feedstock for the production of rayon (via the viscose process), cellulose acetate, celluloid, and nitrocellulose. Chitin has a similar structure, but has nitrogen-containing side branches, increasing its strength. It is found in arthropod exoskeletons and in the cell walls of some fungi. It also has multiple uses, including surgical threads. Other polysa-eccharides include callose or laminarin, chrysolaminarin, xylan, arabinoxylan, mannan, fucoidan, and galactomannan.

## NUTRITION

Foods high in simple carbohydrates include fruits, sweets and soft drinks. Foods high in complex carbohydrates include breads, pastas, beans, potatoes, bran, rice, and cereals. The most common complex carbohydrate in these foods is starch. Carbohydrates are the most common source of energy in living organisms. Proteins and fat are necessary building components for body tissue and cells, and are also a source of energy for most organisms.

Carbohydrates are not essential nutrients in humans: the body can obtain all its energy from protein and fats. The brain and neurons generally cannot burn fat for energy, but can use glucose or ketones; the body can also synthesize some glucose from a few of the amino acids in protein and also from the glycerol backbone in triglycerides. Carbohydrate contains 15.8 kilojoules (3.75 kilocalories) and proteins 16.8 kilojoules (4 kilocalories) per gm., while fats contain 37.8 kilojoules (9 kilocalories) per gm.

In the case of protein, this is somewhat misleading as only some amino acids are usable for fuel. Likewise, in humans, only some carbohydrates are usable for fuel, as in many monosaccharides and some disaccharides. Other carbohydrate types can be used, but only with the assistance of gut bacteria. Ruminants and termites can even process cellulose, which is indigestible to humans.

Based on the effects on risk of heart disease and obesity, the Institute of Medicine recommends that American and Canadian adults get between 45–65 per cent of dietary energy from carbohydrates. The Food and Agriculture Organization and World Health Organization jointly recommend that national dietary guidelines set a goal of 55–75 per cent of total energy from carbohydrates, but only 10 per cent directly from sugars (their term for simple carbohydrates).

**Classification**

For dietary purposes, carbohydrates can be classified as simple (monosaccharides and disaccharides) or complex (oligosaccharides and polysaccharides). The term complex carbohydrate was first used in the U.S. Senate Select Committee on Nutrition and Human Needs publication Dietary Goals for the United States (1977), where it denoted "fruit, vegetables and whole-grains".

Dietary guidelines generally recommend that complex carbohydrates, and such nutrient-rich simple carbohydrate sources such as fruit (glucose or fructose) and dairy products (lactose) make up the bulk of carbohydrate consumption. This excludes such sources of simple sugars as candy and sugary drinks. The USDA's Dietary Guidelines for Americans 2005 dispensed with the simple/complex distinction, instead recommending fibre-rich foods and whole grains.

The glycemic index and glycemic load concepts have been developed to characterize food behaviour during human digestion. They rank carbohydrate-rich foods based on the rapidity of their effect on blood glucose levels.

The insulin index is a similar, more recent classification method that ranks foods based on their effects on blood insulin levels, which are caused by glucose (or starch) and some amino acids in food. Glycemic index is a measure of how quickly food glucose is absorbed, while glycemic load is a measure of the total absorbable glucose in foods.

**Catabolism**

Catabolism is the metabolic reaction cells undergo to extract energy. There are two major metabolic pathways of monosaccharide catabolism: glycolysis and the citric acid cycle. In glycolysis, oligo/polysaccharides are cleaved first to smaller monosaccharides by enzymes called glycoside hydrolases. The monosaccharide units can then enter into monosaccharide catabolism. In some cases, as with humans, not all carbohydrate types are usable as the digestive and metabolic enzymes necessary are not present.

## THE ROLE OF CARBOHYDRATES IN NUTRITION

Carbohydrates are polyhydroxy aldehydes, ketones, alcohols, acids, their simple derivatives and their polymers having linkages of the acetal type. They may be classified according to their degree of polymerization and may be divided initially into three principal groups, namely sugars, oligosaccharides and polysaccharides.

**Table. The Major Dietary Carbohdrates**

| Class (DP*) | Sub-Group | Components |
|---|---|---|
| Sugars (1-2) | Monosaccharides | Glucose, galactose, fructose |
| | Disaccharides | Sucrose, lactose, trehalose |
| | Polyols | Sorbitol, mannitol |
| Oligosaccharides (3-9) | Malto-oligosaccharides | Maltodextrins |
| | Other oligosaccharides | Raffinose, stachyose, fructo-oligosaccharides |
| Polisaccharides (>9) | Starch | Amylose, amylopectin, modified starches |
| | Non-starch polisaccharides | Cellulose, hemicellulose, pectins, hydrocolloids |

DP * = Degree of polymerization

Each of these three groups may be subdivided on the basis of the monosaccharide composition of the individual carbohydrates. Sugars comprise monosaccharides, disacc-harides and polyols (sugar alcohols); oligosaccharides include malto-oligosaccharides, principally those occurring from the hydrolysis of starch, and other oligosaccharides, e.g., a -galactosides (raffinose, stachyose, etc.) and fructo-oligosaccharides; the final group are the polysaccharides which may be divided into starch (a -glucans) and non-starch polysaccharides of which the major components are the polysaccharides of the plant cell wall such as cellulose, hemicellulose and pectin (2,3,4).

## TOTAL CARBOHYDRATE

Although the individual components of dietary carbohydrate are readily identifiable, there is some confusion as to what comprises total carbohydrate as reported in food tables. Two principal measures of total carbohydrate are used, firstly, that derived by "difference" and secondly the direct measurement of the individual components which are then combined to give a total. Calculating carbohydrates by "difference" has been used since the turn of the century.

The protein, fat, ash and moisture content of a food are determined, subtracted from the total weight of the food and the remainder, or "difference", is considered to be carbohydrate. There are, however, a number of problems with this approach to total carbohydrate analysis in that the "by difference" figure includes a number of non-carbohydrate components such as lignin, organic acids, tannins, waxes, and some Maillard products. In addition to this error, it combines all of the analytical errors from the other analyses. Finally, a single global figure for carbohydrates in food is uninformative because it fails to identify the many types of carbohydrates in a food and thus to allow some understanding of the potential physiological properties of those carbohydrates.

## TERMINLOGY

In deciding how to classify dietary carbohydrate the principal problem is to reconcile the various chemical divisions of carbohydrate with that which reflects physiology and health. A classification based purely on chemistry does not allow a ready translation into nutritional terms since each of the major classes of carbohydrate have a variety of physiological effects.

However, a classification based on physiological properties also creates a number of problems in that it requires a single effect to be considered as overridingly important and to be used as the basis of the classification. This dichotomy has led to the introduction of a number of terms to describe various fractions and sub-fractions of carbohydrate.

### Sugars

The term “sugars” is conventionally used to describe the mono and disaccharides. “Sugar”, by contrast, is used to describe purified sucrose as are the terms “refined sugar” and “added sugar”.

### Extrinsic and Intrinsic Sugars

These terms had their origin in a United Kingdom Department of Health committee in 1989, which was looking at the question of sugars in the diet. The terms were developed to help the consumer choose between what were considered to be healthy sugars and those which were not. Intrinsic sugars were defined as sugars occurring within the cell walls of plants, *i.e.*, naturally occurring, while extrinsic sugars were those which were usually added to foods.

Because lactose in milk is also an extrinsic sugar, an additional phrase “non-milk extrinsic sugars” was developed. These terms have not gained wide acceptance either in the U.K. or other countries in the world. There are no current plans to measure these sugars separately in the diet nor to incorporate their use into food tables.

### Complex Carbohydrates

This term was first used in the McGovern report, “Dietary Goals for the United States” in 1977. The term was coined largely to distinguish sugars from other carbohydrates and in the report denotes “fruit, vegetables and whole-grains”. The term has since come to be used to describe either starch alone, or the combination of all polysaccharides.

It was used to encourage consumption of what were considered to be healthy foods such as whole-grain cereals, etc., but becomes meaningless when used to describe fruit and vegetables which are low in starch. Furthermore, it is now realised that starch, which is by any definition a complex carbohydrate, is variable metabolically with some forms being rapidly absorbed and having a high glycemic index and some being resistant to digestion. The term "complex carbohydrate" has encompassed, at various times, starch, dietary fibre and non-digestible oligosaccharides. As a substitute term for starch, however, it would seem to have little merit and, in principle, it is better to discuss carbohydrate components by using their common chemical names.

**Available and Unavailable Carbohydrate**

A major step forward conceptually in our understanding of carbohydrates was made by McCance and Lawrence in 1929 with the division of dietary carbohydrate into available and unavailable. In an attempt to prepare food tables for diabetic diets they realised that not all carbohydrates could be "utilized and metabolized", *i.e.*, provide the body with "carbohydrates for metabolism". Available carbohydrate was defined as "starch and soluble sugars" and unavailable as "mainly hemicellulose and fibre".

This concept proved useful, not the least because it drew attention to the fact that some carbohydrate is not digested and absorbed in the small intestine but rather reaches the large bowel where it is fermented. It suggests that the site of digestion or fermentation in the gut of carbohydrate is of overriding importance.

However, it is misleading to talk of carbohydrate as "unavailable" because some indigestible carbohydrate is able to provide the body with energy through fermentation.

There are many properties of carbohydrate of which digestibility and fermentability are only two. A more appropriate substitute for the terms "available" and "unavailable" today would be to describe carbohydrates as either as glycemic or non-glycemic, which is closer to the original concept of McCance and Lawrence.

**Resistant Starch**

One of the major developments in our understanding of the importance of carbohydrates for health in the past twenty years has been the discovery of resistant starch. Resistant starch is defined as "starch and starch degradation products not absorbed in the small intestine of healthy humans". The main forms of resistant starch are physically enclosed starch, e.g., within intact cell structures ($RS_1$), some raw starch granules ($RS_2$) and retrograded amylose ($RS_3$).

### Modified Starch

The proportions of amylose and amylopectin in a starchy food is variable and can be altered by plant breeding. Techniques using genetic engineering are rapidly emerging, enabling starches to be produced for specific purposes by genetically modifying the crop used for their production. High amylose corn starch and high amylopectin (waxy) corn starch have been available for a long time, and display quite different functional as well as nutritional properties.

High amylose starches require higher temperatures for gelatinization and are more prone to retrograde and to form amylose-lipid complexes. Such properties can be utilized in the formulation of foods with low glycemic index and/or high resistant starch content. Physical modifications of starches include pregelatinization and partial hydrolysis (dextrinization).

Chemical modification is mainly the introduction of side groups and cross-linking or oxidation. These modifications may be used to decrease viscosity and to improve gel stability, mouthfeel, appearance and texture, and resistance for heat treatment. The application of modified starches as fat replacers is another important area. Some modified starches may be partly resistant to digestion in the small intestine, thereby adding to resistant starch.

### Dietary Fibre

The original description of dietary fibre by Trowell in 1972 was "that portion of food which is derived from cellular walls of plants which is digested very poorly by human beings". This is not an exact description of any carbohydrate in the diet but is more a physiological concept. It was linked by Burkitt and Trowell to the etiology of a number of "Western diseases" and on the basis of this a hypothesis relating fibre to health was developed. The use of the term has, however, caused many difficulties over the years because of controversies regarding definition.

Moreover, the proposal that there are a number of dietary fibre deficiency disorders is an over-simplification and needs to be modified now in the light of new knowledge of diet and disease. The main components of dietary fibre are derived from the cell walls of plant material in the diet and comprise cellulose, hemicellulose and pectin. Lignin, a non-carbohydrate component of the cell wall is also often included.

Dietary fibre is a term which is felt to be valuable for the consumer who looks upon this as a healthy component of the diet. At the present time there is no consensus as to which components of carbohydrate should be included as dietary fibre and different authors have variously included non-starch polysaccharides and resistant starch.

More recently it has been suggested that non-digestible oligosaccharides should also be included. Dietary fibre has also been defined by method. While there is general agreement that the non-starch polysaccharides are the principal part of dietary fibre there is currently no consensus as to whether other components should be included in this term. It has been suggested that the use of the term dietary fibre be gradually phased out. Its widespread use and popularity with the consumer has made this difficult in practice and the term has been useful in nutrition education and product development.

### Soluble and Insoluble Fibre

These terms developed out of the early chemistry of non-starch polysaccharides which showed that the fractional extraction of these polysaccharides could be controlled by changing the pH of solutions.

They proved very useful in the initial understanding of the physiological properties of dietary fibre, allowing a simple division into those which principally had effects on glucose and lipid absorption from the small intestine and those which were slowly and incompletely fermented and had more pronounced effects on bowel habit. However, the separation of soluble and insoluble fractions is not chemically very distinct being dependent on the conditions of extraction. Moreover, the physiological differences are not, in fact, so distinct with much insoluble fibre being rapidly and completely fermented while not all soluble fibre has effects on glucose and lipid absorption.

## METHODOLOGY FOR DIETARY CARBOHYDRATE ANALYSIS

### Mono- and Disaccharides

They can be analysed specifically by enzymatic, gas-liquid chromatography (GLC) or high performance liquid chromatography (HPLC) methods. Depending on the food matrix to be analysed, extraction of the low molecular weight carbohydrates in aqueous ethanol, usually 80 per cent (v/v), may be advisable before analysis. The enzymatic procedures are based on specific, highly purified enzymes and have been instrumental in providing means of specific and precise analysis of individual carbohydrates in mixtures without a large investment in instrumentation.

Enzymatic methods are still preferable when one single carbohydrate is to be analysed, e.g., glucose, as the end point of starch analysis. When several different monosaccharides are to be determined simultaneously, HPLC or GLC methods are preferable. HPLC systems using sensitive amperometric detectors are gaining in popularity over GLC, in that the derivatization necessary before the GLC determination is avoided.

### Polyols

Polyols are usually determined by GLC using alditol acetate derivatives. HPLC methods are also available.

### Oligosaccharides

Oligosaccharides can also be determined by GLC or HPLC methods. These methods work well for purified preparations, but in complex foods or diets, enzymatic hydrolysis and determination of liberated monosaccharides is an alternative for specific determination. Malto-oligosaccharides are recovered as "starch" if not extracted before starch analysis.

### Separation of Oligosaccharides from Polysaccharides

By definition, polysaccharides have 10 or more monomeric units, and Oligosaccharides less than 10. Analytically, separation is based on solubility in aqueous ethanol, usually around 80 per cent (v/v). The alcohol solubility of carbohydrates, however, is dependent not only on the degree of polymerization (DP), but also on the molecular structure. For instance, highly branched carbohydrates may be soluble in 80 per cent ethanol in spite of a DP considerably higher than 10. In practice, therefore, the separation of oligosaccharides from polysaccharides is empirical and does not provide an exact division based on DP.

### Starch

Quantitative analysis of starch in foods by most current methods is based on enzymatic degradation and specific determination of liberated glucose. Nutritionally, starch can be divided into glucogenic ("available") and resistant starch, which is not absorbed in the small intestine. Resistant starch is poorly soluble in water and methods aiming at a total starch analysis employ an initial 2M potassium hydroxide (KOH) or dimethylsulfoxide solvent (DMSO) treatment to disperse crystalline starch fractions that would otherwise remain unhydrolyzed.

Methods for measuring resistant starch are still in their infancy and have not yet been tested in formal collaborative studies. They aim at simulating normal starch digestion in the small intestine. A key step is to mimic the normal disintegration of the food which occurs during chewing. One method uses a standardized milling/homogenization technique, whereas others employ standardized chewing by volunteers (19,20). Both approaches have been evaluated against human ileostomy experiments with a limited number of food matrices.

### Non-starch Polysaccharides (NSP)

*The determination of NSP is based on the following steps*:

- Degradation of starch by enzymatic hydrolysis after solublization,
- Removal of low molecular weight carbohydrates, including starch hydrolysis products,

- Hydrolysis of the NSP to their constituent monomers, and
- Quantitative determination of those monomers.

The acid hydrolysis step is a critical one, and it has to be designed as an optimal balance between complete hydrolysis and destruction of the liberated monomers. The most widely-used method today for specific determination of the liberated monomers is GLC with alditol acetate derivatives. HPLC detection is an alternative gaining in popularity.

Colourimetric determination is still preferred for uronic acids, which are derived mainly from pectic substances. A colourimetric method is also available for total NSP. Fractions of NSP, such as cellulose and non-cellulosic polysaccharides, can be separated by using sequential extraction and hydrolysis methods. For instance, cellulose is not hydrolyzed by dilute (1-2M) sulphuric acid, unless it has first been dispersed in concentrated acid.

**Dietary Fibre**

Three methods for dietary fibre analysis have undergone extensive testing in recent years, including collaborative studies satisfactory enough for official approval of bodies such as the AOAC International and the Bureau Communautaire de Reference of the European Community:

- The enzymatic, gravimetric AOAC methods of Prosky and co-workers, and subsequently Lee and co-workers.
- The enzymatic-chemical methods of Englyst and co-workers.
- The enzymatic-chemical method of Theander and co-workers (the Uppsala method).

The enzymatic-gravimetric AOAC methods are derived from methods aiming at simulating the digestion in the human small intestine to isolate an undigested residue as a measure of dietary fibre. This residue is corrected for associated ash and protein. Since no DMSO or KOH dispersion is used, starch that resists the amylases used in the assay will remain as a fibre component. Since the sample has to be milled, and since a heat-stable amylase (termamyl) is used at a temperature close to 100°C, physically enclosed starch ($RS_1$) and resistant starch granules ($RS_2$) will not be included.

Retrograded amylose ($RS_3$) that is included is the main form of resistant starch in processed foods. Lignin, a non-carbohydrate component of the dietary fibre complex is also included, as well as some tannins. These components are a very small proportion of most foods but can be substantial in some unconventional raw materials or special "fibre" preparations. The Englyst method measures the NSP specifically, either as individual monomeric components by GLC or colourimetrically as reducing substances. Accordingly, DMSO is used initially to ensure a complete removal of starch, and lignin is not determined. The difference between estimates with the gravimetric methods and the Englyst method is mainly due to resistant starch and lignin. The Uppsala method employs hydrolysis conditions and GLC determination of monomers in a similar way as in the Englyst method. However, DMSO is not employed for starch dispersion, and a gravimetric estimate of lignin is added to obtain the dietary fibre. The Uppsala method and the gravimetric AOAC methods give very concordant results.

## LABELLING

*Food labelling has two main aims*: to inform the consumer of the composition of the food and to assist them in the selection of a healthy diet. These two aims are not always easy to reconcile because the health benefit of different carbohydrate-containing foods cannot readily be communicated simply from a description of their composition. Labelling should be based on the chemical classification.

Analytical methods should be clearly defined and validated. The principal information should be total carbohydrate, measured as the sum of the individual components. Further information on carbohydrate composition could include terms such as sugars, starch and non-starch polysaccharides. Other terms, such as non-digestible oligosaccharides, polyols, resistant starch and dietary fibre may be used, provided the components included in these terms are clearly defined.

## AVAILABILITY AND CONSUMPTION

*Trends in the supply and intake of carbohydrates can be studied by four principal approaches*:

1. Production.
2. Food balance sheets.
3. Household surveys.
4. Individual assessments.

Food production statistics, which are available from FAO for every country in the world and for every crop, are useful for examining trends in consumption

*From these data it can be seen that the major sources of carbohydrate in the human diet are*:

- Cereals.
- Root crops.
- Sugar crops.
- Pulses.
- Vegetables.
- Fruit.
- Milk products.

**Sustainability**

Trends over the last 20-30 years indicate growth in world production of cereals, sugarcane, vegetables and fruit. On the other hand, production of root crops, pulses and sugar beet has changed little on a world basis. Marked decreases have actually been seen in pulse production in some countries in Asia, and in root crop production in Europe. This suggests a change in food preference away from roots and pulses and towards cereals.

Examination of eating habits in a number of countries indicates that this is the case. Since root crops are an excellent source of carbohydrate, there is concern about this downward trend in production.

Populations continue to grow in most parts of the world and, overall, food production would seem to be keeping pace with population growth. Increased production is due to improved agricultural ractices rather than increased crop area, the major reason for increases being greater use of fertilizer.

There are, however, specific countries where this is not happening. For the entire continent of Africa, cereal production is inadequate.

A major question is how much more improvement and efficiency in production can be achieved, and whether the amount of carbohydrate will be sufficient for the world's population in the future. Projections for future growth suggest problems ahead, particularly in Africa.

**Changing Patterns of Consumption**

Both food balance information and results from individual assessments are used to determine carbohydrate intakes. Food balance data is intended to describe food available for consumption. It is unlikely to do so because it does not include home production, which is variable from country to country, and may be considerable in some developing countries. As a reflection of food consumed, food balance data is questionable, since it does not include food wasted or spoiled, or used for purposes other than human food, the proportion of which may change from year to year.

As a result, food balance data for individual countries has failed to demonstrate the changes in consumption of carbohydrates which are seen using individual surveys. Data from individual surveys also have limitations. Surveys are carried out by a variety of methodologies. While each has advantages and disadvantages, all suffer from a degree of underreporting. This can be intentional or involuntary, most likely due to individuals forgetting food items or not describing foods thought to be undesirable. There is also the failure to record data or the altering of actual diets.

The difference, then, between food balance data and individual assessments, for energy and nutrient intakes, is not only the form of wastage and spoilage on the food balance side of the equation, but also the under-reporting on the individual intake side. True food intakes therefore lie somewhere between food balance and individual intake estimates.

Another major problem is the varied carbohydrate terminology used in different countries. Many countries express total carbohydrate "by difference", rather than as carbohydrate analysed directly, and this results in overestimates of the per cent energy derived from carbohydrate. There is also a great variety in terms used to describe simple sugars, such as "sugars", "sugar", "refined sugar", "added sugar", "sucrose", and "sugars minus lactose". Often there is no description of what is being reported. There is a need to standardize the terminology for carbohydrate and its components in individual surveys and a need for consistency in both reporting and the description of the terms used. In spite of terminology difficulties, it is possible to gain a picture of carbohydrate intakes and trends.

As a per cent of energy, total carbohydrate ranges from about 40 per cent to over 80 per cent, with the developed countries, such as those in North America, Western Europe and Australia at the low end of the range, and developing countries in Asia and Africa at the high end. Starch accounts for 20 per cent-50 per cent or more of energy where the total carbohydrate intake is in the high range. Sugars account for 9 per cent-27 per cent of energy intake; where total carbohydrate is high, sugar intake is generally low. Where data are available, intake of carbohydrate as a per cent of energy is higher for children than for adults.

Trends in consumption indicate a falling carbohydrate intake in developed countries until the last two decades. During that time some increase has been noted as fat intakes fall. The major sources of carbohydrate are cereals, representing over 50 per cent of all carbohydrate consumed in both developed and developing countries, with sugar crops the next major source, followed by root crops, fruits, vegetables, pulses and milk products. In some of the developing countries much of the carbohydrate is derived from a single food source such as rice, cassava or maize. Carbohydrate foods are an important vehicle for protein, micronutrients and other food components, like phytochemicals, which have important benefits for health. Individual food sources vary, however, in the provision of these components.

A single food source of carbohydrate is therefore undesirable and populations whose diets are primarily based on a single food can suffer from micronutrient deficiencies due to lack of variety. It is important, therefore, that a number of different carbohydrate sources be consumed and efforts should be made to encourage a wide variety of carbohydrate foods. Data on intake of sources of sugars is only available for developed countries. These data show similar proportions of sugars are derived from cereal products, milk products and beverages, among these countries. There is some variation in the proportions derived from fruit and confectionery, with the U.K. consuming less fruit and higher amounts of confectionery than countries such as the United States and Australia.

Intakes of non-starch polysaccharides range from about 19gm./day in some countries in Europe and North America, to nearly 30gm./day in rural Africa. Cereals are again the major source of this component. Data on intake of dietary fibre, determined by methods such as that of the AOAC and the older Southgate method are about 15-20 gm./day for North America, Europe and Australia, to 25-40 gm./day for countries in Asia and Africa.

## PHYSIOLOGY

*Carbohydrates have a wide range of physiological effects which may be important to health, such as*:

- Provision of energy.
- Effects on satiety/gastric emptying.
- Control of blood glucose and insulin metabolism.
- Protein glycosylation.
- Cholesterol and triglyceride metabolism.
- Bile acid dehydroxylation.
- Fermentation.
- Hydrogen/methane production.
- Short-chain fatty acids production.
- Control of colonic epithelial cell function.
- Bowel habit/laxation/motor activity.
- Effects on large bowel microflora.

### Carbohydrate as an Energy Source

Dietary carbohydrates have by convention been given an energy value of 4 kcal/gm. (17 kJ/gm), although where carbohydrates are expressed as monosaccharides, the value of 3.75 kcal/gm. (15.7 kJ/gm.) is used. It is now clear, however, that a number of carbohydrates are only partly or not at all digested in the small intestine and are fermented in the large bowel to short chain fatty acids. These include the non-digestible oligosaccharides, resistant starch and non-starch polysaccharides. The process of fermentation is metabolically less efficient than absorption in the small intestine and these carbohydrates provide the body with less energy. In light of a new understanding of the digestion and metabolism of carbohydrate and developments in methodology, the energy value of all carbohydrates in the diet should be reassessed and more accurate energy factors assigned to each group or sub-group. There are a number of potential approaches to accomplish this.

These include the classic calorimetry experiments similar to those first undertaken by Atwater, as well as human balance studies and ileostomy recovery experiments. Knowledge of the chemistry of individual carbohydrates allows a prediction to be made regarding their digestion or fermentation, and an energy value to be assigned. In vitro models of fermentation can be constructed and from these the fermentation stoichiometry can be deduced. Studies using stable isotope tracer techniques may also be of value. While the energy yield of carbohydrate delivered to the colon will vary according to the extent of colonic fermentation (or the assumptions made in the model used), there may be an argument for assigning a single energy value to all such carbohydrate. Published studies suggest that a caloric value of about 2 kcal/ gm. (8 kJ/gm.) would be a reasonable average figure for carbohydrate which reaches the colon. While individual carbohydrates will have different values, in the range of 1-2 kcal/gm., these differences are unlikely to be of importance to health.

## Satiety

The possibility of controlling hunger, satiety and food intake by altering the type of carbohydrate in food has intrigued a number of investigators. At present the variability of the findings and the lack of understanding of a clear relationship to physiologic parametres thought to be involved in the regulation of food intake limit practical application of this approach. It is unlikely that controlling a single dietary component, such as the type of sugar or starch, will lead to significant changes in the amount of food consumed. Also, compensation for small dietary changes made in one meal may often be seen at a subsequent meal. A better approach to controlling hunger and increasing satiety is likely to be associated with changes in the composition of the total diet.

## Glucose and Insulin

The digestion of dietary carbohydrates starts in the mouth, where salivary a-amylase initiates starch degradation. The starch fragments thus formed include maltose, some glucose and dextrins containing the 1,6-a -glycosidic branching points of amylopectin. The a-amylase degradation of starch is completed by the pancreatic amylase active in the small intestine. Dietary disaccharides, as well as degradation products of starch, need to be broken down to monosaccharides in order to be absorbed. This final hydrolysis is accomplished by hydrolases attached to the intestinal brush-border membrane, referred to as "disaccharidases". Disaccharidase deficiencies occur as rare genetic defects, causing malabsorption and intolerance of the corresponding disaccharide. Glucose and galactose are transported actively against a concentration gradient into the intestinal mucosal cells by a sodium dependent transporter. Fructose undergoes facilitated transport by another mechanism.

Fructose taken together with other sugars is better absorbed than fructose alone. When delivered to the circulation, the absorbed carbohydrates cause an elevation of the blood glucose concentration. Fructose and galactose have to be converted to glucose mainly in the liver and therefore produce less pronounced blood glucose elevation. The extent and duration of the blood glucose rise after a meal is dependent upon the rate of absorption, which in turn depends upon factors such as gastric emptying as well as the rate of hydrolysis and diffusion of hydrolysis products in the small intestine. Insulin is secreted as a response to blood glucose elevation but is modified by many neural and endocrine stimuli. Insulin secretion is also influenced by food related factors, especially by the amount and the amino acid composition of dietary proteins. Insulin has important regulatory functions in both carbohydrate and lipid metabolism and is necessary for glucose uptake by most body cells.

**Lactose**

Lactose, a b -linked disaccharide of glucose and galactose, is the principal sugar in milk. At birth, lactase activity is high in the brush-border of the small bowel of infants, but declines after weaning so that most populations of the world have low activity in adult life.

The exceptions are Caucasian peoples and some other population groups in whom the majority retain a high lactase activity throughout life. During the years since 1980, there has been a major change in the way lactose absorption is viewed and a resultant shift away from the concept that lactose "malabsorption" is a pathological state. Low mucosal lactase activity in adults is the norm throughout most of the world. However, such a state usually allows the drinking of modest quantities of milk spaced throughout the day without adverse symptoms. Milk consumption is therefore now being encouraged in many areas of the world because of its value as a source of protein, calcium and riboflavin.

Fermented milk products, which have lower lactose content and contain enzymes and microorganisms that can assist in lactose digestion, are better tolerated than milk. Technology exists to reduce the lactose level in foods and this should be taken into consideration when milk is included as food aid. Cheese, however, has almost no lactose.

Lactose which is not digested, passes into the colon where it is fermented. In some individuals this causes lactose intolerance, the term used to describe the clinical symptoms of abdominal discomfort, flatulence and diarrhoea, associated with the ingestion of lactose containing foods by persons with low lactase activity.

It also occurs as a transient phenomenon when the intestinal mucosa is injured following acute infection in children and in protein-energy malnutrition.

It is also found in adults, particularly in association with coeliac disease and tropical sprue. In these conditions, lactose malabsorption is said to be "secondary" to intestinal mucosal disease. A small proportion of the Caucasian population also exhibits low lactase activity and lactose intolerance.

**Protein Glycosylation**

The non-enzymatic glycation of proteins is dependent on the concentration of glucose and fructose in blood and the half-life of the protein. The initial reaction is between the monosaccharide and the amino group of an amino acid, usually lysine, to form a Shiff base which undergoes rearrangement and formation of Amadori products.

As the reaction progresses, increasingly complex Maillard products are formed with the eventual production of Advanced Glycation End-products or AGEs which are associated with irreversible loss of protein function. The extent of glycation of specific proteins, such as Haemoglobin Ale in diabetics serves as an indication of medium term control of blood glucose.

Examples of functional changes induced by glycation include lens proteins in the eye with resultant cataract formation, increased microvascular complications, abnormal fibrin network formation and impaired fibrinolysis. These changes are most clearly seen in diabetic patients.

**Lipids and Bile Acids**

There has been concern that a substantial increase in carbohydrate-containing food at the expense of fat, might result in a decrease in high-density lipoprotein and a corresponding increase in very low-density lipoprotein and triglycerides in the blood. However, there is no evidence that this happens when the increase in carbohydrates occurs as a result of increased consumption of vegetables, fruits and appropriately processed cereals over prolonged periods.

Polysaccharides like oat b-glucan, guar gum and those from psyllium have been repeatedly shown to lower serum cholesterol levels in those with elevated levels, with little change if serum levels are normal. Proposed mechanisms include impaired bile acid and cholesterol reabsorption through physical entrapment in the small intestine, or inhibitory effects on cholesterol synthesis by products of lower bowel fermentation, particularly propionic acid. Not all fermentable polysaccharides are effective, however, and recent studies have indicated that neither oligosaccharides nor resistant starch have a significant effect on serum lipids in young normolipidemic subjects.

**Fermentation**

Fermentation is the colonic phase of the digestive process and describes the breakdown in the large intestine of carbohydrates not digested and absorbed in the upper gut. This process involves gut microflora and is unique to the colon of humans because it occurs without the availability of oxygen. It thus results in the formation of the gases hydrogen, methane and carbon dioxide, as well as short chain fatty acids (SCFA) (acetate, propionate and butyrate), and stimulates bacterial growth (biomass).

The gases are either absorbed and excreted in breath, or passed out via the rectum. The major products of such fermentation are the SCFA which are rapidly absorbed and metabolized by the body. Acetate passes primarily into the blood and is taken up by liver, muscle and other tissues. Propionate is a major glucose precursor in ruminant animals such as the cow and sheep, but this is not an important pathway in humans.

Butyrate is metabolized primarily by colonocytes and has been shown to regulate cell growth, and to induce differentiation and apoptosis.

**Bowel Habit**

It has long been known that non-starch polysaccharides are the principal dietary component affecting laxation. This occurs through increases in bowel content bulk and a speeding up of intestinal transit time. The extent of the effect depends on the chemical and physical nature of the polysaccharides and the extent to which they are fermented in the colon. Fermentable polysaccharides stimulate increases in microbial biomass in the colon, resulting in some increase in fecal weight, but not to the extent of non-fermentable polysaccharides.

The latter are not significantly degraded in the colon and become consituents of the stool. In so doing, they hold water and produce a marked increase in fecal weight. Similarly, resistant starch can increase fecal weight, but this again depends on the extent of fermentation.

**Microflora**

Carbohydrate which is fermented stimulates the growth of bacteria in the large gut. This is a generalized effect which leads to an increase in the total number of bacteria or biomass. When bacterial growth occurs, thc microflora synthesize protein actively from preformed amino acids and peptides as well as some de-novo synthesis using ammonia as the source of nitrogen. The additional biomass is excreted in faeces and is one of the mechanisms whereby carbohydrate influences bowel habit. The increased biomass excretion is accompanied by increased nitrogen excretion. The efficiency of conversion of carbohydrate to biomass is determined principally by the type of substrate, the rate of breakdown and the transit time through the large intestine. One of the more significant developments in recent years with regard to the gut microflora has been the demonstration that specific dietary carbohydrates selectively stimulate the growth of individual groups or species of bacteria.

An example of this is the effect of fructo-oligosaccharides on the growth of bifidobacteria. The importance of bifidobacteria is that they may be one of the major contributors to colonization resistance in the colon, thereby protecting the host from invasion by pathogenic species. Foods which selectively stimulate the growth of gut bacteria are known as pre-biotics.

## THE ROLE OF CARBOHYDRATES IN MAINTENANCE OF HEALTH

### CARBOHYDRATES IN THE DIET

While the amount of carbohydrate required to avoid ketosis is very small carbohydrate provides the majority of energy in the diets of most people. There are many reasons why this is desirable. In addition to providing easily available energy for oxidative metabolism, carbohydrate-containing foods are vehicles for important micronutrients and phytochemicals.

Dietary carbohydrate is important to maintain glycemic homeostasis and for gastrointestinal integrity and function. Unlike fat and protein, high levels of dietary carbohydrate, provided it is obtained from a variety of sources, is not associated with adverse health effects. Finally, diets high in carbohydrate as compared to those high in fat, reduce the likelihood of developing obesity and its co-morbid conditions. An optimum diet should consist of at least 55 per cent of total energy coming from carbohydrate obtained from a variety of food sources.

The consultation agreed that when carbohydrate consumption levels are at or above 75 per cent of total energy there could be significant adverse effects on nutritional status by the exclusion of adequate quantities of protein, fat and other essential nutrients. In arriving at its recommendation of a minimum of 55 per cent of total energy from carbohydrate, the consultation realised that a significant percentage of total energy needs to be provided by protein and fat, but that their contribution to total energy intakes will vary from one country to another on the basis of food consumption patterns and food availability.

### ENERGY BALANCE

In adults, it is important that the amount of energy ingested be matched to the amount of energy expended. Maintenance of energy balance is important in order to avoid obesity and its associated co-morbidities such as diabetes and cardiovascular disease. Positive energy balance and obesity occur when total energy intake exceeds total energy expenditure, regardless of composition of the excess energy. However, the composition of the diet can affect whether and to what extent positive energy balance occurs. The composition of the diet can also affect the ability to maintain energy balance. In particular, diets containing at least 55 per cent of energy from a variety of carbohydrate sources, as compared to high fat diets, reduce the likelihood that body fat accumulation will occur. Substantial data suggest that diets high in fat content tend to promote consumption of more total energy than diets high in carbohydrates.

This effect may be due to the low energy density of high carbohydrate diets, since total volume of food consumed appears to provide an important satiety cue. There are no data to suggest that different types of carbohydrates differentially affect total energy intake. In addition to affecting the chance of having excess energy available, the composition of the diet also affects the proportion of excess energy that will be stored as body fat.

The body has a large fat storage capacity and excess dietary fat is stored very efficiently in adipose tissue. Alternatively, the body's capacity to store carbohydrate is limited and excess carbohydrate is not efficiently stored as body fat. Instead, excess carbohydrate tends to be oxidized, leading to indirect fat accumulation via reductions in fat oxidation. Excess fat and carbohydrate were previously thought to be equally fattening. This was due to the assumption that *de novo* lipogenesis was a commonly used pathway for disposal of excess carbohydrate.

The available data suggest, however, that this process occurs rarely in human subjects and only in situations of appreciable carbohydrate overfeeding. In most usual circumstances, accumulation of body fat via de novo lipogenesis is quantitatively very low. While noting the low overall contribution of *de novo* lipogenesis to body fat accumulation, it should be noted that *de novo* lipogenesis is increased with insulin resistance and with extremely high consumption of sucrose or fructose.

## PHYSICAL ACTIVITY

Maintenance of energy balance is dependent both on energy intake and energy expenditure. Maintaining regular physical activity greatly reduces the likelihood of creating positive energy balance, regardless of the composition of the diet. There is agreement that the combination of a high carbohydrate diet and regular physical activity is the optimal arrangement to avoid positive energy balance and obesity.

The increased energy needs of physical activity can be supplied by carbohydrate or fat. The importance of carbohydrate in the diet becomes more critical as the amount and intensity of physical activity increases. In many developing countries, the major challenge is to meet daily energy needs created by high levels of daily physical labour. In such cases, any combination of carbohydrate and fat which provides sufficient energy is to be encouraged. Many countries recommend increasing leisure time physical activity. While increased physical activity would clearly increase energy needs, these do not create needs for specific macronutrients.

Rather, the optimum diet identified is considered sufficient to provide for such physical activity. There is substantial evidence that supplemental carbohydrate can improve performance for the elite endurance-trained athlete. A high carbohydrate diet during a few days preceding an endurance event, carbohydrate loading, a high carbohydrate pre-event meal and carbohydrate supplementation in the form of carbohydrate-containing beverages have all been shown to enhance performance during long-distance cycling and running.

There is, however, no evidence that such carbohydrate supplementation would improve performance for the majority of people who engage in recreational physical activity of lower intensity and duration. On the other hand, carbohydrate intake following exercise can help to quickly replenish depleted glycogen stores.

## CARBOHYDRATE AND BEHAVIOUR

It has been suggested that food intake could have important effects on behaviour. While providing breakfast to children who do not typically eat breakfast can increase cognitive performance, it is less clear that the overall composition of the diet can affect behaviour. It has been suggested that sugar consumption leads to hyperactivity in children. However, an extensive review of the literature in this area concluded that there is no evidence to support the claim that refined sugar intake has any significant influence on either behaviour or cognitive performance in children. Because glucose is an essential fuel for the central nervous system, carbohydrate has also been suggested to play a role in memory and cognitive function. While there appears to be a relationship between glucose levels and memory processing, the clinical significance of this relationship remains unclear.

## CARBOHYDRATE THROUGH THE LIFE CYCLE

Energy and nutrient needs are increased in pregnancy and lactation, and the primary challenge for pregnant women is to meet these increased energy needs in order to ensure healthy offspring. It has been observed that where variety in the food supply is low and carbohydrate intake is high, a low birth weight is more common.

This raises concerns about the adequacy of high carbohydrate diets to meet the energy and nutrient needs of pregnancy when food variety is limited. Energy and nutrient needs should be met by consumption of a wide variety of carbohydrate foods. There is also some concern about excessive fat intake in pregnancy since it may be associated with risk of obesity in the mother. In many countries, infants receive 45-55 per cent of energy from fat through breastmilk or formulas and 35-45 per cent of energy from carbohydrate. While specific reductions in fat intake are not recommended below the age of two years, infants in many countries consume lower fat diets. This does not present a problem as long as energy requirements are fulfilled.

From the age of two and on, the optimum diet should be gradually introduced. During the first four to six months of life, exclusive breast feeding is recommended as this tailors the concentration of lactose to the maturing neonatal and infant gut, particularly while colonic microflora and pancreatic amylase production are developing.

For infants fed on formula, the carbohydrate and other nutrient components should usually mimic breastmilk to the extent possible and in accordance with standards of the Codex Alimentarius.

Carbohydrate digestion in the neonate and young infant is significantly influenced by both gastrointestinal maturation and the chemical nature of the carbohydrate ingested.

The establishment of colonic microflora is responsible for colonic carbohydrate scavenging, converting any carbohydrate entering the colon into short chain fatty acids. Any disturbances or inappropriate development of this microflora (incorrect infant formula, antibiotics, infection) leads to colonic carbohydrate overloading and diarrhoea.

Lactose from dairy products can be a major source of carbohydrate for young children. In addition, milk represents an excellent source of high quality protein, calcium, and riboflavin. In most populations, even those with low lactase activity, milk can be ingested in small amounts, especially after meals with dilution by co-ingestion.

Fermented dairy products can be valuable items in the diet of most people irrespective of intestinal lactase status. Often the transition from childhood to adulthood is associated with changes in dietary pattern. In developing countries, children frequently consume very high carbohydrate intakes from a single or a small number of sources, while adults have greater variety. In such cases, the adult diet is preferred. In developed countries, on the other hand, surveys indicate that children have higher intakes of carbohydrate from more sources than adults.

In those countries, the diet consumed by children would seem to be more beneficial. In both situations, at least 55 per cent of carbohydrate energy from a variety of sources is the optimum. Individualization of carbohydrate intake is necessary for elderly populations. Elderly individuals in many countries are at risk as regards both malnutrition and obesity.

Food intake patterns can be altered by changes in taste perception, chronic disease and medication use.

While a high carbohydrate diet is recommended for prevention of weight gain and obesity, it should be recognized that some individuals may need diets higher in energy density (e.g., fats) in order to prevent malnutrition. Optimizing intake of carbohydrate to minimize glucose intolerance in later life is a consideration in countries where such intolerance is a problem.

## DIETARY CARBOHYDRATE AND DISEASE

Carbohydrates may directly influence human diseases by affecting physiological and metabolic processes, thereby reducing risk factors for the disease or the disease process itself. Carbohydrates may also have indirect effects on diseases, for example, by displacing other nutrients or facilitating increased intakes of a wide range of other substances frequently found in carbohydrate-containing foods. Evidence of associations between carbohydrates and diseases comes from epidemiological and clinical studies.

There are relatively few examples in which direct causal links between carbohydrates and diseases have been proven. Thus the nutrient-disease or food-disease associations discussed must be considered in terms of the strength of evidence from a range of observational studies and clinical experiments and the existence of plausible hypotheses.

### OBESITY

The frequency of obesity has increased dramatically in many developed and developing countries. This is of profound public health importance because of the clearly defined negative effect of obesity, especially when centrally distributed, in relation to diabetes, coronary heart disease and other chronic diseases of lifestyle. Genetic and environmental factors play a role in determining the propensity for obesity in populations and individuals. Lack of physical activity is believed to contribute to the increasing rates of obesity observed in many countries and may be a factor in whether an individual who is at risk will become overweight or obese.

High carbohydrate foods promote satiety in the short term. As fat is stored more efficiently than excess carbohydrate, use of high carbohydrate foods is likely to reduce the risk of obesity in the long term. Much controversy surrounds the extent to which sugars and starch promote obesity. There is no direct evidence to implicate either of these groups of carbohydrates in the etiology of obesity, based on data derived from studies in affluent societies. Nevertheless, it is important to reiterate that excess energy in any form will promote body fat accumulation and that excess consumption of low fat foods, while not as obesity-producing as excess consumption of high fat products, will lead to obesity if energy expenditure is not increased. While high carbohydrate diets may help reduce the risk of obesity by preventing overconsumption of energy, there is no evidence to suggest that the macronutrient composition of a low energy diet influences the rate and extent of weight loss in the treatment of obese patients.

### NON-INSULIN DEPENDENT DIABETES MELLITUS (NIDDM)

High rates of NIDDM in all population groups are associated with rapid cultural changes in populations previously consuming traditional diets, and also with increasing obesity, especially when centrally distributed. Although the precise mode of inheritance has not been established, there is no doubt that genetic factors are involved. Certain populations appear to have a strong predisposition to the development of NIDDM to the extent that in some groups about half the adult population have the disease. Within all populations a family history of NIDDM is an important predisposing factor.

Diet and lifestyle-related conditions which may lead to obesity will clearly influence the risk of developing NIDDM in populations and individuals who are susceptible to this condition. Foods rich in non-starch polysaccharides and carbohydrate-containing foods with a low glycemic index appear to protect against diabetes, the effect being independent of body mass index.

In terms of disease prevention, it is not possible on the basis of current data to distinguish the relative merits of different types of non-starch polysaccharides. Some epidemiological evidence suggests particular benefit of appropriately processed cereal foods, while other epidemiological and clinical studies suggest benefits of non-starch polysaccharide from legumes and pectin-rich foods.

Thus, avoiding obesity and increasing intakes of a wide range of foods rich in non-starch polysaccharide and carbohydrate-containing foods with a low glycemic index offers the best means of reducing the rapidly increasing rates of NIDDM in many countries. Consuming a wide range of carbohydrate foods is now regarded as acceptable in the nutritional management of people who have already developed NIDDM. It has been suggested that between 60 and 70 per cent of total energy should be derived from a mix of mono-unsaturated fatty acids and carbohydrates. Carbohydrates should principally be derived from a wide range of appropriately processed cereals, vegetables and fruit, with particular emphasis on those foods which have a low glycemic index.

The goal to achieve and maintain ideal body weight remains paramount, ensuring that foods high in fat which might predispose to obesity are not encouraged, even though they might have a low glycemic index. Sucrose and other sugars have not been directly implicated in the etiology of diabetes and recommendations concerning intake relate primarily to the avoidance of all energy-dense foods in order to reduce obesity.

*Most recommendations for the management of diabetes permit modest (30-50 gm./day) intakes of sucrose and other added sugars in the diabetic dietary prescription provided these are*:

- Consumed within the context of total energy allowance;
- Nutrient-dense foods and foods rich in non-starch polysaccharides are not displaced; and,
- They are incorporated as part of a mixed meal.

In some populations where fat intake is relatively low and sucrose intake high, a reduced intake of sucrose may be considered in the diabetic dietary prescription. Increased meal frequency under iso-energetic conditions does not, in the long term, appear to be associated with any alteration in glycemic control. This suggests that personal preference is the key determinant of meal frequency, provided that body weight and daily (as well as long-term) glycemic control are not adversely influenced. Special diabetic food products are not generally recommended and fructose is not regarded as having any particular merits as a sweetener when compared with other added sugars.

However, low-energy beverages containing alternative non-nutritive sweeteners may be useful for people with diabetes. Dietary factors have not been conclusively shown to be risk factors for insulin-dependent diabetes and the key advice concerning carbohydrates in the management of this condition concerns distribution of intake of carbohydrates during the day. Carbohydrate intake needs to be regularly distributed and balanced with injected insulin. The general principles of the diabetic dietary approach to non-insulin dependent diabetes may also be applied to those with insulin-dependent diabetes.

## CARDIOVASCULAR DISEASE

Many genetic and lifestyle factors are involved in the etiology of coronary heart disease and influence both the atherosclerotic and thrombotic processes underlying the clinical manifestations of this disease. Dietary factors may influence these processes directly or via a range of cardiovascular disease risk factors. Obesity, particularly when centrally distributed, is associated with an appreciable increase in the risk of coronary heart disease. There is also evidence implicating specific nutrients and, in particular, high intakes of some saturated fatty acids appear to be important promoters of coronary heart disease.

On the other hand, there is increasing evidence of a strong protective effect by a range of antioxidant nutrients. Increasing carbohydrate intake can assist in the reduction of saturated fat and many fruits and vegetables rich in carbohydrates are also rich in several antioxidants. Cereal foods rich in non-starch polysaccharides have been shown to be protective against coronary heart disease in a series of prospective studies.

There is no evidence for a causal role of sucrose in the etiology of coronary heart disease. The cornerstone of dietary advice aimed at reducing coronary heart disease risk is to increase the intake of carbohydrate-rich foods, especially cereals, vegetables and fruits rich in non-starch polysaccharide, at the expense of fat. Among those who are overweight or obese it is more important to reduce total fat intake and to encourage the consumption of the most appropriate carbohydrate-containing foods.

There has been concern that a substantial increase in carbohydrate-containing food at the expense of fat, might result in a decrease in high-density lipoprotein and an increase in very low-density lipoprotein and triglycerides in the blood. There is, however, no evidence that this occurs when the increase in carbohydrates results from increased consumption of vegetables, fruits and appropriately processed cereals, over prolonged periods.

Certain non-starch polysaccharides (for example b-glucans) have been shown to have an appreciable effect in lowering serum cholesterol when consumed in naturally occurring foods, or foods which have been enriched by purified forms, or even when fed as dietary supplements. Such polysaccharides may be used in the management of patients with existing hypercholesterolemia but their role, if any, in the prevention of coronary heart disease remains to be established.

Less information is available concerning the role of carbohydrates in other cardiovascular diseases. Plant foods are good sources of potassium and reducing the sodium to potassium ratio may help to reduce the risk of hypertension. Limited data suggest a protective effect of vegetables and fruit in cerebrovascular disease. There has been considerable debate in many developed countries which have high rates of coronary heart disease regarding the age at which children should start to reduce fat intake towards the recommended level for adults.

Clearly children require an adequate intake of energy for growth, and it is important that this does not include an excessive intake of carbohydrates at a very young age. It is generally accepted that dietary carbohydrate should gradually be increased and fat reduced after the age of two years, so that by the age of five years children should have reached a diet in the range of that recommended for adults.

This advice should, of course, include the key dietary guidelines for children and adolescents, which suggest that nutritional adequacy should be achieved by eating a wide variety of foods and that energy intake should be adequate to promote growth and development, and to reach and maintain desirable body weight.

## CANCER

Diet is widely regarded as important in the etiology of colorectal cancer with meat and fat considered the primary risk factors, and fruit, vegetable and cereal foods considered to be protective. Cancer is a disease associated with well-recognized genetic abnormalities and for colorectal cancer in particular, defects in a number of genes have been clearly defined. These genes mostly code for proteins responsible for the control of either cell growth, cell-to-cell communication or DNA repair. They are mainly oncogenes or tumour suppressor genes.

For the development of colorectal cancer an individual must acquire several of these genetic abnormalities in the same cell. The acquisition of gene defects in somatic cells is thought to be through DNA damage and a resultant failure of the DNA repair system (or of apoptosis). Dietary carbohydrate is thought to be protective through mechanisms involving arrest of cell growth, differentiation and selection of damaged cells for cell death (apoptosis).

This is probably achieved primarily through the action of butyric acid which is formed in the colon from fermentation of carbohydrates such as resistant starch and non-starch polysaccharides. Such carbohydrates are found mostly in cereals, fruit and vegetables.

*The process of fermentation may protect the colorectal area against the genetic damage that leads to colorectal cancer through other mechanisms which include*:

- The dilution of potential carcinogens;
- The reduction of products of protein fermentation through stimulation of bacterial growth;
- pH effects;
- Maintenance of the gut mucosal barrier; and,
- Effects on bile acid degradation.

These mechanisms, however, are much less well-established. Carbohydrate staple foods are a source of phytoestrogens which may be protective for breast cancer. Cancer risk is increased for the obese. This applies especially to cancers of the breast and uterus. However, this is a general effect of total energy intake and not specifically of carbohydrates.

Dietary carbohydrates do not have a known role in the etiology of lung, breast, stomach, prostate, pancreas, oesophagus, liver or cervical cancers. There is, however, some evidence that there is an increased risk of ovarian cancer in women with mild galactosemia.

## GASTROINTESTINAL DISEASES OTHER THAN CANCER

Intakes of non-starch polysaccharides and resistant starch are the most important contributors to stool weight. Therefore, increasing consumption of foods rich in these carbohydrates is a very effective means of preventing and treating constipation, as well as haemorrhoids and anal fissures. Bran and other cereal sources containing non-starch polysaccharide also appear to protect against diverticular disease and have an important role in the treatment of this condition. Obesity is an important risk factor for gallstones. High intakes of carbohydrate may facilitate the colonization of bifidobacteria and lactobacilli in the gut and thus reduce the risk of acute infective gastrointestinal illnesses.

### 50gm. Carbohydrate Portion

The portion of food tested should contain 50gm. of glycemic (available) carbohydrate. In practice, glycemic carbohydrate is often measured as total carbohydrate minus dietary fibre, as determined by the AOAC method. Since this method does not include RS 1 and RS2 when they are present, they will be mistakenly included as glycemic carbohydrate.

**Blood Glucose Response**

This is normally measured in capillary whole blood. Plasma glucose can be used to determine the glycemic index and gives similar values.

However, capillary blood is preferred because it is easier to obtain, the rise in blood glucose is greater than in venous plasma and the results for capillary blood glucose are less variable than those for venous plasma glucose. Thus, differences between foods are larger and easier to detect statistically using capillary blood glucose. An illustration of the difference between glucose as measured in simultaneously-obtained venous plasma and capillary whole blood is shown in Table 2.

**Table. Glucose Response from Capillary Blood and Venous Plasma**

| | 0 min | 15 min | 30 min | 45 min | 60 min | 90 min | 120 min | IAUC |
|---|---|---|---|---|---|---|---|---|
| Capillary blood | 4.1 | 6.3 | 9.0 | 8.7 | 6.7 | 5.7 | 3.9 | 279 |
| Venous plasma | 5.0 | 7.1 | 8.8 | 8.0 | 5.6 | 5.4 | 4.2 | 155 |

**Standard Food**

Either white bread or glucose can be used as the standard food. The GI values obtained if white bread is used are about 1.4 times those obtained if glucose is the standard food. Other standard foods could be used, but to enable comparison with data in the literature, the GI of the new standard food relative to standardized white bread or glucose should be established.

## FACTORS INFLUENCING THE BLOOD GLUCOSE RESPONSES OF FOODS

Starchy foods with a low GI are digested and absorbed more slowly than foods with a high GI. Some factors that influence glycemic properties of foods are listed in Table 3.

**Table. Food Factors Influencing Glycemic Responses**

| Amount of carbohydrate |
|---|

- *Nature of the monosaccharide components*:
  - Glucose
  - Fructose
  - Galactose
- *Nature of the starch*:
  - Amylose

- Amylopectin
- Starch-nutrient interaction
- Resistant starch

- *Cooking/food processing*:
  - Degree of starch gelatinization
  - Particle size
  - Food form
  - Cellular structure
- *Other food components*:
  - Fat and protein
  - Dietary fibre
  - Antinutrients
  - Organic acids

## CALCULATION OF GLYCEMIC INDEX OF MEALS OR DIETS

The GI can be applied in a detailed fashion to mixed meals or whole diets by calculating the weighted GI value of the meal or diet. For example, the way to calculate the GI of a meal containing bread, cereal, sucrose, milk and orange juice is shown in Table 4.

**Table. 4: Calculation of the Glycemic Index of Meals**

| Food | Grams Glycemic Carbohydrate | Proportion of total Glycemic Carbohydrate | Food Glycemic Index | Meal Glycemic Index * |
|---|---|---|---|---|
| Bread | 25 | 0.342 | 100 | 34.2 |
| Cereal | 25 | 0.342 | 72 | 24.6 |
| Milk | 6 | 0.082 | 39 | 3.2 |
| Sucrose | 5 | 0.068 | 87 | 5.9 |
| Orange juice | 12 | 0.164 | 74 | 12.1 |
| Total | 73 | | | 80.0 |

* Values for each food equals the proportion of total glycemic carbohydrate multiplied by the food GI. The sum of these values is the meal GI.

Using this type of calculation, there is a good correlation between meal GI and the observed glycemic responses of meals of equal nutrient composition. Blood glucose responses are also influenced by the amount of carbohydrate in the meal. To compare the expected glycemic load of meals with different carbohydrate contents, a non-linear adjustment can be applied but this has only been tested in normal subjects. For detailed application of the GI, a value of the GI for every food in the diet or meal needs to have been assigned (for many foods the value has to be estimated). The accuracy of the calculation depends upon the accuracy of the GI values ascribed to foods, which may vary from place to place due to local factors such as variety, cooking, processing, etc. Foods particularly prone to such variation include rice, potatoes and bananas.

## PRACTICAL APPLICATION OF THE GLYCEMIC INDEX

The glycemic index can be used, in conjunction with information about food composition, to guide food choices. For practical application, the glycemic index is useful to rank foods by developing exchange lists of categories of low glycemic index foods, such as legumes, pearled barley, lightly refined grains (e.g., whole grain pumpernickel bread, or breads made from coarse flour), pasta, etc. Specific local foods should be included in such lists where information is available (e.g. green bananas in the Caribbean and specific rice varieties in Southeast Asia).

In choosing carbohydrate foods, both glycemic index and food composition must be considered. Some low GI foods may not always be a good choice because they are high in fat. Conversely, some high GI foods may be a good choice because of convenience or because they have low energy and high nutrient content. It is not necessary or desirable to exclude or avoid all high GI foods.

## PHYSIOLOGIC AND THERAPEUTIC EFFECTS OF LOW GLYCEMIC INDEX FOODS

Meals containing low GI foods reduce both postpr-andial blood glucose and insulin responses. Animal studies suggest that incorporating slowly digested starch into the diet delays the onset of insulin resistance. Some epidemiologic studies suggest that a low GI diet is associated with reduced risk of developing non-insulin diabetes in men and women. Clinical trials in normal, diabetic and hyperlipidemic subjects show that low GI diets reduce mean blood glucose concentrations, reduce insulin secretion and reduce serum triglycerides in individuals with hypertrigly-ceridemia.

In addition, the digestibility of the carbohydrate in low GI foods is generally less than that of high GI foods. Thus, low GI foods increase the amount of carbohydrate entering the colon and increase colonic fermentation and short chain fatty acid production. This has implications for systemic nitrogen and lipid metabolism, and for local events within the colon.

# GOALS AND GUIDELINES FOR CARBOHYDRATE FOOD CHOICES

## RATIONALE AND FRAMEWORK

Although the scientific basis for dietary guidelines requires an understanding of physiology and health relationships, the guidance most helpful to consumers uses food-based terms. In preparing such guidelines, food traditions and beliefs must be taken into account and the total food intake should reflect practical issues, such as meal patterns, food status, celebratory or usual role, seasonal availability, affordability and sustainability. These, including the health priorities, are matters for national policy makers.

## PRINCIPLES OF CARBOHYDRATE FOOD CHOICES

*The principles are*:

- To acknowledge the socio-cultural context, lifestyle and stage of life-cycle, in food carbohydrate choice;
- To give preference to food choices rather than to nutrient goals in carbohydrate food choices, and in so doing:
  - Use food categories as a guide to chemically defined carbohydrate type.
  - Use numbers of portions (serving sizes) of foods from designated food categories in order to provide semi-quantitative food-based advice. This may imply that meal frequency would need to increase in some cultures, because the accommodation of enough carbohydrate food in the course of the day, without an excessive amount on any one occasion, requires more frequent servings and consumption;
- To appreciate that many of the world's health problems are associated with inadequate carbo-hydrate intake, and potentially also associated with inappropriate carbohydrate intake;
- To ensure the acceptability and practicality of any recommended change in carbohydrate food intake;
- To acknowledge that there may be unintended consequences involved in carbohydrate food intake change, and also to ensure that risks involved in dietary changes from traditional diets is considered;
- To monitor the intake of carbohydrate foods and, wherever possible, of chemically defined carbohydrate components of those foods in relation to health issues; and
- To ascertain whether food carbohydrate choices encourage biodiversity and are sustainable.

## CARBOHYDRATE NUTRIENT AND FOOD GOALS

### Nutrient Goals

The minimum amount of carbohydrate in the human diet that is needed to avoid ketosis is of the order of 50 g/day in adults. Beyond this, additional energy needs are best met by nutrient-dense carbohydrate foods. There must, of course, be adequate intakes of protein (with essential amino acids) and essential fatty acids from fat. Moderate intake of sugar-rich foods can also provide for a palatable and nutritious diet.

**Food Goals**

*There are a number of approaches to translating nutrient recommendations to food goal*s:

- Recommending the total weight of food groups to be consumed. Various national food guides have suggested quantities of specific foods to be consumed, such as fruits and vegetables, and pulses, nuts and seeds.
- Examining sources of carbohydrate foods in various diets, particularly diets which have desirable total carbohydrate intakes or from countries where the incidence of lifestyle diseases is low. Recommendations can then be made on the basis of intakes.
- Examining major food groups which contain carbohydrate foods and recommending numbers of servings of those food groups. Numerous countries around the world, both developed and developing, have produced food guides with such groupings, and considering the level of agreement that exists for carbohydrate as a per cent energy, these food guides are remarkably consistent in their advice.
- Examining indices which exist to describe various physiological properties of carbohydrate-containing foods, such as glycemic index values and values from other indices which are presently being developed.

On the basis of the approaches, and taking into account the principles for carbohydrate food choice, the following recommendations can be made:

- A variety of foods should provide the carbohydrate in the diet, not a single or small number of sources.
- Cereals, roots, pulses, fruit and vegetables are all components of a healthy diet throughout the world.
- Cereal foods or root crops, where this is the main staple, should provide the major source of carbohydrate energy.
- Intake of fruits and vegetables (including potatoes in developed countries) should be high. As well as being a valuable source of carbohydrate, fruit and vegetables are an important source of antioxidant vitamins and other food components.
- Consumption of pulses, nuts and seeds should be encouraged. While this group often represents only a small amount of carbohydrate energy, these foods are a good source of protein and micronutrients. They should be consumed with cereals to optimize protein quality.

- At least small quantities of milk products are desirable, even when low lactase activity exists, since these are a good source of protein and micro-nutrients.
- These recommendations apply to all individuals over the age of two years, with adjustments as necessary for growth and the increased demand of pregnancy and lactation.

## TRANSLATION FROM CARBOHYDRATE NUTRIENTS TO FOODS

Achieving goals for intake of carbohydrates does not ensure nutritional adequacy. Carbohydrate foods provide a range of nutrients and other substances essential for health in addition to energy. It is therefore essential to consume a variety of foods in order to derive the full benefits of a high carbohydrate diet. Nutrients from foods require monitoring. For example, in Iran carbohydrate foods include vegetables (250 gm./day), fruits (210 gm./day), pulses (20 gm./day) and cereals (wheat at about 250 gm./day and rice 110 gm./day, uncooked). Wheat has mostly been consumed as bread with traditional pastries being festive foods.

Recently, consumption of the latter has increased substantially with potential reduction of nutritionally useful food groups traditionally accompanying bread. This may not significantly impact on total carbohydrate intake, but could influence nutritional adequacy. Traditional methods of food preparation and preservation facilitate food choice variety, and promote nutritional benefits. Alteration of traditional practices may compromise such benefits. Ongoing monitoring may be required to guard against nutritional inadequacy.

## CONSIDERATIONS FOR TARGET AUDIENCES

*Planners and policy makers need to*:

- Recognize dietary goals of at least 55 per cent of total energy from a variety of carbohydrate sources.
- Recognize the extent of change necessary in order to meet these goals (e.g. it may take considerable change in food production and consumption to meet goals in Western countries).
- Understand that there must be a gradual transition in meeting new dietary guidelines and that new terminology will need to be gradually accepted.
- Consider the effects of economic and cultural factors in achieving dietary goals.
- Develop clear guides about the types and quantities of food recommended.
- Develop methods to monitor food consumption to meet dietary goals.

*Primary producers and processors need to*:

- Consider how existing and new technologies can be used to help meet dietary goals regarding the quantity and nutritional properties of food carbohydrates, as well as levels of micronutrients and other desirable food components.
- Provide foods, such as breakfast cereals and snack foods that are high in NSP, low in energy density, and with a low glycemic index.
- Increase the availability and convenience of fruits and vegetables.
- Provide appropriate information to the consumer on food labels.

*To facilitate individual choice:*

- Provide easily understandable food-based guides for the consumer.

# 7

# Tubers and Fruits

## TUBERS

The two tubers that are of chief interest are the Irish potato and the sweet potato. The former is easily and cheaply grown on vast areas of land and therefore forms a large part of the food of many people. Properly prepared it is easily digested and very nourishing.

| | Water | Protein | Fat | Carbohydrates | Ash | Calories per lb. |
|---|---|---|---|---|---|---|
| Potato | 78.3 | 2.2 | 0.1 | 18.0 | 1.0 | 375 |
| Sweet potato | 51.9 | 3.0 | 2.1 | 42.1 | .9 | 925 |
| Jerusalem artichoke | 78.7 | 2.5 | 0.2 | 17.5 | 1.1 | |

The sweet potato is a richer food than the Irish potato, but on account of its high sugar contents people soon weary of it. The southern negroes are very fond of this food. Like all other starches, potatoes must be thoroughly masticated, or they will disagree in time.

Potatoes are of such consistency that they are easily bolted without proper mouth preparation. In time the digestive organs object. A new tuber is receiving considerable attention. It is the dasheen. It is said to be of very agreeable flavour, mealy after cooking, and produces tops that can be used in the same manner as asparagus. The dasheen requires a rather warm climate for its growth.

### TUBERS PREPARATION

All the tubers may be baked. Clean and place in the oven; bake until tender. A medium sized potato will bake in about an hour. If the potatoes are soggy after being baked they are not well flavoured.

To remedy this, run a fork into them after they have been in the oven for a while; this allows some of the steam to escape and the potatoes become mealy.

When a fork can easily be run into the potato, it is well enough done. If the potatoes are well cleaned, there is no objection to eating a part of the jacket after they are baked.

The finest flavouring is right under the jacket. This part contains a large portion of the salts. All tubers may be boiled. It is best to keep the jacket on, otherwise a great deal of both the salts and the nourishment is lost. If the potatoes boiled in the jacket seem too highly flavoured, cut off one of the ends before placing them in the water. It takes about thirty or forty minutes to boil a medium sized Irish potato. Test with a fork, the same as baked potato, to find if done.

Potatoes should never be peeled and soaked. If they are to be boiled without the jacket, they should be cooked immediately after being peeled. Steamed potatoes are good.

There is no objection to mashing potatoes and adding milk, cream or butter, provided they are thoroughly masticated when eaten. If the potatoes are mashed, this should be so thoroughly done that not a lump is to be found. Potatoes cooked in grease are an abomination. The grease ruins a part of the potato and makes the rest more difficult to digest. Potato chips, French fried potatoes and German fried potatoes are too hard to digest for people who live mostly indoors. They should be used very seldom.

### COMBINATIONS

Potatoes are best eaten in combinations such as given for cereals. They are commonly taken with meat and bread. This combination is one of the causes of overeating. Occasionally they may be eaten with flesh, but this should not be a habit. Take them as the main part of the meal. Baked potatoes and butter with a glass of milk make a very satisfying meal. A good dinner can be made of potatoes with cooked succulent vegetables and one or two of the raw salad vegetables, with the usual dressings.

It is best not to eat potatoes and acid fruits in the same meal. In selecting food it is well to remember that as a general rule but one heavy, concentrated food should be eaten at a meal, for when two, three or even four concentrated foods are partaken of, the appetite is so tempted and stimulated by each new dish that before one is aware of it an excessive amount of food has been ingested.

## FRUITS

Apricots, avocados, blackberries, cherries, cranberries, currants, gooseberries, grapes, huckleberries, mulberries, nectarines, olives, pineapples, plums, raspberries and whortleberries are some of the other juicy fruits. They are much like the apple in composition, containing much water and generally from 6 to 15 per cent of carbohydrates. Olives and avocados are rich in oil.

You may classify rhubarb, watermelons and muskmelons as vegetables, if you wish. On the table they seem more like fruit, which is the reason they are given here. Melons are fine hot weather food.

| | Water | Pro-tein | Etherial Extracts | Carbohy-drates | Ash | Calories per lb. |
|---|---|---|---|---|---|---|
| Apples...... | 84.6 | 0.4 | 0.5 | 14.2 | 0.3 | 290 |
| Bananas..... | 75.3 | 1.3 | 0.6 | 22.0 | 0.8 | 460 |
| Figs, fresh... | 79.1 | 1.5 | .. | 18.8 | 0.6 | 380 |
| Lemons...... | 89.3 | 1.0 | 0.7 | 8.5 | 0.5 | 205 |
| Muskmelons.... | 89.5 | 0.6 | .. | 9.3 | 0.6 | 185 |
| Oranges..... | 86.9 | 0.8 | 0.2 | 11.6 | 0.5 | 240 |
| Peaches..... | 89.4 | 0.7 | 0.1 | 9.4 | 0.4 | 190 |
| Pears...... | 80.9 | 1.0 | 0.5 | 17.2 | 0.4 | .. |
| Persimmons.... | 66.1 | 0.8 | 0.7 | 31.5 | 0.9 | 630 |
| Rhubarb, stalk. | 94.4 | 0.6 | 0.7 | 3.6 | 0.7 | 105 |
| Strawberries... | 90.4 | 1.0 | 0.6 | 7.4 | 0.6 | 180 |
| Watermelon.... | 92.4 | 0.4 | 0.2 | 6.7 | 0.3 | 140 |
| *"Dried Fruits":* | | | | | | |
| Apples...... | 26.1 | 1.6 | 2.2 | 68.1 | 2.0 | 1350 |
| Apricots..... | 29.4 | 4.7 | 1.0 | 62.5 | 2.4 | 1290 |
| Citrons..... | 19.0 | 0.5 | 1.5 | 78.1 | 0.9 | 1525 |
| Dates...... | 15.4 | 2.1 | 2.8 | 78.4 | 1.3 | 161 |
| Figs....... | 18.8 | 4.3 | 0.3 | 74.2 | 2.4 | 1475 |
| Prunes...... | 22.3 | 2.1 | .. | 73.3 | 2.3 | 1400 |
| Raisins..... | 14.6 | 2.6 | 3.3 | 76.1 | 3.4 | 1605 |
| Currants..... | 17.2 | 2.4 | 1.7 | 74.2 | 4.5 | 1495 |

They are mostly water, which is pure. During hot weather it is all right to make a meal of melons and nothing else, at any time. The melons are so watery that they dilute the gastric juice very much. The result is that when eaten with concentrated foods they are liable to repeat, which indicates indigestion.

Fruits are not generally eaten for the great amount of nourishment to be obtained from them.

They are very pleasant in flavour and contain salts and acids which are needed by the body. The various fluids of the body are alkaline, and the fruits furnish the salts that help to keep them so. A few secretions and excretions are naturally acid.

Sometimes the body gets into a too acid state, but that is very rarely due to overeating of fruit. It is generally caused by pathological fermentation of food in the alimentary tract. The salts and acids of fruits are broken up in the stomach and help to form alkaline substances.

The water of the fruit is very pure, distilled by nature. The acid fruits are refreshing and helpful to those who have a tendency to be bilious. Fruits are cleansers, both of the alimentary tract and of the blood. Fruits grow most abundantly in warm climates and that is where they should be used most. In temperate climates they should be eaten most freely during warm weather. Young, vigourous people can eat all the fruit they wish at all seasons, within reason. Thin, nervous people, and those who are well advanced in years should do most of their fruit eating in summer.

In winter there is a tendency to be chilly after a meal of acid fruit. In summer such meals do not add to the burden of life by making the partaker unduly warm. The apple is perhaps the best all-round fruit of all. It is grown in many lands and climates.

It is possible to get apples of various kinds, from those that are very tart to those that are so mild that the acid is hardly perceptible to the taste. Stout people can eat sour apples with benefit. Thin, fidgety ones should use the milder varieties.

The juice from apples, sweet cider, freshly expressed, is a very pleasant drink, and may be taken with fruit meals. The avocado is a good salad fruit. It is quite oily. A combination of avocado and lettuce makes a good salad. Thanks to rapid transportation, the banana has become a staple. It is quite commonly believed that bananas are very starchy and rather indigestible. This may be true when they are green, but not when they are ripe. Green bananas are no more fit for food than are green apples. Ripe bananas are neither starchy nor indigestible.

When the banana is ripe it contains a trace of starch, all the rest having been changed to sugar. A ripe banana is mellow and sweet, but firm. The skin is either entirely black, or black in spots, but the flesh is unspotted. The best bananas can often be purchased for one-half of the price of those that are not yet fit to eat. Bananas are a rich food.

Weight for weight they contain more nourishment than Irish potatoes. A few nuts or a glass of milk and bananas make a good meal. Bananas contain so much sugar that it is not necessary to eat bread or other starches with them. Those with normal taste will not spoil good bananas by adding sugar and cream. When well masticated the flavour is excellent and can not be improved by using dressings.

Be sure that the children have learned to masticate well before giving bananas, and then give only ripe ones. The flesh of the banana is so smooth and slippery that children often swallow it in big lumps, and then they frequently suffer. Lemonade may be taken with fruit or flesh meals. As usually made it is quite nourishing, for it contains considerable sugar. Those who are troubled with sluggish liver may take it with benefit, but the less sugar used the better.

Other fruit juices may be used likewise, but they should be fresh. If they are bottled, be sure that no fermentation is taking place in them. These juices may be served with the same kind of meals as lemonade. Most of them require dilution. Grape juice is very rich and a large glassful of the pure juice makes a good summer lunch.

It should be sipped slowly. Those who like the combination may make a meal of fruit juice mixed with milk, half and half. Grapes and strawberries, which are relished by most, disagree with some people. The skin of the Concord grape should be rejected, for it irritates many. If they are relished, the skins of most fruits may be eaten. When peeled apples lose a part of their flavour.

Olives are generally eaten pickled. The fruit in its natural state tastes very disagreeable to most people. The ripe olive is superior in flavour to the green, which is not usually relished at first. The sweet fruits, by which we mean dried currants, raisins, figs and dates, and bananas should be classed with them, serve the body in the same way as do the breadstuffs, and may be substituted for starches at any time.

They may be eaten at all seasons of the year, but are used most during cold weather. A moderate amount of them may be eaten with breadstuffs, or they may be taken alone, or with milk, or with nuts, or with acid fruit. They are very nourishing so it does not take much of them to make a meal. To get the full benefit, masticate thoroughly. They contain sugar in its best form, sugar that not impoverished by being deprived of its salts. Grape sugar needs very little preparation before it enters the blood. Starch and sugar are of equal value as nourishment. It seems that the sugar is available for energy sooner than the starch.

Americans generally weary quickly of sweet foods, though they consume enormous quantities of refined sugar, but in tropical countries figs and dates are staple in many places and the inhabitants relish them day in and day out as we relish some of out staples. It is a matter of habit. Those who do not surfeit themselves do not weary quickly of any particular substance of diet.

## FRUIT PREPARATION

Most fruits are best raw. Then their acids and salts are in their most available form. Those who become uncomfortable after eating acid fruit may know that they have abused their digestive organs and they should take it as an indication to reduce their food intake, simplify their diet, masticate better and eat more raw food.

Those who overeat of starch or partake of much alcohol cultivate irritable stomachs, which object to the bracing fruit juices.

For the sake of a change fruits may be cooked. The more plainly they are cooked the better. Always use sugar in moderation, no matter whether the fruit is to be stewed or baked. To stew fruit, clean and if necessary peel. Stew in sufficient water until tender. When almost done add what sugar is needed. When stewed thus less sugar is required than if the sweetening is done at the start. Stewed fruit can be sweetened by adding raisins, figs or dates. This is relished by many. Figs and dates stewed by themselves are too sweet for many tastes. This can be remedied by making a sauce of figs or dates with tart apples or any other acid fruit that appeals in such combinations.

**"Baked Apple"**

Place whole apples in large, deep pan; add about one-third cup of water and one and one-half teaspoonfuls sugar to each apple. Put into oven and bake until skins burst and the apples are well done. Serve with all the juice.

**"Boiled Apple"**

Place whole apples in a stewing pan; add two teaspoonfuls sugar and one cup or more of water to each apple; use less sugar if desired. Cover the vessel tightly and boil moderately until the skins burst and the apples are well done. All stewed fruits should be well done. Avoid making the fruit sauces too sweet.

**"Stewed Prunes"**

A good prune needs no sweetening. Stew until tender. It is a good plan to let the prunes soak a few hours before stewing them. Raisins may be treated in the same way. Prunes may be washed and put into a dish; then add hot water enough to about half cover them; cover the dish very tightly and put aside over night. The prunes need no further preparation before being eaten. If the covering is not tight it will be necessary to use more water.

Raisins and sundried figs may be treated in the same way. Unfortunately, most of our dried fruit is sulphured. Sulphurous acid fumes are employed, and you may be sure that this does the fruit no good. If you can get unsulphured fruit, do so. The sulphuring process is popular because it acts as a preservative and it is profitable because it allows the fruit to retain more water without spoiling than would be possible otherwise.

**"Canning Fruit"**

It is very easy to can fruit, but it requires care. Select fruit that is not overripe. The work room should be clean and so should the cans and covers. It is not sufficient to rinse the cans in clean water. Both the jars and the covers should be taken from boiling water immediately before being used.

Use only sound fruit, cook it sufficiently, adding the sugar when the fruit is almost done. If you cook the fruit in syrup, do not have a heavy syrup. Put into jar while piping hot, filling the jar as full as possible, put on the cover immediately, turning until it fits snugly; turn jar upside down for a few hours to see if it leaks; tighten again and put in cool place. An even better way, especially for berries, is to fill the jar with fruit, pour syrup over them, put the jars into a receptacle containing water and let this water boil until the berries are done; then fill the jars properly and seal. Some berries that lose their colour when cooked in syrup retain it when treated this way. Canned fruits are not as good as the fresh ones, but better than none. Be sure that they are not fermenting when opened. When proper care is exercised a spoiled jar is a rarity. If there is any doubt about the fruit, scald and cool before using. This destroys the ferments. Fresh fruit is the best. Next comes fruit recently stewed or baked. If other fruit cannot be obtained, get good dried fruit and stew it.

## FRUIT COMBINATIONS

Fruits may be combined with almost any food, except that which is rich in starch, and even that combination may be used occasionally, although it is not the best. We have seen people who were supposed to be incurable get well when their breakfasts were mostly apple sauce and toast. However, sick people should avoid such combining entirely and healthy ones most of the time. Breakfasting on cereals and fruit is a mistake. Those who eat thus may say that they feel no bad results, but time will tell. Nowhere in our manner of feeding does nature demand of a healthy human being that he walk the chalk line. All she/he asks is that he be reasonable. So if you feel fine and want a shortcake for dinner take it. But the shortcake should be the meal, not the end of one that has already furnished too much food. Fruit combines well with both milk and cheese. The impression to the contrary that has been gained from both medical and lay writers is due to false deductions based on premises not founded on facts. Milk and fruit, and nothing else, make very good meals in summer.

### "Fruit Salads"

A great variety of these salads can be made. Take two or three of the juicy fruits, slice and mix. Dress with a little sugar, or salt and olive oil, or simply olive oil, or no dressing. Some like a dressing of sour cream or of cottage cheese rather well thinned out. Raisins and other sweet fruits may also be used. Ripe banana may be one of the ingredients. Such a salad may be eaten with a flesh or nut meal, or it may be used as a meal by itself. Fruit and cottage cheese make a meal that is both delicious and nourishing. A fruit salad strewed with nuts does the same. Strawberries and sliced tomatoes dressed with cottage cheese make a good meal. Lettuce, celery and tomatoes may be used in fruit salads. A few fruit salads to serve as examples are: Apples, grapes and lettuce; peaches, strawberries and celery; bananas, pineapples and nuts; strawberries, tomatoes and lettuce. Combine to suit taste and dress likewise, but avoid large quantities of cream and sugar, not only on your salads, but on all fruits. No acid should be necessary, but if it is desired, use lemon juice or incorporate oranges as a part of the salad.

# 8

# Vitamins, Minerals and Calcium in Food

## VITAMIN A

Vitamin A (retinol) is an essential nutrient needed in small amounts by humans for the normal functioning of the visual system; growth and development; and maintenance of epithelial cellular integrity, immune function, and reproduction. These dietary needs for vitamin A are normally provided for as preformed retinol (mainly as retinyl ester) and pro-vitamin A carotenoids.

### OVERVIEW OF VITAMIN A METABOLISM

Preformed vitamin A in animal foods occurs as retinyl esters of fatty acids in association with membrane-bound cellular lipid and fat-containing storage cells. Pro-vitamin A carotenoids in foods of vegetable origin are also associated with cellular lipids but are embedded in complex cellular structures such as the cellulose-containing matrix of chloroplasts or the pigment-containing portion of chromoplasts. Normal digestive processes free vitamin A and carotenoids from embedding food matrices, a more efficient process from animal than from vegetable tissues. Retinyl esters are hydrolysed and the retinol and freed carotenoids are incorporated into lipid-containing, water-miscible micellar solutions.

Products of fat digestion (*e.g.*, fatty acids, monoglycerides, cholesterol, and phospholipids) and secretions in bile (*e.g.*, bile salts and hydrolytic enzymes) are essential for the efficient solubilisation of retinol and especially for solubilisation of the very lipophilic carotenoids (*e.g.*, aa- and bb-carotene, bb-cryptoxanthin, and lycopene) in the aqueous intestinal milieu. Micellar solubilisation is a prerequisite to their efficient passage into the lipid-rich membrane of intestinal mucosal cells (*i.e.*, enterocytes). Diets critically low in dietary fat (under about 5-10 g daily) or disease conditions that interfere with normal digestion and absorption leading to steatorrhea (*e.g.*, pancreatic and liver diseases and frequent gastroenteritis) can therefore impede the efficient absorption of retinol and carotenoids. Retinol and some carotenoids enter the intestinal mucosal brush border by diffusion in accord with the concentration gradient between the micelle and plasma membrane of enterocytes. Some carotenoids pass into the enterocyte and are solubilized into chylomicrons without further change whereas some of the pro-vitamin A carotenoids are converted to retinol by a cleavage enzyme in the brush border. Retinol is trapped intracellularly by re-esterification or binding to specific intracellular binding proteins. Retinyl esters and unconverted carotenoids together with other lipids are incorporated into chylomicrons, excreted into intestinal lymphatic channels, and delivered to the blood through the thoracic duct.

Tissues extract most lipids and some carotenoids from circulating chylomicrons, but most retinyl esters are stripped from the chylomicron remnant, hydrolysed, and taken up primarily by parenchymal liver cells. If not immediately needed, retinol is re-esterified and retained in the fat-storing cells of the liver (variously called adipocytes, stellate cells, or Ito cells).

The liver parenchymal cells also take in substantial amounts of carotenoids. Whereas most of the body's vitamin A reserve remains in the liver, carotenoids are also deposited elsewhere in fatty tissues throughout the body. Usually, turnover of carotenoids in tissues is relatively slow, but in times of low dietary carotenoid intake, stored carotenoids are mobilised. A recent study in one subject using stable isotopes suggests that retinol can be derived not only from conversion of dietary pro-vitamin carotenoids in enterocytes–the major site of bioconversion, but also from hepatic conversion of circulating pro-vitamin carotenoids. The quantitative contribution to vitamin A requirements of carotenoid converted to retinoids beyond the enterocyte is unknown.

Following hydrolysis of stored retinyl esters, retinol combines with a plasma-specific transport protein, retinol-binding protein (RBP). This process, including synthesis of the unoccupied RBP (apo-RBP), occurs to the greatest extent within liver cells but it may also occur in some peripheral tissues. The RBP-retinol complex (holo-RBP) is secreted into the blood where it associates with another hepatically synthesised and excreted larger protein, transthyretin.

The transthyretin-RBP-retinol complex circulates in the blood, delivering the lipophilic retinol to tissues; its large size prevents its loss through kidney filtration. Dietary restriction in energy, proteins, and some micronutrients can limit hepatic synthesis of proteins specific to mobilisation and transport of vitamin A. Altered kidney functions or fever associated with infections can increase urinary vitamin A loss.

Holo-RBP transiently associates with target-tissue membranes, and specific intracellular binding proteins then extract the retinol. Some of the transiently sequestered retinol is released into the blood unchanged and is recycled. A limited reserve of intracellular retinyl esters is formed, that subsequently can provide functionally active retinol and its oxidation products (*i.e.*, isomers of retinoic acid) as needed intracellularly. These biologically active forms of vitamin A are associated with specific cellular proteins which bind with retinoids within cells during metabolism and with nuclear receptors that mediate retinoid action on the genome. Retinoids modulate the transcription of several hundreds of genes. In addition to the latter role of retinoic acid, retinol is the form required for functions in the visual and reproductive systems and during embryonic development.

Holo-RBP is filtered into the glomerulus but recovered from the kidney tubule and recycled. Normally vitamin A leaves the body in urine only as inactive metabolites which result from tissue utilisation and as potentially recyclable active glucuronide conjugates of retinol in bile secretions. No single urinary metabolite has been identified which accurately reflects tissue levels of vitamin A or its rate of utilisation. Hence, at this time urine is not a useful biologic fluid for assessment of vitamin A nutriture.

**Biochemical Mechanisms for Vitamin A Functions**

Vitamin A functions at two levels in the body. The first is in the visual cycle in the retina of the eye; the second is in all body tissues systemically to maintain growth and the soundness of cells. In the visual system, carrier-bound retinol is transported to ocular tissue and to the retina by intracellular binding and transport proteins. Rhodopsin, the visual pigment critical to dim-light vision, is formed in rod cells after conversion of all-*trans* retinol to retinaldehyde, isomerization to the 11-*cis*-form, and binding to opsin.

Alteration of rhodopsin through a cascade of photochemical reactions results in ability to see objects in dim light. The speed at which rhodopsin is regenerated relates to the availability of retinol. Night blindness is usually an indicator of inadequate available retinol, but it can also be due to a deficit of other nutrients, which are critical to the regeneration of rhodopsin, such as protein and zinc, and to some inherited diseases, such as retinitis pigmentosa.

The growth and differentiation of epithelial cells throughout the body are especially affected by vitamin A deficiency (VAD). Goblet cell numbers are reduced in epithelial tissues. The consequence is that mucous secretions with their antimicrobial components diminish. Cells lining protective tissue surfaces fail to regenerate and differentiate, hence flatten and accumulate keratin.

Both factors–the decline in mucous secretions and loss of cellular integrity–diminish resistance to invasion by potentially pathogenic organisms. The immune system is also compromised by direct interference with production of some types of protective secretions and cells.

Classical symptoms of xerosis (drying or nonwetability) and desquamation of dead surface cells as seen in ocular tissue (*i.e.*, xerophthalmia) are the external evidence of the changes also occurring to various degrees in internal epithelial tissues.

Current understanding of the mechanism of vitamin A action within cells outside the visual cycle is that cellular functions are mediated through specific nuclear receptors. These receptors are activated by binding with specific isomers of retinoic acid (*i.e.*, all-*trans* and 9-*cis* retinoic acid). Activated receptors bind to DNA response elements located upstream of specific genes to regulate the level of expression of those genes. The synthesis of a large number of proteins vital to maintaining normal physiologic functions is regulated by these retinoid-activated genes. There also may be other mechanisms of action that are as yet undiscovered.

**UNITS OF EXPRESSION**

In blood, tissues, and human milk, vitamin A levels are conventionally expressed in μg/dL or μmol/l of all-*trans* retinol. Except for postprandial conditions, most of the circulating vitamin A is retinol whereas in most tissues (such as the liver), secretions (such as human milk), and other animal food sources it exists mainly as retinyl esters, that are usually hydrolysed before analytical detection.

To express the vitamin A activity of carotenoids in diets on a common basis, a joint FAO/WHO Expert Group in 1967 introduced the concept of the retinol equivalent (RE) and established the following relationships among food sources of vitamin A:

1 μg retinol = 1 RE

1 μg b-carotene = 0.167 μg RE

1 μg other pro-vitamin A carotenoids = 0.084 μg RE

These equivalencies were derived from balance studies to account for the less-efficient absorption of carotenoids (thought to be about one-third that of retinol) and their bioconversion to vitamin A (one-half for b-carotene and one-fourth for other pro-vitamin carotenoids). It was recognised at the time that the recommended conversion factors (*i.e.*, 1:6 for vitamin A:b-carotene and 1:12 for vitamin A: all other pro-vitamin carotenoids) were only average estimates for a mixed diet. Recently there has been renewed interest in examining bio-availability factors by using more quantitative stable isotope techniques for measuring whole-body stores in response to controlled intakes and by following postabsorption carotenoids in the triacylglycerol-rich lipoprotein fraction. The data are inconsistent but in general suggests that revision towards lower bio-availability estimates is likely.

Until additional definitive data are available, however, the above conversion factors will be used.

Retinol equivalents in a diet are calculated as the sum of the weight of the retinol portion of preformed vitamin A with the weight of b-carotene divided by its conversion factor and with the weight of other carotenoids divided by their conversion factor. Most recent food composition tables report b-carotene and sometimes other pro-vitamin A carotenoids as $\mu$g/g edible portion. However, older food composition tables frequently report vitamin A as international units (IUs). The following applies to determining comparable values as $\mu$g:

1 IU retinol = 0.3 $\mu$g retinol

1 IU b-carotene = 0.6 $\mu$g b-carotene

1 IU retinol = 3 IU b-carotene

It is strongly recommended that weight or molar units replace the use of IU to decrease confusion and overcome limitations in the non-equivalence of the IU values for retinol and beta-carotene.

## DIETARY SOURCES

Preformed vitamin A is found almost exclusively in animal products, such as human milk, glandular meats, liver and fish liver oils (especially), egg yolk, and whole milk and dairy products. Preformed vitamin A is also used to fortify processed foods, that may include sugar, cereals, condiments, fats, and oils. Pro-vitamin A carotenoids are found in green leafy vegetables (*e.g.*, spinach, amaranth, and young leaves from various sources), yellow vegetables (*e.g.*, pumpkins, squash, and carrots), and yellow and orange noncitrus fruits (*e.g.*, mangoes, apricots, and papaya). Red palm oil produced in several countries worldwide is especially rich in pro-vitamin A. Some other indigenous plants also may be unusually rich sources of pro-vitamin A. Such examples are the palm fruit known in Brazil as *buriti*, that is found in areas along the Amazon, and the fruit known as *gac* in Vietnam, that is used to colour rice, particularly on ceremonial occasions. Foods containing pro-vitamin A carotenoids tend to be less biologically available but more affordable than animal products. It is mainly for this reason that carotenoids provide most of the vitamin A activity in the diets of economically deprived populations.

### Dietary Intake and Patterns

Vitamin A status cannot be assessed from dietary intake alone, but dietary intake assessment can provide evidence of risk of an inadequate status. Quantitative collection of dietary information is fraught with measurement problems. These problems arise both from obtaining representative quantitative dietary histories from individuals, communities, or both and from interpreting these data while accounting for differences in bio-availability, preparation losses, and variations in food composition data among population groups. This is especially difficult in populations consuming most of their dietary vitamin A from pro-vitamin carotenoid sources. Simplified guidelines have been developed recently in an effort to improve the obtaining of reliable dietary intake information from individuals and communities.

**World and Regional Supply and Patterns**

In theory the world's food supply is sufficient to meet global requirements. Great differences exist, however, in the available sources (animal and vegetable) and in per capita consumption of the vitamin among different countries, age categories, and socio-economic groups. VAD as a global public health problem, therefore, is largely due to inequitable food distribution among and within countries and households in relation to need for ample bio-available vitamin A sources.

Earlier FAO global estimates in 1984 indicated that preformed vitamin A constituted about one-third of total dietary vitamin A. World availability of vitamin A for human consumption at that time was approximately 220 $\mu$g of preformed retinol per capita daily and 560 $\mu$g RE from pro-vitamin carotenoids per person per day, for a total of about 790 $\mu$g RE. These values are based on supply estimates and not consumption estimates. Losses commonly occur during food storage and processing, both industrially and in the home.

The estimated available regional supply of vitamin A from a more recent global evaluation the variability in amounts and sources of vitamin A. The variability is further complicated by access to the available supply, that varies with household income, poverty being a yardstick for risk of VAD. VAD is most prevalent in Southeast Asia, Africa, and the Western Pacific, where vegetable sources contribute nearly 80 per cent or more of the available supply of retinol equivalents.

Furthermore, in Southeast Asia the total available supply is about half of that of most other regions and is particularly low in animal sources. In contrast, the Americas, Europe, and Eastern Mediterranean regions have a supply ranging from 800 to 1000 mmg RE/day, one-third of which comes from animal sources.

Recent national data from the USA Continuing Survey of Food Consumption and the National Health and Nutrition Examination Survey included mean dietary intakes of children 0-6 years of age of 864 ± 497 and 921 ± 444 mmg RE daily. In the Dietary and Nutritional Survey of British Adults, the median intake of men and women 35-49 years old was 1118 mmg RE and 926 mmg RE, respectively, which corresponded to serum retinol concentrations of 2.3 mmol/l and 1.8 mmol/l, respectively. In another selected survey in the United Kingdom, median intakes for nonpregnant women who did not consume liver or liver products during the survey week were reported to be 686 mmg RE daily.

The available world supply figures were recently reassessed based on a bio-availability ratio of 1:30 for retinol to other pro-vitamin A carotenoids. This conversion factor was justified on the basis of one published controlled intervention study conducted in Indonesia and a limited number of other studies not yet published in full. Applying the unconfirmed conversion factor would lead to the conclusion that regional and country needs for vitamin A could not be met from predominantly vegetarian diets. This is inconsistent with the preponderance of epidemiologic evidence.

Most studies report a positive response when vegetable sources of pro-vitamin A are given under controlled conditions to deficient subjects freed of confounding parasite loads and provided with sufficient dietary fat. Emerging data are likely to justify a lower biologic activity for pro-vitamin A carotenoids because of the mix of total carotenoids found in food sources in a usual meal. This Consultation concluded that the 1:6 bioconversion factor originally derived on the basis of balance studies should be retained until there is firm confirmation from ongoing studies that use more precise methodologies.

## VITAMIN $B_{12}$

### VITAMIN $B_{12}$ IN HUMAN METABOLIC PROCESSES

Although the nutritional literature still uses the term vitamin $B_{12}$, a more specific name for vitamin $B_{12}$ is cobalamin. Vitamin $B_{12}$ is the largest of the B complex vitamins, with a molecular weight of over 1000. It consists of a corrin ring made up of four pyrroles with cobalt at the centre of the ring).

There are several vitamin $B_{12}$-dependent enzymes in bacteria and algae, but no species of plants have the enzymes necessary for vitamin $B_{12}$ synthesis. This fact has significant implications for the dietary sources and availability of vitamin $B_{12}$. In mammalian cells there are only two vitamin $B_{12}$-dependent enzymes.

One of these enzymes, methionine synthase, uses the chemical form of the vitamin which has a methyl group attached to the cobalt and is called methylcobalamin. The other enzyme, methylmalonyl CoA mutase, uses vitamin $B_{12}$ with a 5'-adeoxyadenosyl moiety attached to the cobalt and is called 5'-deoxyaldenosylcobalamin, or coenzyme $B_{12}$. In nature there are two other forms of vitamin $B_{12}$: hydroxycobalamin and aquacobalamin, where hydroxyl and water groups, respectively, are attached to the cobalt. The synthetic form of vitamin $B_{12}$ found in supplements and fortified foods is cyanocobalamin, which has cyanide attached to the cobalt. These three forms of $B_{12}$ are enzymatically activated to the methyl- or deoxyadenosylcobalamins in all mammalian cells.

### POPULATIONS AT RISK FOR AND CONSEQUENCES OF VITAMIN $B_{12}$ DEFICIENCY

Because plants do not synthesise vitamin $B_{12}$, individuals who consume diets completely free of animal products (vegan diets) are at risk of vitamin $B_{12}$ deficiency. This is not true of lacto-ovo-vegetarians, who consume the vitamin in eggs, milk, and other dairy products.

### Pernicious Anaemia

Malabsorption of vitamin $B_{12}$ can occur at several points during digestion. By far the most important condition resulting in vitamin $B_{12}$ malabsorption is the auto-immune disease called pernicious anaemia (PA). In most cases of PA, antibodies are produced against the parietal cells causing them to atrophy, lose their ability to produce intrinsic factor, and secrete hydrochloric acid. In some forms of PA the parietal cells remain intact but auto-antiobodies are produced against the intrinsic factor itself and attach to it, thus preventing it from binding vitamin $B_{12}$.

In another less common form of PA, the antibodies allow vitamin $B_{12}$ to bind to the intrinsic factor but prevent the absorption of the intrinsic factor-vitamin $B_{12}$ complex by the ileal receptors. As is the case with most auto-immune diseases, the incidence of PA increases markedly with age. In most ethnic groups it is virtually unknown to occur before the age of 50, with a progressive rise in incidence thereafter.

However, African American populations are known to have an earlier age of presentation. In addition to causing malabsorption of dietary vitamin $B_{12}$, PA also results in an inability to reabsorb the vitamin $B_{12}$ which is secreted in the bile. Biliary secretion of vitamin $B_{12}$ is estimated to be between 0.3 and 0.5 $\mu$g/day. Interruption of this so-called enterohepatic circulation of vitamin $B_{12}$ causes the body to go into a significant negative balance for the vitamin.

Although the body typically has sufficient vitamin $B_{12}$ stores to last 3-5 years, once PA has been established the lack of absorption of new vitamin $B_{12}$ is compounded by the loss of the vitamin because of negative balance. When the stores have been depleted, the final stages of deficiency are often quite rapid, resulting in death in a period of months if left untreated.

### Atrophic Gastritis

Historically, PA was considered to be the major cause of vitamin $B_{12}$ deficiency, but it was a fairly rare condition, perhaps affecting 1 per cent to a few per cent of elderly populations. More recently it has been suggested that a far more common problem is that of hypochlorhydria associated with atrophic gastritis, where there is a progressive reduction with age of the ability of the parietal cells to secrete hydrochloric acid. It is claimed that perhaps up to one-quarter of elderly subjects could have various degrees of hypochlorhydria as a result of atrophic gastritis.

It has also been suggested that bacterial overgrowth in the stomach and intestine in individuals suffering from atrophic gastritis may also reduce vitamin $B_{12}$ absorption. This absence of acid is postulated to prevent the release of protein-bound vitamin $B_{12}$ contained in food but not to interfere with the absorption of the free vitamin $B_{12}$ found in fortified foods or supplements.

Atrophic gastritis does not prevent the reabsorption of bilary vitamin $B_{12}$ and therefore does not result in the negative balance seen in individuals with PA. However, it is agreed that with time, a reduction in the amount of vitamin $B_{12}$ absorbed from the diet will eventually deplete even the usually adequate vitamin $B_{12}$ stores, resulting in overt deficiency.

When considering recommended nutrient intakes (RNIs) for vitamin $B_{12}$ for the elderly, it is important to take into account the absorption of vitamin $B_{12}$ from sources such as fortified foods or supplements as compared with dietary vitamin $B_{12}$. In the latter instances, it is clear that absorption of intakes of less than 1.5-2.0 $\mu$g/day is complete–that is, for intakes of less than 1.5-2.0 $\mu$g of free vitamin $B_{12}$, the intrinsic factor–mediated system absorbs all of that amount.

It is probable that this is also true of vitamin $B_{12}$ in fortified foods, although this has not specifically been examined. However, absorption of food-bound vitamin $B_{12}$ has been reported to vary from 9 per cent to 60 per cent depending on the study and the source of the vitamin, which is perhaps related to its incomplete release from food. This has led many to estimate absorption as being up to 50 per cent to correct for bio-availability of absorption from food.

## VITAMIN $B_{12}$ INTERACTION WITH FOLIC ACID

One of the vitamin $B_{12}$-dependent enzymes, methionine synthase, functions in one of the two folate cycles–the methylation cycle. This cycle is necessary to maintain availability of the methyl donor *S*-adenosylmethionine; interruption reduces the wide range of methylated products. One such important methylation is that of myelin basic protein. Reductions in the level of *S*-adenosylmethionine seen in PA and other causes of vitamin $B_{12}$ deficiency produce demyelination of the peripheral nerves and the spinal column, called sub-acute combined degeneration.

This neuropathy is one of the main presenting conditions in PA. The other principal presenting condition in PA is a megaloblastic anaemia morphologically identical to that seen in folate deficiency. Disruption of the methylation cycle should cause a lack of DNA biosynthesis and anaemia.The methyl trap hypothesis is based on the fact that once the cofactor 5,10-methylenetetrahydrofolate is reduced by its reductase to form 5-methyltetrahydrofolate, the reverse reaction cannot occur. This suggests that the only way for the methyltetrahydrofolate to be recycled to tetrahydrofolate, and thus to participate in DNA biosynthesis and cell division, is through the vitamin $B_{12}$-dependent enzyme methionine synthase. When the activity of this synthase is compromised, as it would be in PA, the cellular folate will become progressively trapped as 5-methyltetrahydrofolate.

This will result in a cellular pseudo folate deficiency where despite adequate amounts of folate an anaemia will develop that is identical to that seen in true folate deficiency. Clinical symptoms of PA, therefore, include neuropathy, anaemia, or both. Treatment with vitamin $B_{12}$, if given intramuscularly, will reactivate methionine synthase, allowing myelination to restart. The trapped folate will be released and DNA synthesis and generation of red cells will cure the anaemia. Treatment with high concentrations of folic acid will treat the anaemia but not the neuropathy of PA. It should be stressed that the so-called masking of the anaemia of PA is generally agreed not to occur at concentrations of folate found in food or at intakes of the synthetic form of folic acid found at usual RNI levels of 200 or 400 $\mu$g/day.

However, there is some evidence that amounts less than 400 $\mu$g may cause a haematologic response and thus potentially treat the anaemia. The masking of the anaemia definitely occurs at high concentrations of folic acid (>1000 $\mu$g/day). This becomes a concern when considering fortification with synthetic folic acid of a dietary staple such as flour. In humans the vitamin $B_{12}$-dependent enzyme methylmalonyl coenzyme A (CoA) mutase functions in the metabolism of propionate and certain of the amino acids, converting them into succinyl CoA, and in their subsequent metabolism via the citric acid cycle. It is clear that in vitamin $B_{12}$ deficiency the activity of the mutase is compromised, resulting in high plasma or urine concentrations of methylmalonic acid (MMA), a degradation product of methylmalonyl CoA.

In adults this mutase does not appear to have any vital function, but it clearly has an important role during embryonic life and in early development. Children deficient in this enzyme, through rare genetic mutations, suffer from mental retardation and other developmental defects.

## ASSESSMENT OF VITAMIN $B_{12}$ STATUS

Traditionally it was thought that low vitamin $B_{12}$ status was accompanied by a low serum or plasma vitamin $B_{12}$ level. Recently this has been challenged by Lindenbaum *et al*, who suggested that a proportion of people with normal vitamin $B_{12}$ levels are in fact vitamin $B_{12}$ deficient. They also suggested that elevation of plasma homo-cysteine and plasma MMA are more sensitive indicators of vitamin $B_{12}$ status. Although plasma homo-cysteine may also be elevated because of folate or vitamin $B_6$ deficiency, elevation of MMA apparently always occurs with poor vitamin $B_{12}$ status. There may be other reasons why MMA is elevated, such as renal insufficiency, so the elevation of itself is not diagnostic. Many would feel that low or decreased plasma vitamin $B_{12}$ levels should be the first indication of poor status and that this could be confirmed by an elevated MMA if this assay was available.

## VITAMIN C

Vitamin C (chemical names: ascorbic acid and ascorbate) is a six-carbon lactone which is synthesised from glucose by many animals. Vitamin C is synthesised in the liver in some mammals and in the kidney in birds and reptiles. However, several species–including humans, non-human primates, guinea pigs, Indian fruit bats, and Nepalese red-vented bulbuls are unable to synthesise vitamin C. When there is insufficient vitamin C in the diet, humans suffer from the potentially lethal deficiency disease scurvy. Humans and primates lack the terminal enzyme in the biosynthetic pathway of ascorbic acid, l-gulonolactone oxidase, because the gene encoding for the enzyme has undergone substantial mutation so that no protein is produced.

## VITAMIN D

Vitamin D is required to maintain normal blood levels of calcium and phosphate, that are in turn needed for the normal mineralisation of bone, muscle contraction, nerve conduction, and general cellular function in all cells of the body. Vitamin D achieves this after its conversion to the active form 1,25-dihydroxyvitamin D [1,25-$(OH)_2D$], or calcitriol. This active form regulates the transcription of a number of vitamin D-dependent genes coding for calcium-transporting proteins and bone matrix proteins.

Vitamin D also modulates the transcription of cell cycle proteins, that decrease cell proliferation and increase cell differentiation of a number of specialised cells of the body (*e.g.*, osteoclastic precursors, enterocytes, keratinocytes, etc.).

This property may explain the actions of vitamin D in bone resorption, intestinal calcium transport, and skin. Vitamin D also possesses immuno-modulatory properties that may alter responses to infections *in vivo*. The cell differentiating and immuno-modulatory properties underlie the reason why vitamin D derivatives are now used successfully in the treatment of psoriasis and other skin disorders.

Clinical assays measure 1,25-$(OH)_2D_2$ and 1,25-$(OH)_2D_3$, collectively called 1,25-$(OH)_2D$. Similarly, calcidiol is measured as 25-OH-D but it is a mixture of 25-OH-$D_2$ and 25-OH-$D_3$. For the purposes of this document, 1,25-$(OH)_2D$ and 25-OH-D will be used to refer to calcitriol and calcidiol, respectively.

## VITAMIN D IN HUMAN METABOLIC PROCESSES

Vitamin D, a seco-steroid, can either be made in the skin from a cholesterol-like precursor (7-dehydrocholesterol) by exposure to sunlight or can be provided pre-formed in the diet (*1*).

The version made in the skin is referred to as vitamin $D_3$ whereas the dietary form can be vitamin $D_3$ or a closely related molecule of plant origin known as vitamin $D_2$. Because vitamin D can be made in the skin, it should not strictly be called a vitamin, and some nutritional texts refer to the substance as a prohormone and to the two forms as cholecalciferol ($D_3$) or ergocalciferol ($D_2$).

From a nutritional perspective, the two forms are metabolised similarly in humans, are equal in potency, and can be considered equivalent. It is now firmly established that vitamin $D_3$ is metabolised first in the liver to 25-hydroxyvitamin-D (25-OH-D or calcidiol) (*2*) and subsequently in the kidneys to 1,25-$(OH)_2D$ to produce a biologically active hormone. The 1,25-$(OH)_2D$, like all vitamin D metabolites, is present in the blood complexed to vitamin D binding protein, a specific a-globulin. The 1,25-$(OH)_2D$ is believed to act on target cells similarly to the way a steroid hormone would act.

Free hormone crosses the plasma membrane and interacts with a specific nuclear receptor known as the vitamin D receptor, a DNA-binding, zinc-finger protein with a molecular weight of 55,000. This ligand-receptor complex binds to a specific vitamin D-responsive element and, with associated transcription factors (*e.g.*, retinoid X receptor), enhances transcription of mRNAs which code for calcium-transporting proteins, bone matrix proteins, or cell cycle-regulating proteins. As a result of these processes,1,25-$(OH)_2D$ stimulates intestinal absorption of calcium and phosphate and mobilises calcium and phosphate by stimulating bone resorption. These functions serve the common purpose of restoring blood levels of calcium and phosphate to normal when concentrations of the two ions are low.

Lately, interest has focused on other cellular actions of 1,25-$(OH)_2D$. With the discovery of 1,25-$(OH)_2D$ receptors in many classical non-target tissues such as brain, various bone marrow-derived cells, skin, thymus, etc, the view has been expressed that 1,25-$(OH)_2D$ induces fusion and differentiation of macrophages. This effect has been widely interpreted to mean that the natural role of 1,25-$(OH)_2D$ is to induce osteoclastogenesis from colony forming units-granulatory monocytes in the bone marrow.

The 1,25-$(OH)_2D$ also suppresses interleukin 2 production in activated T lymphocytes, an effect which suggests the hormone might play a role in immuno-modulation *in vivo*. Other tissues (*e.g.*, skin) are directly affected by exogenous administration of vitamin D, though the physiologic significance of these effects is poorly understood. The pharmacologic effects of 1,25-$(OH)_2D$ are profound and have resulted in the development of vitamin D analogues, that are approved for use in hyper-proliferative conditions such as psoriasis.

In calcium homeostasis 1,25-$(OH)_2D$ works in conjunction with parathyroid hormone (PTH) to produce its beneficial effects on the plasma levels of ionised calcium and phosphate.

The physiologic loop starts with calcium sensing by the calcium receptor of the parathyroid gland. When the level of ionised calcium in plasma falls, PTH is secreted by the parathyroid gland and stimulates the tightly regulated renal enzyme 25-OH-D-1-aa-hydroxylase to make more 1,25-$(OH)_2D$ from the large circulating pool of 25-OH-D.

## VITAMIN E

A large body of scientific evidence indicates that reactive free radicals are involved in many diseases, including heart disease and cancers. Cells contain many potentially oxidizable substrates such as polyunsaturated fatty acids (PUFAs), proteins, and DNA. Therefore, a complex antioxidant defence system normally protects cells from the injurious effects of endogenously produced free radicals as well as from species of exogenous origin such as cigarette smoke and pollutants.

Should our exposure to free radicals exceed the protective capacity of the antioxidant defence system, a phenomenon often referred to as oxidative stress, then damage to biologic molecules may occur. There is considerable evidence that disease causes an increase in oxidative stress; therefore, consumption of foods rich in antioxidants, which are potentially able to quench or neutralise excess radicals, may play an important role in modifying the development of such diseases.

Vitamin E is the major lipid-soluble antioxidant in the cell antioxidant defence system and is exclusively obtained from the diet. The term "vitamin E" refers to a family of eight naturally occurring homologues that are synthesised by plants from homogentisic acid. All are derivatives of 6-chromanol and differ in the number and position of methyl groups on the ring structure. The four tocopherol homologues (*d*-a-, *d*-b-, *d*-g-, and *d*-d-) have a saturated 16-carbon phytyl side chain, whereas the tocotrienols homologues (*d*-a-, *d*-b-, *d*-g-, and *d*-d-) have three double bonds on the side chain. There is also a widely available synthetic form, *dl*-a-tocopherol, prepared by coupling trimethylhydroquinone with isophytol.

This consists of a mixture of eight stereoisomers in approximately equal amounts; these isomers are differentiated by rotations of the phytyl chain in various directions that do not occur naturally. For dietary purposes, vitamin E activity is expressed as a-tocopherol equivalents (a-TEs). One a-TE is the activity of 1 mg *RRR*-a-tocopherol (*d*-a-tocopherol). To estimate the a-TE of mixed diet containing natural forms of vitamin E, the number of milligrams of b-tocopherol should be multiplied by 0.5, g-tocopherol by 0.1, and a-tocotrienol by 0.3. Any of the synthetic all-*rac*-a-tocopherol (*dl*-a-tocopherol) should be multiplied by 0.74. One milligram of the latter compound in the acetate form is equivalent to 1 IU of vitamin E.

Vitamin E is an example of a phenolic antioxidant. Such molecules readily donate the hydrogen from the hydroxyl (-OH) group on the ring structure to free radicals, which then become unreactive. On donating the hydrogen, the phenolic compound itself becomes a relatively unreactive free radical because the unpaired electron on the oxygen atom is usually delocalised into the aromatic ring structure thereby increasing its stability.

The major biologic role of vitamin E is to protect PUFAs and other components of cell membranes and low-density lipoprotein (LDL) from oxidation by free radicals. Vitamin E is located primarily within the phospholipid bilayer of cell membranes.

It is particularly effective in preventing lipid peroxidation, a series of chemical reactions involving the oxidative deterioration of PUFAs. Elevated levels of lipid peroxidation products are associated with numerous diseases and clinical conditions. Although vitamin E is primarily located in cell and organelle membranes where it can exert its maximum protective effect, its concentration may only be one molecule for every 2000 phospholipid molecules. This suggests that after its reaction with free radicals it is rapidly regenerated, possibly by other antioxidants.

Absorption of vitamin E from the intestine depends on adequate pancreatic function, biliary secretion, and micelle formation. Conditions for absorption are like those for dietary lipid, that is, efficient emulsification, solubilisation within mixed bile salt micelles, uptake by enterocytes, and secretion into the circulation via the lymphatic system. Emulsification takes place initially in the stomach and then in the small intestine in the presence of pancreatic and biliary secretions.

The resulting mixed micelle aggregates the vitamin E molecules, solubilises the vitamin E, and then transports it to the brush border membrane of the enterocyte probably by passive diffusion. Within the enterocyte, tocopherol is incorporated into chylomicrons and secreted into the intracellular space and lymphatic system and subsequently into the blood stream. Tocopherol esters, present in processed foods and vitamin supplements, must be hydrolysed in the small intestine before absorption.

Vitamin E is transported in the blood by the plasma lipoproteins and erythrocytes. Chylomicrons carry tocopherol from the enterocyte to the liver, where they are incorporated into parenchymal cells as chylomicron remnants. The catabolism of chylomicrons takes place in the systemic circulation through the action of cellular lipoprotein lipase. During this process tocopherol can be transferred to high-density lipoproteins (HDLs).

The tocopherol in HDLs can transfer to other circulating lipoproteins, such as LDLs and very low-density lipoproteins (VLDLs). During the conversion of VLDL to LDL in the circulation, some a-tocopherol remains within the core lipids and thus is incorporated in LDL. Most a-tocopherol then enters the cells of peripheral tissues within the intact lipoprotein through the LDL receptor pathway, although some may be taken up by membrane binding sites recognising apolipoprotein A-I and A-II present on HDL.

Although the process of absorption of all the tocopherol homologues in our diet is similar, the a form predominates in blood and tissue. This is due to the action of binding proteins that preferentially select the a form over the others. In the first instance, a 30-kDa binding protein unique to the liver cytoplasm preferentially incorporates a-tocopherol in the nascent VLDL. This form also accumulates in non-hepatic tissues, particularly at sites where free radical production is greatest, such as in the membranes of mitochondria and endoplasmic reticulum in the heart and lungs.

Hepatic intracellular transport may be expedited by a 14.2-kDa binding protein that binds a-tocopherol in preference to the other homologues. Other proteinaceous sites with apparent tocopherol-binding abilities have been found on erythrocytes, adrenal membranes, and smooth muscle cells. These may serve as vitamin E receptors which orient the molecule within the membrane for optimum antioxidant function.

These selective mechanisms explain why vitamin E homologues have markedly differing antioxidant abilities in biologic systems and illustrates the important distinction between the *in vitro* antioxidant effectiveness of a substance in the stabilisation of, for example, a food product and its *in vivo* potency as an antioxidant. From a nutritional perspective, the most important form of vitamin E is a-tocopherol; this is corroborated in animal model tests of biopotency which assess the ability of the various homologues to prevent foetal absorption and muscular dystrophies.

Plasma vitamin E concentrations vary little over a wide range of dietary intakes. Even daily supplements of the order of 1600 IU/day for 3 weeks only increased plasma levels 2-3 times and on cessation of treatment plasma levels returned to pretreatment levels in 5 days. Likewise, tissue concentrations only increased by a similar amount when patients undergoing heart surgery were given 300 mg/day of the natural stereoisomer for 2 weeks preoperatively.

Kinetic studies with deuterated tocopherol suggest that there is rapid equilibration of new tocopherol in erythrocytes, liver, and spleen but that turnover in other tissues such as heart, muscle, and adipose tissue is much slower. The brain is markedly resistant to depletion and repletion with vitamin E. This presumably reflects an adaptive mechanism to avoid detrimental oxidative reactions in this key organ.

The primary oxidation product of a-tocopherol is a tocopheryl quinone that can be conjugated to yield the glucuronate after prior reduction to the hydroquinone.

This is excreted in the bile or further degraded in the kidneys to a-tocopheronic acid and hence excreted in the bile. Those vitamin E homologues not preferentially selected by the hepatic binding proteins are eliminated during the process of nascent VLDL secretion in the liver and probably excreted via the bile. Some vitamin E may also be excreted via skin sebaceous glands.

## VITAMIN K

Vitamin K is an essential fat-soluble micronutrient which is needed for a unique post-translational chemical modification in a small group of proteins with calcium-binding properties, collectively known as vitamin K dependent proteins or Gla-proteins. Thus far, the only unequivocal role of vitamin K in health is in the maintenance of normal coagulation.

The vitamin K dependent coagulation proteins are synthesised in the liver and comprise factors II, VII, IX, and X, which have a haemostatic role (*i.e.*, they are procoagulants that arrest and prevent bleeding), and proteins C and S, which have an anticoagulant role (*i.e.*, they inhibit the clotting process). Despite this duality of function, the overriding effect of nutritional vitamin K deficiency is to tip the balance in coagulation towards a bleeding tendency caused by the relative inactivity of the procoagulant proteins. Vitamin K dependent proteins synthesised by other tissues include the bone protein osteocalcin and matrix Gla protein; their functions remain to be clarified.

## BIOLOGICAL ROLE OF VITAMIN K

Vitamin K is the family name for a series of fat-soluble compounds, which have a common 2-methyl-1, 4-naphthoquinone nucleus but differ in the structures of a side chain at the 3-position. They are synthesised by plants and bacteria. In plants the only important molecular form is phylloquinone (vitamin $K_1$), which has a phytyl side chain. Bacteria synthesise a family of compounds called menaquinones (vitamin $K_2$), which have side chains based on repeating unsaturated 5-carbon (prenyl) units.

These are designated menaquinone-n (MK-n) according to the number (n) of prenyl units. Some bacteria also synthesise menaquinones in which one or more of the double bonds is saturated. The compound 2-methyl-1,4-naphthoquinone (common name menadione) may be regarded as a provitamin because vertebrates can convert it to MK-4 by adding a 4-prenyl side chain at the 3-position.

The biologic role of vitamin K is to act as a cofactor for a specific carboxylation reaction that transforms selective glutamate (Glu) residues to gg-carboxyglutamate (Gla) residues. The reaction is catalysed by a microsomal enzyme, gg-glutamyl, or vitamin K dependent carboxylase, which in turn is linked to a cyclic salvage pathway known as the vitamin K epoxide cycle.

Scheme shows the cyclic metabolism of vitamin K in relation to the conversion of glutamate (Glu) to gg-carboxyglutamate (Gla) residues for the coagulation protein prothrombin.

A general term for the glutamate precursors of vitamin K-dependent proteins is proteins induced by vitamin K absence, abbreviated PIVKA. For prothrombin (factor II) the glutamate precursor is known as PIVKA-II. The active form of vitamin K needed for carboxylation is the reduced form, vitamin K quinol.

When coagulation is initiated, the zymogens of the four vitamin K-dependent clotting factors are cleaved to yield the active protease clotting factors. Two other vitamin K-dependent proteins called protein C and protein S play a regulatory role in the inhibition of coagulation. The function of protein C is to degrade phospholipid-bound activated factors V and VIII in the presence of calcium. Protein S acts as a synergistic cofactor to protein C by enhancing the binding of activated protein C to negatively charged phospholipids. Yet another vitamin K-dependent plasma protein (protein Z) is suspected to have a haemostatic role but its function is currently unknown.

Apart from the coagulation proteins, several other vitamin K-dependent proteins have been isolated from bone, cartilage, kidney, lungs, and other tissues. Only two, osteocalcin and matrix Gla protein (MGP), have been well characterised. Both are found in bone but MGP also occurs in cartilage, blood vessel walls, and other soft tissues.

There is evidence that protein S is synthesised by several tissues including the vessel wall and bone and may have other functions besides its well-established role as a coagulation inhibitor.

It also seems likely that one function of MGP is to inhibit mineralisation. Thus far, no clear biologic role for osteocalcin has been established despite its being the major non-collagenous bone protein synthesised by osteoblasts. This failure to establish a biologic function for osteocalcin has hampered studies of the possible detrimental effects of vitamin K deficiency on bone health. Evidence of a possible association of a suboptimal vitamin K status with increased fracture risk remains to be confirmed.

## POPULATIONS AT RISK

### Vitamin K-deficiency Bleeding in Infants

In infants up to around age 6 months, vitamin K deficiency, although rare, represents a significant public health problem throughout the world. The deficiency syndrome is traditionally known as haemorrhagic disease of the newborn or more recently, to give a better definition of the cause, vitamin K deficiency bleeding (VKDB).

The time of onset of VKDB is more unpredictable than previously supposed and it is now useful to recognise three syndromes: early, classic, and late. Until the 1960s, VKDB was considered to be solely a problem of the first week of life. Then, in 1966, came the first reports from Thailand of a new vitamin K deficiency syndrome that typically presented between 1 and 2 months of life and is now termed late VKDB. In 1977 Bhanchet and colleagues, who had first described this syndrome, summarised their studies of 93 affected Thai infants, establishing the idiopathic history, preponderance of breast-fed infants (98 per cent), and high incidence of intracranial bleeding (63 per cent).

More reports from South East Asia and Australia followed, and in 1983 McNinch *et al.* reported the return of VKDB in the United Kingdom. This increased incidence was ascribed to a decrease in the practice of vitamin K prophylaxis and to an increased trend towards exclusive human milk feeding. Human milk has lower concentrations of vitamin K than do infant milk formulas.

Without vitamin K prophylaxis, the incidence of late VKDB (per 100,000 births), based on acceptable surveillance data, has been estimated to be 4.4 in the United Kingdom, 7.2 in Germany, and as high as 72 in Thailand. Of real concern is that late VKDB, unlike the classic form, has a high incidence of death or severe and permanent brain damage resulting from intracranial haemorrhage.

Epidemiologic studies worldwide have identified two major risk factors for both classic and late VKDB: exclusive human milk feeding and the failure to give any vitamin K prophylaxis. The increased risk for infants fed human milk compared with formula milk is probably related to the relatively low concentrations of vitamin K (phylloquinone) in breast milk compared with formula milks.

## DIETARY SOURCES

High-performance liquid chromatography can be used to accurately determine the major dietary form of vitamin K (phylloquinone) in foods, and food tables are being compiled for Western diets. Phylloquinone is distributed ubiquitously throughout the diet, and the range of concentrations in different food categories is very wide. In general, the relative values in vegetables confirm the known association of phylloquinone with photosynthetic tissues, with the highest values (normally in the range 400-700 $\mu$g/100 g) being found in green leafy vegetables.

The next best sources are certain vegetable oils (*e.g.*, soybean, rapeseed, and olive oils) which contain 50-200 $\mu$g/100 g. Some vegetable oils, such as peanut, corn, sunflower and safflower oils, have a much lower phylloquinone content (1-10 $\mu$g/100 g). The great differences between vegetable oils obviously presents problems for calculating the phylloquinone contents of oil-containing foods when the type of oil (or its storage condition) is not known.

Menaquinones seem to have a more restricted distribution in the diet than does phylloquinone. In the Western diet nutritionally significant amounts of long-chain menaquinones have been found in animal livers and fermented foods such as cheeses. Yeasts do not synthesise menaquinones and menaquinone-rich foods are those with a bacterial fermentation stage. The Japanese food *natto* (fermented soybeans) has a menaquinone content even higher than that of phylloquinone in green leafy vegetables.

The relative dietary importance of MK-4 is more difficult to evaluate because concentrations in foods may well depend on geographic differences in the use of menadione in animal husbandry, menadione from which MK-4 may be synthesised in animal tissues. Another imponderable factor is the evidence that animal tissues and dairy produce may contain some MK-4 as a product of tissue synthesis from phylloquinone itself.

Knowledge of the vitamin K content of human milk has been the subject of methodologic controversies with a 10-fold variation in reported values of phylloquinone concentrations of mature human milk. Where milk sampling and analytical techniques have met certain criteria for their validity, the phylloquinone content of mature milk have generally ranged between 1 and 4 $\mu$g/l, with average concentrations near the lower end of this range.

However, there is considerable intra- and inter-subject variation, and levels higher are in colostral milk than in mature milk. Menaquinone concentrations in human milk have not been accurately determined but appear to be much lower than those of phylloquinone. Phylloquinone concentrations in infant formula milk range from 3 to 16 $\mu$g/l in unsupplemented formulas and up to 100 $\mu$g/l in fortified formulas. Nowadays most formulas are fortified; typical phylloquinone concentrations are about 50 mg/l.

**BIO-AVAILABILITY OF VITAMIN K FROM FOODS**

Very little is known about the bio-availability of the K vitamins from different foods. It has been estimated that the efficiency of absorption of phylloquinone from boiled spinach (eaten with butter) is no greater than 10 per cent compared with an estimated 80 per cent when phylloquinone is given in its free form. This poor absorption of phylloquinone from green leafy vegetables may be explained by its location in chloroplasts and tight association with the thylakoid membrane, where this naphthoquinone plays a role in photosynthesis. In comparison, the bio-availability of MK-4 from butter artificially enriched with this vitamer was more than twofold higher than that of phylloquinone from spinach.

The poor extraction of phylloquinone from leafy vegetables, which as a category represents the single greatest food source of phylloquinone, may place a different perspective on the relative importance of other foods with lower concentrations of phylloquinone (*e.g.*, containing soybean and rapeseed oils) but in which the vitamin is not tightly bound and its bio-availability is likely to be greater. Even before bio-availability was taken into account, fats and oils that are contained in mixed dishes were found to make an important contribution to the phylloquinone content of the US diet and in a UK study contributed 30 per cent of the total dietary intake.

No data exist on the efficiency of intestinal absorption of dietary long-chain menaquinones. Because the lipophilic properties of menaquinones are greater than those of phylloquinone, it is likely that the efficiency of their absorption, in the free form, is low, as suggested by animal studies.

**Intestinal Bacterial Synthesis as a Source of Vitamin K**

Intestinal microflora synthesise large amounts of menaquinones, which are potentially available as a source of vitamin K. Quantitative measurements at different sites of the human intestine have demonstrated that most of these menaquinones are present in the distal colon. Major forms produced are MK-10 and MK-11 by *Bacteroides*, MK-8 by *Enterobacter*, MK-7 by *Veillonella,* and MK-6 by *Eubacterium lentum*. It is noteworthy that menaquinones with very long chains (MKs 10-13) are known to be synthesised by members of the anaerobic genus *Bacteroides* and are major inhabitants of the intestinal tract but have not been detected in significant amounts in foods. The widespread presence of MKs 10-13 in human livers at high concentrations therefore suggests that these forms, at least, originate from intestinal synthesis.

It is commonly held that animals and humans obtain a significant fraction of their vitamin K requirement from direct absorption of menaquinones produced by microfloral synthesis, but hard experimental evidence documenting the site and extent of any absorption is singularly lacking. The most promising site of absorption is the terminal ileum, where there are some menaquinone-producing bacteria as well as bile salts. The evidence overall suggests that the bio-availability of bacterial menaquinones is poor because they are mostly tightly bound to the bacterial cytoplasmic membrane and the largest pool is present in the colon, which lacks bile salts for their solubilisation.

**Assessment of Vitamin K Status**

Conventional coagulation assays are useful for detecting overt vitamin K-deficient states which are associated with a risk of bleeding. However, they offer only a relatively insensitive insight into vitamin K nutritional status and the detection of sub-clinical vitamin K-deficient states. A more sensitive measure of vitamin K sufficiency can be obtained from tests that detect under-carboxylated species of vitamin K-dependent proteins. In states of vitamin K deficiency, under-carboxylated species of the vitamin K-dependent coagulation proteins are released from the liver into the blood; their levels increase with the degree of severity of vitamin K deficiency.

These under-carboxylated forms (PIVKA) are unable to participate in the normal coagulation cascade because they are unable to bind calcium. The measurement of under-carboxylated prothrombin (PIVKA-II) is the most useful and sensitive homeostatic marker of sub-clinical vitamin K deficiency. Importantly, PIVKA-II is detectable in plasma before any changes occur in conventional coagulation tests. Several types of assay for PIVKA-II have been developed which vary in their sensitivity.

In the same way that vitamin K deficiency causes PIVKA-II to be released into the circulation from the liver, a deficit of vitamin K in bone will cause the osteoblasts to secrete under-carboxylated species of osteocalcin (ucOC) into the bloodstream. It has been proposed that the concentration of circulating ucOC reflects the sufficiency of vitamin K for the carboxylation of this Gla protein in bone tissue. Most assays for ucOC have been indirect because they rely on the differential absorption of carboxylated and under-carboxylated forms to hydroxyapatite and are difficult to interpret.

Other criteria of vitamin K sufficiency that have been used are plasma measurements of phylloquinone and the measurement of urinary Gla. It is expected and found that the excretion of urinary Gla is decreased in vitamin K deficiency.

## Dietary Intakes in Infants and Their Adequacy

The average intake of phylloquinone in infants fed human milk during the first 6 months of life has been reported to be less than 1 μg/day; this is approximately 100-fold lower than the intake in infants fed a typical supplemented formula.

This big disparity between intakes is reflected in plasma levels. Using the detection of PIVKA-II as a marker of sub-clinical deficiency, a study from Germany concluded that a minimum daily intake of about 100 ml of colostral milk (that supplies about 0.2-0.3 μg of phylloquinone) is sufficient for normal haemostasis in a baby of about 3 kg during the first week of life.

Similar conclusions were reached in a Japanese study which showed a linear correlation between the prevalence of PIVKA-II and the volume of breast milk ingested over 3 days; 95 per cent of infants with detectable PIVKA-II had average daily intakes of less than about 120 ml, but the marker was not detectable when intakes reached 170 ml/day.

## Vitamin K Deficiency Bleeding

The natural tendency for human-milk-fed infants to develop a sub-clinical vitamin K deficiency in the first 2-3 days of life is self-limiting. Comparisons between untreated human-milk-fed infants with others who had received vitamin K or supplementary feeds clearly suggest that this improvement in vitamin K-dependent clotting activity is due to an improved vitamin K status. After the first week, vitamin K-dependent clotting factor increases are more gradual, and it is not possible from clotting factor assays to differentiate between the natural post-natal increase in the synthesis of the core proteins from an improved vitamin K status leading to greater functional activity.

Use of the most sensitive assays for PIVKA-II shows that there is still evidence of suboptimal vitamin K status in infants solely fed human milk between the ages of 1 and 2 months. Deficiency signs are less common in infants who have received adequate vitamin K supplementation or who have been formula fed.

**Dietary Intakes in Older Infants, Children and Adults**

The only comprehensive national survey of phylloquinone intakes across all age groups (except infants aged 0-6 months) is that of the US Food and Drug Administration Total Diet Study, which was based on the 1987-88 Nationwide Food Consumption Survey. For infants and children from the age of 6 months to 16 years, average phylloquinone intakes were above the current US recommended dietary allowance (RDA) values for their respective age groups, more so for children up to 10 years than from 10 to 16 years. There have been no studies of intakes in children in relation to functional markers of vitamin K sufficiency in children.

Intakes for adults in The Total Diet Study were also close to or slightly higher than the current US RDA values of 80 $\mu$g for men and 65 $\mu$g for women, although intakes were slightly lower than the RDA in the 25-30 years age group. There is some evidence from an evaluation of all the US studies that older adults have higher dietary intakes of phylloquinone than do younger adults.

The US results are very comparable with a detailed, seasonality study in the United Kingdom in which mean intakes in men and women (aged 22-54 years) were 72 and 64 $\mu$g/day, respectively; no significant sex or seasonal variations were found. Another UK study suggested that intakes were lower in manual workers and in smokers, reflecting their lower intakes of green vegetables and high-quality vegetable oil.

Several dietary restriction and repletion studies have attempted to assess the adequacy of vitamin K intakes in adults. It is clear from these studies that volunteers consuming less than 10 $\mu$g/day of phylloquinone do not show any changes in conventional coagulation tests even after several weeks unless other measures to reduce the efficiency of absorption are introduced. However, a diet containing only 2-5 $\mu$g/day of phylloquinone fed for 2 weeks did result in an increase of PIVKA-II and a 70 per cent decrease in plasma phylloquinone.

Similar evidence of a sub-clinical vitamin K deficiency together with an increased urinary excretion of Gla was found when dietary intakes of phylloquinone were reduced from about 80 to about 40 $\mu$g/day for 21 days. A repletion phase in this study was consistent with a human dietary vitamin K requirement (for its coagulation role) of about 1 $\mu$g/kg body weight/day.

The most detailed and controlled dietary restriction and repletion study in healthy human subjects is that by Ferland *et al.* In this study 32 healthy subjects in two age groups (20-40 and 60-80 years) were fed a mixed diet containing about 80 $\mu$g/day of phylloquinone, which is the RDA for adult males in the United States. After 4 days on this baseline diet there was a 13-day depletion period during which the subjects were fed a diet containing about 10 μg/day.

After this depletion phase the subjects entered a 16-day repletion period during which, over 4-day intervals, they were sequentially repleted with 5, 15, 25, and 45 μg phylloquinone. The depletion protocol had no effect on conventional coagulation and specific factor assays but did induce a significant increase in PIVKA-II in both age groups.

The most dramatic change was in plasma levels of phylloquinone, which fell to about 15 per cent of the values on day 1. The drop in plasma phylloquinone also suggested that the average dietary intake of these particular individuals before they entered the study had been greater than the baseline diet of 80 μg/day.

The repletion protocol failed to bring the plasma phylloquinone levels of the young subjects back above the lower limit of the normal range (previously established in healthy, free-living adults) whereas the plasma levels in the elderly group only rose slightly above this lower limit in the last 4 days.

Another indication of a reduced vitamin K status in the young group was the fall in urinary output of Gla (90 per cent of baseline) that was not seen in the elderly group; this suggested that younger subjects are more susceptible to the effects of an acute deficiency than are older subjects.

## MINERALS IN FOOD

### ZINC

Zinc is present in all body tissues and fluids. The total body zinc content has been estimated to be 30 mmol (2 g). Skeletal muscle accounts for approximately 60 per cent of the total body content and bone mass, with a zinc concentration of 1.5-3 mmol/g (100-200 mg/g), for approximately 30 per cent. Zinc concentration of lean body mass is approximately 0.46 mmol/g (30 mg/g). Plasma zinc has a rapid turnover rate and it represents only about 0.1 per cent of total body zinc content.

This level appears to be under close homeostatic control. High concentrations of zinc are found in the choroid of the eye 4.2 mmol/g (274 μg/g) and in prostatic fluids 4.6-7.7 mmol/l (300-500 mg/l).

Zinc is an essential component of a large number (>300) of enzymes participating in the synthesis and degradation of carbohydrates, lipids, proteins, and nucleic acids as well as in the metabolism of other micronutrients. Zinc stabilises the molecular structure of cellular components and membranes and contributes in this way to the maintenance of cell and organ integrity. Furthermore, zinc has an essential role in polynucleotide transcription and thus in the process of genetic expression. Its involvement in such fundamental activities probably accounts for the essentiality of zinc for all life forms.

Zinc plays a central role in the immune system, affecting a number of aspects of cellular and Humoral immunity. The role of zinc in immunity was reviewed extensively by Shanglar *et al.*.

The clinical features of severe zinc deficiency in humans are growth retardation, delayed sexual and bone maturation, skin lesions, diarrhoea, alopecia, impaired appetite, increased susceptibility to infections mediated via defects in the immune system, and the appearance of behavioural changes. The effects of marginal or mild zinc deficiency are less clear. A reduced growth rate and impairments of immune defence are so far the only clearly demonstrated signs of mild zinc deficiency in humans. Other effects, such as impaired taste and wound healing, which have been claimed to result from a low zinc intake, are less consistently observed.

**Zinc Metabolism and Homeostasis**

Zinc absorption is concentration dependent and occurs throughout the small intestine. Under normal physiologic conditions, transport processes of uptake are not saturated. Zinc administered in aqueous solutions to fasting subjects is absorbed efficiently (60-70 per cent), whereas absorption from solid diets is less efficient and varies depending on zinc content and diet composition.

Zinc is lost from the body through the kidneys, skin, and intestine. The endogenous intestinal losses can vary from 7 mmol/day (0.5 mg/day) to more than 45 mmol/day (3 mg/day), depending on zinc intake. Urinary and skin losses are of the order of 7-10 mmol/day (0.5-0.7 mg/day) each and depend less on normal variations in zinc intake. Starvation and muscle catabolism increase zinc losses in urine. Strenuous exercise and elevated ambient temperatures could lead to losses by perspiration.

The body has no zinc stores in the conventional sense. In conditions of bone resorption and tissue catabolism, zinc is released and may be re-utilised to some extent. Human experimental studies with low-zinc diets 2.6-3.6 mg/day (40-55 mmol/day) have shown that circulating zinc levels and activities of zinc-containing enzymes can be maintained within normal range over several months, which highlights the efficiency of the zinc homeostasis mechanism.

Controlled depletion-repletion studies in humans have shown that changes in the endogenous excretion of zinc through the kidneys, intestine, and skin and changes in absorptive efficiency are how body zinc content is maintained. The underlying mechanisms are poorly understood.

Sensitive indexes for assessing zinc status are unknown at present. Static indexes, such as zinc concentration in plasma, blood cells, and hair, and urinary zinc excretion are decreased in severe zinc deficiency. A number of conditions that are unrelated to zinc status can affect all these indexes, especially zinc plasma levels.

Infection, stress situations such as fever, food intake, and pregnancy lower plasma zinc concentrations whereas, for example, long-term fasting increases it. However, on a population basis, reduced plasma zinc concentrations seem to be a marker for zinc-responsive growth reductions. Experimental zinc depletion studies suggest that changes in immune response occur before reductions in plasma zinc concentrations are apparent. So far, it has not been possible to identify zinc-dependent enzymes which could serve as early markers for zinc status.

A number of functional indexes of zinc status have been suggested, for example, wound healing, taste acuity, and dark adaptation. Changes in these functions are, however, not specific to zinc and these indexes have so far not been proven useful for identifying marginal zinc deficiency in humans.

The introduction of stable isotope techniques in zinc research has created possibilities for evaluating the relationship between diet and zinc status and is likely to lead to a better understanding of the mechanisms underlying the homeostatic regulations of zinc. Estimations of turnover rates of administered isotopes in plasma or urine have revealed the existence of a relatively small rapidly exchangeable body pool of zinc of about 1.5-3 mmol (100-200 mg).

The size of the pool seems to be correlated to habitual dietary intake and it is reduced in controlled depletion studies. The exchangeable zinc pool was also found to be correlated to endogenous faecal excretion of zinc and to total daily absorption of zinc. These data suggest that the size of the exchangeable pool depends on recently absorbed zinc and that a larger exchangeable pool results in larger endogenous excretion. Changes in endogenous intestinal excretion of zinc seem to be more important than changes in absorptive efficiency for maintenance of zinc homeostasis.

**Populations at Risk for Zinc Deficiency**

The central role of zinc in cell division, protein synthesis, and growth makes infants, children, adolescents, and pregnant women especially at risk for an inadequate zinc intake. Zinc-responsive stunting has been identified in several studies, and a more rapid body weight gain in malnourished children supplemented with zinc was reported. Other studies have failed to show a growth-promoting effect of zinc supplementation.

A recent meta-analysis of 25 intervention trials comprising 1834 children under 13 years of age, with a mean duration of approximately 7 months and a mean dose of zinc of 14 mg/day (214 mmol/day), showed a small but significant positive effect of zinc supplementation on height and weight increases.

The initial presence of stunting was significantly associated with an effect of zinc supplementation on height, whereas initial low plasma zinc concentrations were associated with a more pronounced effect on weight gain.

Results from zinc supplementation studies suggest that a low zinc status in children not only affects growth but is also associated with an increased risk of severe infectious diseases.

Episodes of acute diarrhoea with shorter duration and less severity and reductions in incidence of diarrhoea in zinc-supplemented groups have been reported. Other studies indicate that the incidence of acute lower respiratory tract infections and malaria may also be reduced by zinc supplementation. Prevention of sub-optimal zinc status and zinc deficiency in children by an increased intake and availability of zinc could consequently have a significant effect on child health in developing countries.

The role of maternal zinc status on pregnancy outcome is still unclear. Positive as well as negative associations between plasma zinc concentration and foetal growth or labour and delivery complications have been reported. Results of zinc supplementation studies also remain inconclusive. Interpretation of plasma zinc concentrations in pregnancy is complicated by the effect of hemodilution, and low plasma zinc levels may reflect other metabolic disturbances.

Zinc supplementation studies of pregnant women have been performed mainly in relatively well-nourished populations, which may be one of the reasons for the mixed results. A recent study in low-income American women with plasma zinc concentrations below the mean at enrolment in prenatal care showed that a zinc intake of 25 mg/day resulted in greater infant birth weights and head circumferences and a reduction in very low birth weights among non-obese women compared with the placebo group.

**Dietary Sources and Availability of Zinc**

Lean red meat, whole-grain cereals, pulses, and legumes provide the highest concentrations of zinc 25-50 mg/kg (380-760 mmol/kg) raw weight. Processed cereals with low extraction rates, polished rice, and lean meat or meat with high fat content have a moderate zinc content 10-25 mg/kg (150-380 mmol/kg). Fish, roots and tubers, green leafy vegetables, and fruits are only modest sources of zinc <10 mg/kg (<150 mmol/kg). Separated fats and oils, sugar, and alcohol have a very low zinc content.

The utilisation of zinc depends on the overall composition of the diet. Experimental studies have identified a number of dietary factors as potential promoters or antagonists of zinc absorption. Soluble low-molecular-weight organic substances, such as amino and hydroxy acids, facilitate zinc absorption. In contrast, organic compounds forming stable and poorly soluble complexes with zinc can impair absorption. In addition, competitive interactions between zinc and other ions with similar physicochemical properties can affect the uptake and intestinal absorption of zinc.

The risk for competitive interactions seems mainly to be related to high doses in the form of supplements or in aqueous solutions. However, at levels present in food and at realistic fortification levels, zinc absorption appears not to be affected, for example, by iron and copper.

Isotope studies with human subjects have identified two factors which together with the total zinc content of the diet are major determinants of absorption and utilisation of dietary zinc. The first is the content of inositol hexaphosphate (phytate) and the second is the level and source of dietary protein. Phytates are present in whole-grain cereals and legumes and in smaller amounts in other vegetables. They have a strong potential for binding divalent cations and their depressive effect on zinc absorption has been demonstrated in humans.

The molar ratio between phytates and zinc in meals or diets is a useful indicator of the effect of phytates in depressing zinc absorption. At molar ratios above the range of 6-10, zinc absorption starts to decline; at ratios above 15 absorption is typically less than 15 per cent. The effect of phytate is, however, modified by the source and amount of dietary proteins consumed. Animal proteins improve zinc absorption from a phytate-containing diet. Zinc absorption from some legume-based diets is comparable with that from animal-protein-based diets despite a higher phytate content in the former. High dietary calcium potentiated the antagonistic effects of phytates on zinc absorption in experimental studies. The results from human studies are less consistent and any effects seem to depend on the source of calcium and the composition of the diet.

Some examples of recently published absorption studies illustrate the effect of zinc content and diet composition on fractional zinc absorption. The results from the total diet studies, where all main meals of a day's intake have been extrinsically labelled, show a remarkable consistency in fractional absorption despite relatively large variations in meal composition and zinc content. Thus, approximately twice as much zinc was absorbed from a non-vegetarian or high-meat die than from a diet in rural China based on rice and wheat flour. Data are lacking on zinc absorption from typical diets of developing countries, which usually have a high phytate content.

The availability of zinc from the diet can be improved by reductions in the phytate content and inclusion of animal protein sources. Lower extraction rates of cereal grains will result in lower phytate content but at the same time the zinc content is reduced, so that the net effect on zinc supply is limited. The phytate content can be reduced by activating the phytase present in most phytate-containing foods or through the addition of microbial or fungal phytases.

Phytases hydrolyse the phytate to lower inositol phosphates, resulting in an improved zinc absorption. The activity of phytases in tropical cereals such as maize and sorghum is lower than that in wheat and rye. Germination of cereals and legumes increases phytase activity and addition of some germinated flour to ungerminated maize or sorghum followed by soaking at ambient temperature for 12-24 hours can reduce the phytate content substantially.

Additional reduction can be achieved by the fermentation of porridge for weaning foods or doughs for bread making. Commercially available phytase preparations could also be used but may not be economically accessible in many populations.

## IODINE

At present, the only physiologic role known for iodine in the human body is in the synthesis of thyroid hormones by the thyroid gland. Therefore, the dietary requirement of iodine is determined by normal thyroxine ($T_4$) production by the thyroid gland without stressing the thyroid iodide trapping mechanism or raising thyroid stimulating hormone (TSH) levels.

Iodine from the diet is absorbed throughout the gastrointestinal tract. Dietary iodine is converted into the iodide ion before it is absorbed. The iodide ion is bio-available and absorbed totally from food and water. This is not true for iodine within thyroid hormones ingested for therapeutic purposes. Iodine enters the circulation as plasma inorganic iodide, which is cleared from circulation by the thyroid and kidney.

The iodide is used by the thyroid gland for synthesis of thyroid hormones, and the kidney excretes iodine with urine. The excretion of iodine in the urine is a good measure of iodine intake. In a normal population with no evidence of clinical iodine deficiency either in the form of endemic goitre or endemic cretinism, urinary iodine excretion reflects the average daily iodine requirement. Therefore, for determining the iodine requirements, the important indexes are serum $T_4$ and TSH levels (indicating normal thyroid status) and urinary iodine excretion.

### Dietary Sources

The iodine content of food depends on the iodine content of the soil in which it is grown. The iodine present in the upper crust of earth is leached by glaciation and repeated flooding and is carried to the sea. Sea water is, therefore, a rich source of iodine. The seaweed located near coral reefs has an inherent biologic capacity to concentrate iodine from the sea. The reef fish which thrive on seaweed are rich in iodine.

Thus, a population consuming seaweed and reef fish has a high intake of iodine, as the case in Japan. The amount of iodine intake by the Japanese is in the range of 2-3 mg/day. In several areas of Asia, Africa, Latin America, and parts of Europe, iodine intake varies from 20 to 80 mg/day. In the United States and Canada and some parts of Europe, the intake is around 500 mg/day.

**Table : Average iodine content of foods (in mg/g)**

| Food | Fresh basis | | Dry basis | |
|---|---|---|---|---|
| | Mean | Range | Mean | Range |
| Fish (fresh water) | 30 | 17-40 | 116 | 68-194 |
| Fish (marine) | 832 | 163-3180 | 3715 | 471-4591 |
| Shellfish | 798 | 308-1300 | 3866 | 1292-4987 |
| Meat | 50 | 27-97 | - | - |
| Milk | 47 | 35-56 | - | - |
| Eggs | 93 | - | - | - |
| Cereal grains | 47 | 22-72 | 65 | 34-92 |
| Fruits | 18 | 10-29 | 154 | 62-277 |
| Legumes | 30 | 23-36 | 234 | 223-245 |
| Vegetables | 29 | 12-201 | 385 | 204-1636 |

## Iodine Fortification

Iodine deficiency is present in almost all parts of the developed and developing world, and environmental iodine deficiency is the main cause of iodine deficiency disorders. Iodine is irregularly distributed over the earth's crust, resulting in acute deficiencies in areas such as mountainous regions and flood plains. The problem is aggravated by accelerated deforestation and soil erosion. Thus, the food grown in iodine-deficient regions can never provide enough iodine for the people and livestock living there.

The iodine deficiency results from geologic rather than social and economic conditions. It cannot be eliminated by changing dietary habits or by eating specific kinds of foods but must be corrected by supplying iodine from external sources. It has, therefore, been a common practice to use common salt as a vehicle for iodine fortification for the past 75 years. Salt is consumed at approximately the same level throughout the year by the entire population of a region. Universal salt iodisation is now a widely accepted strategy for preventing and correcting iodine deficiency disorders.

There are areas where consumption of goitrogens in the staple diet (*e.g.*, cassava) affects the proper utilisation of iodine by the thyroid gland. For example, in Congo, Africa, as a result of cassava diets there is an overload of thiocyanate. To overcome this problem, appropriate increases in salt iodisation are required to ensure the recommended dietary intake. The iodisation of salt is done either by spraying potassium iodate or potassium iodide in amounts that ensure a minimum of 150 $\mu$g iodine/day. Both of these forms of iodine are absorbed as iodide ions and are completely bio-available. Other methods of iodine prophylaxis are also used: iodised oil (capsule and injections), iodised water, iodised bread, iodised soya sauce, iodoform compounds used in dairy and poultry, and certain food additives.

Iodine loss occurs as a result of improper packaging, Humidity and moisture, and transport in open trucks and railway wagons exposed to sunlight. To compensate for these losses, higher levels of iodine are used during the production of iodised salt. Losses during the cooking process vary from 20 per cent to 40 per cent depending on the type of cooking used.

To ensure the consumption of recommended levels of iodine, the iodine content of salt at the production level should be monitored with proper quality assurance programmes. Regular evaluation of the urinary iodine excretion pattern in the population consuming iodised salt or exposed to other iodine prophylactic measures would help the adjusting of iodine intake.

## IRON

Iron has several vital functions in the body. It serves as a carrier of oxygen to the tissues from the lungs by red blood cell haemoglobin, as a transport medium for electrons within cells, and as an integrated part of important enzyme systems in various tissues. The physiology of iron has been extensively reviewed.

Most of the iron in the body is present in the erythrocytes as haemoglobin, a molecule composed of four units, each containing one heme group and one protein chain. The structure of haemoglobin allows it to be fully loaded with oxygen in the lungs and partially unloaded in the tissues (*e.g.*, in the muscles). The iron-containing oxygen storage protein in the muscles, myoglobin, is similar in structure to haemoglobin but has only one heme unit and one globin chain. Several iron-containing enzymes, the cytochromes, also have one heme group and one globin protein chain. These enzymes act as electron carriers within the cell and their structures do not permit reversible loading and unloading of oxygen.

Their role in the oxidative metabolism is to transfer energy within the cell and specifically in the mitochondria. Other key functions for the iron-containing enzymes (*e.g.*, cytochrome) include the synthesis of steroid hormones and bile acids; detoxification of foreign substances in the liver; and signal controlling in some neurotransmitters, such as the dopamine and serotonin systems in the brain. Iron is reversibly stored within the liver as ferritin and hemosiderin whereas it is transported between different compartments in the body by the protein transferrin.

### Iron Requirements

Iron is not actively excreted from the body in urine or in the intestines. Iron is only lost with cells from the skin and the interior surfaces of the body intestines, urinary tract, and airways. The total amount lost is estimated at 14 $\mu$g/kg body weight/day. In children, it is probably more correct to relate these losses to body surface. A non-menstruating 55-kg women loses about 0.8 mg

Fe/day and a 70-kg man loses about 1 mg. The range of individual variation has been estimated to be ±15 per cent.

Earlier studies suggested that sweat iron losses could be considerable, especially in a hot, Humid climate. However, new studies which took extensive precautions to avoid the interference of contamination of iron from the skin during the collection of total body sweat have shown that these sweat iron losses are negligible.

**Growth**

The newborn term infant has an iron content of about 250-300 mg (75 mg/kg body weight). During the first 2 months of life, haemoglobin concentration falls because of the improved oxygen situation in the newborn infant compared with the intrauterine foetus. This leads to a considerable redistribution of iron from catabolised erythrocytes to iron stores.

This iron will cover the needs of the term infant during the first 4-6 months of life and is why iron requirements during this period can be provided by human milk, that contains very little iron. Because of the marked supply of iron to the foetus during the last trimester of pregnancy, the iron situation is much less favourable in the premature and low-birth-weight infant than in the term infant. An extra supply of iron is therefore needed in these infants even during the first 6 months of life.

In the full-term infant, iron requirements will rise markedly after age 4-6 months and amount to about 0.7-0.9 mg/day during the remaining part of the first year. These requirements are therefore very high, especially in relation to body size and energy intake.

In the first year of life, the full-term infant almost doubles its total iron stores and triple its body weight. The change in body iron during this period occurs mainly during the first 6-12 months of life. Between 1 and 6 years of age, the body iron content is again doubled. The requirements for absorbed iron in infants and children are very high in relation to their energy requirements. For example, in infants 6-12 months of age, about 1.5 mg of iron need to be absorbed per 4.184 MJ and about half of this amount is required up to age 4 years.

In the weaning period, the iron requirements in relation to energy intake are the highest of the lifespan except for the last trimester of pregnancy, when iron requirements to a large extent have to be covered from the iron stores of the mother. The rapidly growing weaning infant has no iron stores and has to rely on dietary iron. It is possible to meet these high requirements if the diet has a consistently high content of meat and foods rich in ascorbic acid.

In most developed countries today, infant cereal products are the staple foods for that period of life. Commercial products are regularly fortified with iron and ascorbic acid, and they are usually given together with fruit juices and solid foods containing meat, fish, and vegetables. The fortification of cereal products with iron and ascorbic acid is important in meeting the high dietary needs, especially considering the importance of an optimal iron nutrition during this phase of brain development.

**Iron Absorption**

With respect to the mechanism of absorption, there are two kinds of dietary iron: heme iron and non-heme iron. In the human diet the primary sources of heme iron are the haemoglobin and myoglobin from consumption of meat, poultry, and fish whereas non-heme iron is obtained from cereals, pulses, legumes, fruits, and vegetables. The average absorption of heme iron from meat-containing meals is about 25 per cent.

The absorption of heme iron can vary from about 40 per cent during iron deficiency to about 10 per cent during iron repletion. Heme iron can be degraded and converted to non-heme iron if foods are cooked at a high temperature for too long. Calcium is the only dietary factor that negatively influences the absorption of heme iron and does so to the same extent that it influences non-heme iron.

Non-heme iron is the main form of dietary iron. The absorption of non-heme iron is influenced by individual iron status and by several factors in the diet. Iron compounds used for the fortification of foods will only be partially available for absorption. Once iron is dissolved, its absorption from fortificants and food contaminants is influenced by the same factors as the iron native to the food substance. Iron originating from the soil (*e.g.*, from various forms of clay) is sometimes present in considerable amounts on the surface of foods as a contaminant originating from dust on air-dried foods or from water used in irrigation. Even if the fraction of iron that is available is often small, contamination iron may still be nutritionally important because of the great amounts present.

Reducing substances (*i.e.*, substances that keep iron in the ferrous form) must be present for iron to be absorbed. The presence of meat, poultry, and fish in the diet enhance iron absorption. Other foods contain factors (ligands) that strongly bind ferrous ions that subsequently inhibit absorption. Examples are phytates and certain iron-binding polyphenols.

**Inhibition of Iron Absorption**

Phytates are found in all kinds of grains, seeds, nuts, vegetables, roots (*e.g.*, potatoes), and fruits. Chemically, phytates are inositol hexaphosphate salts and are a storage form of phosphates and minerals. Other phosphates have not been shown to inhibit non-heme iron absorption. In North American and European diets, about 90 per cent of phytates originate from cereals. Phytates strongly inhibit iron absorption in a dose-dependent fashion and even small amounts of phytates have a marked effect.

Bran has a high content of phytate and strongly inhibits iron absorption. Whole-wheat flour, therefore, has a much higher content of phytates than does white wheat flour. In bread some of the phytates in bran are degraded during the fermentation of the dough. Fermentation for a couple of days (sourdough fermentation) can therefore almost completely degrade the phytate and increase the bio-availability of iron in bread made from whole-wheat flour. Oats strongly inhibit iron absorption because of their high phytate content, that results from native phytase in oats being destroyed by the normal heat process used to avoid rancidity. Sufficient amounts of ascorbic acid can counteract this inhibition. By contrast, non-phytate-containing dietary fibre components have almost no influence on iron absorption.

Almost all plants contain phenolic compounds as part of their defence system against insects, animals, and humans. Only some of the phenolic compounds (mainly those containing galloyl groups) seem to be responsible for the inhibition of iron absorption. Tea, coffee, and cocoa are common plant products that contain iron-binding polyphenols. Many vegetables, especially green leafy vegetables (*e.g.*, spinach), and herbs and spices (*e.g.*, oregano) contain appreciable amounts of galloyl groups, that strongly inhibit iron absorption. Consumption of betel leaves, common in areas of Asia, also has a marked negative effect on iron absorption.

Calcium, consumed as a salt or in dairy products interferes significantly with the absorption of both heme and non-heme iron. Because calcium and iron are both essential nutrients, calcium cannot be considered to be an inhibitor in the same way as phytates or phenolic compounds. The practical solution for this competition is to increase iron intake, increase its bio-availability, or avoid the intake of foods rich in calcium and foods rich in iron at the same meal.

The mechanism of action for absorption inhibition is unknown, but the balance of evidence strongly suggest that the inhibition is located within the mucosal cell itself at the common final transfer step for heme and non-heme iron.

Recent analyses of the dose-effect relationship show that no inhibition is seen from the first 40 mg of calcium in a meal. A sigmoid relationship is then seen, reaching a 60 per cent maximal inhibition of iron absorption by 300-600 mg calcium. The form of this curve suggests a one-site competitive binding of iron and calcium. This relationship explains some of the seemingly conflicting results obtained in studies on the interaction between calcium and iron.

For unknown reasons, the addition of soy protein to a meal reduces the fraction of iron absorbed. This inhibition is not solely explained by the high phytate content of soy protein. However, because of the high iron content of soy proteins, the net effect on iron absorption of an addition of soy products to a meal is usually positive. In infant foods containing soy proteins, the inhibiting effect can be overcome by the addition of sufficient amounts of ascorbic acid. Some fermented soy sauces, however, have been found to enhance iron absorption.

**Enhancement of Iron Absorption**

Ascorbic acid is the most potent enhancer of non-heme iron absorption. Synthetic vitamin C increases the absorption of iron to the same extent as the native ascorbic acid in fruits, vegetables, and juices. The effect of ascorbic acid on iron absorption is so marked and essential that this effect could be considered as one of vitamin C's physiologic roles. Each meal should preferably contain at least 25 mg of ascorbic acid and possibly more if the meal contains many inhibitors of iron absorption. Therefore, a requirement of ascorbic acid for iron absorption should be taken into account when establishing the requirements for vitamin C, that are set only to prevent vitamin C deficiency (especially scurvy).

Meat, fish, and seafood all promote the absorption of non-heme iron. The mechanism for this effect has not been determined. It should be pointed out that meat also enhances the absorption of heme iron to about the same extent. Meat promotes iron nutrition in two ways: it stimulates the absorption of both heme and non-heme iron and it provides the well-absorbed heme iron. Epidemiologically, the intake of meat has been found to be associated with a lower prevalence of iron deficiency.

Organic acids, such as citric acid, have in some studies been found to enhance the absorption of non-heme iron. This effect is not observed as consistently as is the effect of ascorbic acid. Sauerkraut and other fermented vegetables and even some fermented soy sauces enhance iron absorption. The nature of this enhancement has not yet been determined.

**Iron Absorption from Meals**

The pool concept in iron absorption implies that there are two main pools in the gastrointestinal lumen–one pool of heme iron and another pool of non-heme iron–and that iron absorption takes place independently from these two pools. The pool concept also implies that the absorption of iron from the non-heme iron pool results from all ligands present in the mixture of foods included in a meal.

The absorption of non-heme iron from a certain meal not only depends on its iron content but also, and to a marked degree, on the composition of the meal (*i.e.*, the balance among all factors enhancing and inhibiting the absorption of iron). The bio-availability can vary more than 10-fold among meals with a similar content of iron, energy, protein, fat, etc. Just the addition of certain spices (*e.g.*, oregano) or a cup of tea may reduce the bio-availability by one-half or more. However, the addition of certain vegetables or fruits containing ascorbic acid may double or even triple iron absorption, depending on the other properties of the meal and the amounts of ascorbic acid present.

**Iron Absorption from the Whole Diet**

There is limited information about the total amounts of iron absorbed from the diet because no simple method is available to measure iron absorption from the whole diet. It has been measured by chemical balance studies using long balance periods or by determining the haemoglobin regeneration rate in subjects with induced iron deficiency anaemia and a well-controlled diet over a long period of time.

A method was recently developed to measure iron absorption from the whole diet. In the first studies all non-heme iron in all meals over periods of 5-10 days was homogeneously labelled to the same specific activity with an extrinsic inorganic radioiron tracer. Heme iron absorption was then estimated. In a further study, heme and non-heme iron were separately labelled with two radioiron tracers as biosynthetically labelled haemoglobin and as an inorganic iron salt. New information could be obtained, for example, about the average bio-availability of dietary iron in different types of diets, overall effects of certain factors (*e.g.*, calcium) on iron nutrition, and regulation of iron absorption in relation to iron status.

Iron absorption from the whole diet is the sum of the absorption of iron from the single meals included in the diet. It has been suggested that the iron absorption of single meals may exaggerate the absorption of iron from the diet. Iron absorption from single meals can never represent iron absorption from the whole diet, but iron absorption from a single meal was the same when the meal was served in the morning after an overnight fast or at lunch or supper. The same observation was made in another study when a hamburger meal was served in the morning or 2-4 hours after a breakfast.

Because energy expenditure and energy intake set the limit for the amount of food eaten and for meal size, it is practical to relate the bio-availability of iron in different meals to energy content (bio-available nutrient density). The use of bio-available nutrient density is a feasible way to compare different meals, construct menus, and calculate recommended intakes.

Intake of energy and essential nutrients such as iron was probably considerably higher for early humans than it is today. The present low iron intake associated with a low-energy lifestyle implies that the interaction between different factors influencing iron absorption, will be more critical. For example, the interaction between calcium and iron absorption probably had no importance in the nutrition of early humans, who had a diet with ample amounts of both iron and calcium.

**Iron Balance and Regulation of Iron Absorption**

The body has three unique mechanisms for maintaining iron balance and preventing iron deficiency and iron overload. The first is the continuous re-utilisation of iron from catabolised erythrocytes in the body. When an erythrocyte dies after about 120 days, it is usually degraded by the macrophages of the reticular endothelium. The iron is released and delivered to transferrin in the plasma, which brings the iron back to red blood cell precursors in the bone marrow or to other cells in different tissues.

Uptake and distribution of iron in the body is regulated by the synthesis of transferrin receptors on the cell surface. This system for internal iron transport not only controls the rate of flow of iron to different tissues according to their needs but also effectively prevents the appearance of free iron and the formation of free radicals in the circulation.

The second mechanism is the access of the specific storage protein, ferritin, which can store and release iron to meet excessive iron demands. This iron reservoir is especially important in the third trimester of pregnancy.

The third mechanism involves the regulation of absorption of iron from the intestines, with an increased iron absorption in the presence of decreasing body iron stores and a decreased iron absorption when iron stores increase. Iron absorption decreases until an equilibrium is established between absorption and requirements. For a given diet this regulation of iron absorption, however, can only balance losses up to a certain critical point beyond which iron deficiency will develop.

About half of the basal iron losses are from blood, primarily in the gastrointestinal tract. Both these losses and the menstrual iron losses are influenced by the haemoglobin level; during the development of an iron deficiency, menstrual and basal iron losses will successively decrease when the haemoglobin level decreases. In a state of more severe iron deficiency, skin iron losses may also decrease. Iron balance (absorption equals losses) may be present not only in normal subjects but also during iron deficiency and iron overload.

The three main factors that affect iron balance are absorption (intake and bio-availability of iron), losses, and amount in stores. The interrelationship among these factors was recently been described in mathematical terms, making it possible to predict, for example, the amount of stored iron when iron losses and bio-availability of dietary iron are known. With increasing iron requirements or decreasing bio-availability, the regulatory capacity to prevent iron deficiency is limited. However, to prevent iron overload with increasing dietary iron intake or bio-availability, the regulatory capacity seems to be extremely good.

**Effects of Iron Deficiency**

Studies in animals have clearly shown that iron deficiency has several negative effects on important functions in the body. Physical working capacity in rats has been shown to be significantly reduced in iron deficiency, that is especially valid for endurance activities. This negative effect seems to be less related to the degree of anaemia than to impaired oxidative metabolism in the muscles with an increased formation of lactic acid, that in turn is due to a lack of iron-containing enzymes which are rate limiting for the oxidative metabolism.

The relationship between iron deficiency and brain function is of great importance for the choice of strategy in combating iron deficiency. Several structures in the brain have a high iron content of the same magnitude as observed in the liver. Of great importance is the observation that the lower iron content of the brain in iron-deficient growing rats cannot be increased by giving iron later on. This fact strongly suggests that the supply of iron to brain cells takes place during an early phase of brain development and that, as such, early iron deficiency may lead to irreparable damage to brain cells.

In humans about 10 per cent of brain iron is present at birth; at the age of 10 years the brain has only reached half its normal iron content, and optimal amounts are first reached at the age of 20-30 years. In populations with long-standing iron deficiency, a reduction of physical working capacity has been demonstrated by several groups with improvement in working capacity after iron administration.

Iron deficiency also negatively influences the normal defence systems against infections. The cell-mediated immunologic response by the action of T lymphocytes is impaired as a result of a reduced formation of these cells. This in turn is due to a reduced DNA synthesis depending on the function of ribonucleotide reductase, which requires a continuous supply of iron for its function. The phagocytosis and killing of bacteria by the neutrophil leukocytes is an important component of the defence mechanism against infections. These functions are impaired in iron deficiency. The killing function is based on the formation of free hydroxyl radicals within the leukocytes, the respiratory burst, and results from the activation of the iron-sulphur enzyme NADPH oxidase and probably also cytochrome b (a heme enzyme).

The impairment of the immunologic defence against infections that was found in animals is also regularly found in humans. Administration of iron normalises these changes within 4-7 days. It has been difficult to demonstrate, however, that the prevalence of infections is higher or that their severity is more marked in iron-deficient subjects than in control subjects. This may well be ascribed to the difficulty in studying this problem with an adequate experimental design.

A relationship between iron deficiency and behaviour such as attention, memory, and learning, has been demonstrated in infants and small children by several groups. In the most recent well-controlled studies, no effect was noted from the administration of iron. This finding is consistent with the observations in animals.

Therapy-resistant behavioural impairment and the fact that there is an accumulation of iron during the whole period of brain growth should be considered strong arguments for the more active and effective combating of iron deficiency. This is valid for women, especially during pregnancy, for infants and children, and up through the period of adolescence and early adulthood. In a recent well-controlled study, administration of iron to non-anaemic but iron-deficient adolescent girls improved verbal learning and memory.

Well-controlled studies in adolescent girls show that iron-deficiency without anaemia is associated with reduced physical endurance and changes in mood and ability to concentrate. A recent careful study showed that there was a reduction in maximum oxygen consumption in non-anaemic women with iron deficiency that was unrelated to a decreased oxygen-transport capacity of the blood.

**Iron during Pregnancy and Lactation**

Iron requirements during pregnancy are well established. Most of the iron required during pregnancy is used to increase the haemoglobin mass of the mother, which occurs in all healthy pregnant women who have sufficiently large iron stores or who are adequately supplemented with iron. The increased haemoglobin mass is directly proportional to the increased need for oxygen transport during pregnancy and is one of the important physiologic adaptations that occurs in pregnancy.

A major problem for iron balance in pregnancy is that iron requirements are not equally distributed over its duration. The exponential growth of the foetus implies that iron needs are almost negligible in the first trimester and that more than 80 per cent relates to the last trimester.

The total daily iron requirements, including the basal iron losses (0.8 mg), increase during pregnancy from 0.8 mg to about 10 mg during the last 6 weeks of pregnancy.

Iron absorption during pregnancy is determined by the amount of iron in the diet, its bio-availability (meal composition), and the changes in iron absorption that occur during pregnancy. There are marked changes in the fraction of iron absorbed during pregnancy. In the first trimester there is a marked, somewhat paradoxical, decrease in the absorption of iron, which is closely related to the reduction in iron requirements during this period as compared with the non-pregnant state.

In the second trimester iron absorption is increased by about 50 per cent, and in the last trimester it may increase by up to about four times. Even considering the marked increase in iron absorption, it is impossible for the mother to cover her iron requirements from diet alone, even if its iron content and bio-availability are very high. It can be calculated that with diets prevailing in most industrialized countries, there will be a deficit of about 400-500 mg in the amount of iron absorbed during pregnancy.

An adequate iron balance can be achieved if iron stores of 500 mg are available. However, it is uncommon for women today to have iron stores of this size. It is therefore recommended that iron supplements in tablet form, preferably together with folic acid, be given to all pregnant women because of the difficulties in correctly evaluating iron status in pregnancy with routine laboratory methods. In the non-anaemic pregnant woman, daily supplements of 100 mg of iron (*e.g.*, as ferrous sulphate) given during the second half of pregnancy are adequate.

**Nutrient Intake for Iron**

To translate physiologic iron requirements, into dietary iron requirements, the bio-availability of iron in different diets must be calculated. It is therefore necessary to choose an iron status where the supply of iron to the erythrocyte precursors and other tissues starts to be compromised. A state of iron-deficient erythropoiesis occurs when iron can no longer be mobilised from iron stores; iron can no longer be mobilised when stores are almost completely empty.

A reduction then occurs, for example, in the concentration of haemoglobin and in the average content of haemoglobin in the erythrocytes (a reduction in mean corpuscular haemoglobin). At the same time the concentration of transferrin in the plasma increases because of an insufficient supply of iron to liver cells. These changes were recently shown to occur rather suddenly at a level of serum ferritin of £15 μg/l. A continued negative iron balance will further reduce the level of haemoglobin. Symptoms related to iron deficiency are less related to the haemoglobin level and more to the fact that there is a compromised supply of iron to tissues.

The bio-availability of iron in meals consumed in countries with a Western-type diet has been measured by using different methods. Numerous single-meal studies have shown absorption of non-heme iron ranging from 5 per cent to 40 per cent. Attempts have also been made to estimate the bio-availability of dietary iron in populations consuming Western-type diets by using indirect methods (*e.g.*, calculation of the coverage of iron requirements in groups of subjects with known dietary intake). Such estimations suggest that in borderline iron-deficient subjects the bio-availability from good diets may reach a level around 14-16 per cent (15 per cent relates to subjects who have a serum ferritin value of $<15$μg/l or a reference dose absorption of 56.5 per cent).

Recently, direct measurements were made of the average bio-availability of iron in different Western-type diets. Expressed as total amounts of iron absorbed from the whole diet, it was found that 53.2 $\mu$g Fe/kg/day could be absorbed daily from each of the two main meals of an experimental diet which included ample amounts of meat or fish.

For a body weight of 55 kg and an iron intake of 14 mg/day, this corresponds to a bio-availability of 21 per cent in subjects with no iron stores and an iron-deficient erythropoiesis. A diet common among women in Sweden contained smaller portions of meat and fish, higher phytates, and some vegetarian meals each week was found to have a bio-availability of 12 per cent. Reducing the intake of meat and fish further will reduce the bio-availability to about 10 per cent (25$\mu$g Fe/kg/day).

In vegetarians the bio-availability is usually low because of the absence of meat and fish and a high intake of phytate and polyphenols. An average good Western-type whole diet has a bio-availability of about 15 per cent but for common diets, especially among women, the bio-availability is around 12 per cent or even 10 per cent. In countries or for certain groups in a population with a very high meat intake, the bio-availability may rather be around 18 per cent. In Western countries, a high bio-availability is mainly associated with a high meat intake, a high intake of ascorbic acid with meals, a low intake of phytate-rich cereals, and no coffee or tea within 2 hours of the main meals.

## MAGNESIUM

The human body contains about 760 mg of magnesium at birth, approximately 5 g at age 4-5 months, and 25 g when adult. Of the body's magnesium, 30-40 per cent is found in muscles and soft tissues, 1 per cent is found in extracellular fluid, and the remainder is in the skeleton, where it accounts for up to 1 per cent of bone ash.

Soft tissue magnesium functions as a co-factor of many enzymes involved in energy metabolism, protein synthesis, RNA and DNA synthesis, and maintenance of the electrical potential of nervous tissues and cell membranes. Of particular importance with respect to the pathologic effects of magnesium depletion is the role of this element in regulating potassium fluxes and its involvement in the metabolism of calcium. Magnesium depletion depresses both cellular and extracellular potassium and exacerbates the effects of low-potassium diets on cellular potassium content. Muscle potassium becomes depleted as magnesium deficiency develops, and tissue repletion of potassium is virtually impossible unless magnesium status is restored to normal. Low plasma calcium develops frequently as magnesium status declines. It is not clear whether this occurs because parathyroid hormone release is inhibited or, more probably, because of a reduced sensitivity of the bone to parathyroid hormone, thus restricting withdrawal of calcium from the skeletal matrix.

Between 50 per cent and 60 per cent of body magnesium is located within bone, where it is thought to form a surface constituent of the hydroxyapatite (calcium phosphate) mineral component. Initially much of this magnesium is readily exchangeable with serum and therefore represents a moderately accessible magnesium store, which can be drawn on in times of deficiency. However, the proportion of bone magnesium in this exchangeable form declines significantly with increasing age.

Significant increases in bone mineral density of the femur have been associated positively with rises in erythrocyte magnesium when the diets of subjects with gluten-sensitive enteropathy were fortified with magnesium. Little is known of other roles for magnesium in skeletal tissues.

**Effects of Magnesium Deficiency**

Pathologic effects of primary nutritional deficiency of magnesium occur infrequently in infants but are even less common in adults unless a relatively low magnesium intake is accompanied by prolonged diarrhoea or excessive urinary magnesium losses. Susceptibility to the effects of magnesium deficiency rises when demands for magnesium increase markedly with the resumption of tissue growth during rehabilitation from general malnutrition. Studies have shown that a decline in urinary magnesium excretion during protein-energy malnutrition (PEM) is accompanied by a reduced intestinal absorption of magnesium. The catch-up growth associated with recovery from PEM is achieved only if magnesium supply is increased substantially.

Most of the early pathologic consequences of magnesium depletion are neurologic or neuromuscular defects, some of which probably reflect the influence of the element on potassium flux within tissues. Thus, a decline in magnesium status produces anorexia, nausea, muscular weakness, lethargy, staggering, and, if deficiency is prolonged, weight loss. Progressively increasing with the severity and duration of depletion are manifestations of hyperirritability, hyperexcitability, muscular spasms, and tetany, leading ultimately to convulsions. An increased susceptibility to audiogenic shock is common in experimental animals. Cardiac arrhythmia and pulmonary oedema frequently have fatal consequences. It has been suggested that a sub-optimal magnesium status may be a factor in the aetiology of coronary heart disease and hypertension but additional evidence is needed.

**Magnesium Requirements**

In 1996 Shils and Rude published a constructive review of past procedures used to derive estimates of magnesium requirements. They questioned the arguments of many authors that metabolic balance studies are probably the only practicable, non-invasive techniques for assessing the relationships of magnesium intake to magnesium status. At the same time, they emphasised the great scarcity of data on variations in urinary magnesium output and on magnesium levels in serum, erythrocytes, lymphocytes, bone, and soft tissues. Such data are needed to verify current assumptions that pathologic responses to a decline in magnesium supply are not likely occur to if magnesium balance remains relatively constant.

In view of the recent conclusion that many estimates of dietary requirements for magnesium were "based upon questionable and insufficient data", a closer examination is needed of the value of biochemical criteria for defining the adequacy of magnesium status. Attention could be paid to the effects of changes in magnesium intake on urinary magnesium-creatinine ratios, the relationships between serum magnesium-calcium and magnesium-potassium concentrations, and other functional indicators of magnesium status.

**Estimated Allowances of Magnesium**

The scarcity of studies from which to derive estimates of dietary allowances for magnesium has been emphasised by virtually all the agencies faced with this task. One United Kingdom agency commented particularly on the scarcity of studies with young subjects, and circumvented the problem of discordant data from work with adolescents and adults by restricting the range of studies considered.

Using experimental data virtually identical to those used for a detailed critique of the basis for US estimates, the Scientific Committee for Food of the European Communities did not propose magnesium allowances (or population reference intakes, PRIs) because of inadequate data. Instead, they offered an acceptable range of intakes for adults of 150-500 mg/day and described a series of quasi-PRI values for specific age groups, including an increment of 30 per cent to allow for individual variations in growth. Statements of acceptable intakes leave uncertainty as to the extent of overestimation of derived recommended intakes.

It is questionable whether more reliable estimates of magnesium requirements can be made until data from balance studies are supported by the use of biochemical indexes of adequacy that could reveal the development of manifestations of sub-optimal status. Such indexes have been examined, for example, by Nichols *et al.* in their studies of the metabolic significance of magnesium depletion during PEM.

A loss of muscle and serum magnesium resulted if total body magnesium retention fell below 2 mg/kg/day and was followed by a fall in the myofibrillar nitrogen-collagen ratio of muscle and a fall in muscle potassium content. Repletion of tissue magnesium status preceded a threefold increase in muscle potassium content. It accelerated by 7-10 days at the rate of recovery of muscle mass and composition initiated by restitution of nitrogen and energy supplies to infants previously deficient.

Neurologic signs such as hyper-irritability, apathy, tremors, and occasional ataxia accompanied by low concentrations of potassium and magnesium in skeletal muscle and strongly negative magnesium balances were reported by many other studies of protein calorie deficiency in infants. Particularly noteworthy is evidence that all these effects are ameliorated or eliminated by increased oral magnesium, as were specific anomalies in the electrocardiographic T-wave profiles of such malnourished subjects. Evidence that the initial rate of growth at rehabilitation is influenced by dietary magnesium intake indicates the significance of this element for those involved in the aetiology of the PEM syndromes.

Regrettably, detailed studies have yet to be carried out to define the nature of changes resulting from a primary deficiency of dietary magnesium. Definition of magnesium requirements must continue to be based on the limited information provided by balance techniques, which give little or no indications of responses to inadequacy in magnesium supply which may induce covert pathologic changes.

Reassurance must thus be sought from the application of dietary standards for magnesium in communities consuming diets differing widely in magnesium content. The inadequate definition of lower acceptable limits of magnesium intakes raises concern in communities or individuals suffering malnutrition or from a wider variety of nutritional or other diseases which influence magnesium metabolism adversely.

## SELENIUM

Our understanding of the significance of selenium in the nutrition of human subjects has grown rapidly during the past 20 years. Demonstrations of its essentiality to rats and farm animals were followed by appreciation that the development of selenium-responsive diseases often reflected the distribution of geochemical variables which restricted the entry of the element from soils into food chains. Such findings were the stimulus to in-depth investigations of the regional relevance of selenium in human nutrition. These studies have now yielded an increased understanding of the complex metabolic role of this trace nutrient. Selenium has been implicated in the protection of body tissues against oxidative stress, maintenance of defences against infection, and modulation of growth and development.

The selenium content of normal adult humans can vary widely. Values from 3 mg in New Zealanders to 14 mg in some Americans reflect the profound influence of the natural environment on the selenium contents of soils, crops, and human tissues. Approximately 30 per cent of tissue selenium is contained in the liver, 15 per cent in kidney, 30 per cent in muscle, and 10 per cent in blood plasma. Much of tissue selenium is found in proteins as seleno-analogues of sulphur amino acids; other metabolically active forms include selenotrisulphides and other acid-labile selenium compounds. At least 15 selenoproteins have now been characterised.

**Table : A Selection of Characterised Selenoproteins**

| Protein | Selenocysteine residues | Tissue distribution |
|---|---|---|
| Cytosolic glutathione peroxidase (GSHPx) | 1 | All, including thyroid |
| Phospholipid hydroperoxide GSHPx | 1 | All, including thyroid |
| Gastrointestinal GSHPx | 1 | Gastrointestinal tract |
| Extracellular GSHPx | 1 | Plasma, thyroid |
| Thioredoxin reductase | 1 or 2 | All including thyroid |
| Iodothyronine-deiodinase (type 1) | 1 | Liver, kidneys, and thyroid |
| Iodothyronine-deiodinase (type 2) | 1 | Central nervous system (CNS), and pituitary |
| Iodothyronine-deiodinase (type 3) | 1 | Brown adipose tissue, CNS, and placenta |
| Selenoprotein P | 10 | Plasma |
| Selenoprotein W | 1 | Muscle |
| Sperm capsule selenoprotein | 3 | Sperm tail |

Functionally, there appear to be at least two distinct families of selenium-containing enzymes. The first includes glutathione peroxidases and thioredoxin reductase, which are involved in controlling tissue concentrations of highly reactive oxygen-containing metabolites. These metabolites are essential at low concentrations for maintaining cell-mediated immunity against infections but highly toxic if produced in excess.

The role of selenium in the cytosolic enzyme glutathione peroxidase (GSHPx) was first illustrated in 1973. During stress, infection, or tissue injury, selenoenzymes may protect against the damaging effects of hydrogen peroxide or oxygen-rich free radicals. This family of enzymes catalyses the destruction of hydrogen peroxide or lipid hydroperoxides according to the following general reactions:

$$H_2O_2 + 2GSH \rightarrow 2H_2O + GSSG$$

$$ROOH + 2GSH \rightarrow ROH + H_2O + GSSG$$

where GSH is glutathione and GSSG is its oxidized form. At least four forms of GSHPx exist; they differ both in their tissue distribution and in their sensitivity to selenium depletion. The GSHPx enzymes of liver and blood plasma fall in activity rapidly at early stages of selenium deficiency. In contrast, a form of

GSHPx associated specifically with phospholipid-rich tissue membranes is preserved against selenium deficiency and is believed to have broader metabolic roles (*e.g.*, in prostaglandin synthesis). In concert with vitamin E, selenium is also involved in the protection of cell membranes against oxidative damage. The selenoenzyme thioredoxin reductase is involved in disposal of the products of oxidative metabolism. It contains two selenocysteine groups per molecule and is a major component of a redox system with a multiplicity of functions, among which is the capacity to degrade locally excessive and potentially toxic concentrations of peroxide and hydroperoxides likely to induce cell death and tissue atrophy.

Another group of selenoproteins is essential in the conversion of thyroxin, or tetraiodothyronine ($T_4$), to its physiologically active form, triiodothyronine ($T_3$). Three types of these iodothyronine deiodinases, differing both in tissue distribution and sensitivity to selenium deficiency, have been characterised. The consequences of a low selenium status on physiologic responses to a shortage of iodine are complex. The influence of a loss of selenium-dependent iodothyronine deiodinase differs in its severity depending on whether a target tissue needs a preformed supply of $T_3$ (*e.g.*, via plasma) or whether, as with the brain, pituitary gland, and placenta, it can rely upon local synthesis of $T_3$ from $T_4$.

Despite this, marked changes in the $T_3$-$T_4$ ratio as a consequence of a reduced selenium status (when iodine supplies are also marginal) indicate the modifying influence of selenium on thyroid hormone balance in both animal models and human subjects. Their possible significance can be anticipated from the fact that whereas thyroid weights increase typically by 50 per cent in rats offered an iodine-deficient diet, thyroid weight is increased 154 per cent by diets concurrently deficient in both selenium and iodine.

Between 60 per cent and 80 per cent of selenium in human plasma is accounted for by a well-characterised fraction designated selenoprotein P, the function of which has yet to be determined. It is thought to be a selenium storage protein because there is limited evidence that it also has an antioxidant role. At least 10 other selenoproteins exist, including one which is a component of the mitochondrial capsule of sperm cells, damage to which may account for the development of sperm abnormalities during selenium deficiency. Other aspects of the function and metabolism of selenium are reviewed elsewhere.

### Selenium Deficiency

Biochemical evidence of selenium depletion (*e.g.*, a decline in blood GSHPx activity) is not uncommon in subjects maintained on parenteral or enteral feeding for long periods. Blood selenium values declining to one-tenth of normal values have been reported when the selenium content of such preparations has not been maintained by fortification. Low selenium contents of some commercial formulas for infants resulting in a fall in daily selenium intake to approximately 0.5 μg/day have been shown to strongly exacerbate the fall in serum selenium and GSHPx activity normally experienced from 2 to 8 months of age even in human-milk-fed infants typically receiving threefold higher selenium intakes. The importance of maintaining trace element levels in such preparations was reviewed elsewhere.Clinical manifestations of deficiency arising from such situations are uncommon and poorly defined. They include muscular weakness and myalgia with, in several instances, the development of congestive heart failure. In at least one instance such pathologic signs have developed as a consequence of a generally inadequate diet providing selenium at less than 10 μg/day. The 2-year-old subject recovered rapidly after selenium administration. With this last exception, virtually all of the above reports describe observations with subjects under close medical supervision. This may well be relevant to the scarcity of consistent pathologic findings.

### *Kaschin-beck Disease*

A selenium-responsive bone and joint disease (osteoarthropathy) has been detected in children aged 5-13 years in China and less extensively in south-east Siberia. The disease is characterised by joint necrosis–epiphyseal degeneration of the arm and leg joints resulting in structural shortening of the fingers and long bones with consequent growth retardation and stunting. Although not identical to Keshan disease, Kaschin-Beck disease also occurs in areas where the availability of soil selenium for crop growth is low.

The selenium contents of hair and of whole blood are abnormally low and the blood content of GSHPx is reduced. Although it is ameliorated by selenium therapy, other factors such as the frequent presence of mycotoxins in cereal grains grown in the area may be involved. A spontaneous decrease in incidence from 1970 (44 per cent) to 1980 (14 per cent) to 1986 (1 per cent) has been attributed to general improvements in the nutritional status of Chinese rural communities.

### *Selenium Status and Susceptibility to Infection*

As stated earlier, the expressions of the cardiac lesions of Keshan disease probably involve not only the development of selenium deficiency but also the presence of a Coxsackie virus (BA) infection. Animal studies have confirmed that selenium-deficient mice infected with Coxsackie virus (CVB/0) were particularly susceptible to the virus. These studies also illustrated that passage of the virus through selenium-deficient subjects enhanced its virulence. Myocarditic virulence developed even in strains such as CVB/0 which normally were not myopathogenic. The enhancement of virulence in this RNA virus involves modifications to the nucleotide sequence of the phenotype. These modifications were maintained and expressed even during subsequent passage through animals with normal selenium status. Enhancing the virulence of a virus with a selenium deficiency (resulting either from a nutritional challenge or an increased metabolic demand on tissue selenium depots) appears not to be unique to the Coxsackie viruses. The early pre-clinical stages of development of human immunodeficiency virus (HIV) infection are accompanied by a very marked decline in plasma selenium. Sub-clinical malnutrition assumes increased significance during the development of acquired immune deficiency syndrome (AIDS). However, for the nutrients affected, there are strong indications that only the extent of the decline in selenium status has predictive value with respect to both the rate of development of AIDS and its resulting mortality.

The virulence of other RNA viruses such as hepatitis B and those associated with the development of haemolytic anaemias are enhanced similarly by a decline in selenium status. The mechanisms underlying these effects are not yet resolved.

There are indications that the loss of protective antioxidant functions dependent on selenium and vitamin E are both involved and that the resulting structural changes in viral nucleotide sequences are reproducible and appear to provoke additional selenoprotein synthesis. It is suspected that this further depletes previously diminished pools of physiologically available selenium and accelerates pathologic responses.

Whatever mechanisms are involved, further understanding is needed of the influence of selenium status on susceptibility to viral diseases ranging from cardiomyopathies to haemolytic anaemias. The relationship already illustrates the difficulty of defining nutritional essentiality for nutrients which may primarily maintain defences against infection. Studies of the effects of selenium deficiency in several experimental animal species have shown that the microbicidal activity of blood neutrophils is severely impaired even though phagocytic activity remains unimpaired. The complexity of species differences in the influence of selenium status on the effectiveness of cell-mediated immune processes is summarised elsewhere.

The possibility that increased intakes of selenium might protect against the development of cancer in humans has generated great interest. However, a number of epidemiologic studies have now been reported which show no relationship between selenium and cancer risk. Moreover, an analysis of the relationship between selenium and cancer suggests that "the question of whether selenium protects against cancer is still wide open".

An increased intake of selenium appears to stimulate tumorigenesis in some animal models of pancreatic and skin cancer. In contrast, the protective effect of higher exposures to selenium observed in several animal studies, together with small but statistically significant differences in selenium blood plasma levels detected in some retrospective-prospective studies of subgroups of people developing cancer, explains the continuing interest in the anticarcinogenic potential of selenium.

However, the results of prospective-retrospective studies had no predictive value for individuals and could have reflected non-specific influences on groups. The association between low selenium intake and high cancer risk, although clearly of some interest, is in need of further investigation before a conclusion can be reached.

Although a biochemical mechanism can be postulated whereby selenium could protect against heart disease by influencing platelet aggregation (through an effect on the prostacyclin-thromboxane ratio), the epidemiologic evidence linking selenium status and risk of cardiovascular disease is still equivocal.

***Criteria for Assessing Selenium Requirements***

Levander convincingly illustrated the impracticability of assessing selenium requirements from input-output balance data because the history of selenium nutrition influences the proportion of dietary selenium absorbed, retained, or excreted. The changing equilibria when selenium intake is varied experimentally yield data which are of limited value for estimating minimal requirements.

Examples are cited of estimates of selenium requirement for adults of 7.4 and 80 μg/day derived from Chinese and United States studies, respectively. Such discrepancies reflect differences in the usual daily selenium intakes of the experimental subjects and the extent to which this was changed experimentally. This situation, not unique to selenium, emphasises the importance of basing requirement estimates on functional criteria derived from evidence describing the minimum levels of intake which, directly or indirectly, reflect the normality of selenium-dependent processes.

A detailed review of 36 reports describing serum selenium values in healthy subjects indicated that they ranged from a low of 0.52 μmol/l in Serbia to a high of 2.5 μmol/l in Wyoming and South Dakota in the United States. It was suggested that mean values within this range derived from 75.02 apparently healthy individuals should be regarded tentatively as a standard for normal reference. This survey clearly illustrated the influence of crop management on serum selenium level; in Finland and New Zealand, selenium fortification of fertilisers for cereals increased serum selenium from 0.6 to 1.5 μmol/l. These include reports from studies of Keshan disease, Kaschin-Beck disease, and specific studies of cretinism, hypothyroidism, and HIV and AIDS where clinical outcome or prognosis has been related to selenium status.

This report and the report by the World Health Organization (WHO), FAO, and IAEA use virtually identical approaches to derive their estimates of basal requirements for selenium ($SE_R^{basal}$). As yet there are no published reports suggesting that these basal estimates using Se or GSHPx activity as criteria of adequacy are invalid. Some modification is necessary however to estimate population minimum intakes with adequate allowance for the variability (CV) associated with estimates of the average selenium intakes from the typical diets of many communities.

In the WHO-FAO-IAEA report a CV of 16 per cent was assumed for the selenium conventional diets and 12.5 per cent for the milk-based diets of infants to limit the risks of inadequacy arising from unexpectedly low selenium contents. More recent studies suggest that the variability of selenium intake from diets for which the selenium content has been predicted rather than measured may be substantially greater than estimated previously.

## CALCIUM IN FOOD

Calcium is a divalent cation with an atomic weight of 40. In the elementary composition of the human body, it ranks fifth after oxygen, carbon, hydrogen, and nitrogen, and it makes up 1.9 per cent of the body by weight. Carcass analyses show that it constitutes 0.1-0.2 per cent of early foetal fat-free weight, rising to about 2 per cent of adult fat-free weight. In absolute terms, this represents a rise from about 24 g (600 mmol) at birth to 1300 g (32.5 mol) at maturity, requiring an average daily positive calcium balance of 180 mg (4.5 mmol) during the 20 years of growth.

Ninety-nine per cent of the body calcium is located in the skeleton. The remaining 1 per cent is equally distributed between the teeth and soft tissues, with only 0.1 per cent in the extracellular fluid (ECF). In the skeleton it constitutes 25 per cent of the dry weight and 40 per cent of the ash weight. The ECF contains ionised calcium at about 4.8 mg/100 ml (1.20 mmol/l) maintained by the parathyroid–vitamin D system as well as complexed calcium at about 1.6 mg/100 ml (0.4 mmol/l). In the plasma there is an additional protein-bound calcium fraction of 3.2 mg/100 ml (0.8 mmol/l). In the cellular compartment the total calcium concentration is comparable with that in the ECF, but the free calcium concentration is lower by several orders of magnitude.

Calcium salts provide rigidity to the skeleton and calcium ions play a role in many if not most metabolic processes. In the primitive exoskeleton and in shells, rigidity is generally provided by calcium carbonate, but in the vertebrate skeleton it is provided by a form of calcium phosphate which approximates hydroxyapatite [$Ca_{10}(OH)_2(PO_4)_6$] and is embedded in collagen fibrils.

Bone mineral serves as the ultimate reservoir for the calcium circulating in the ECF. Calcium enters the ECF from the gut by absorption and from bone by resorption. Calcium leaves the ECF via the gastrointestinal tract, kidneys, and skin and enters into bone via bone formation. In addition, calcium fluxes occur across all cell membranes. Many neuromuscular and other cellular functions depend on the maintenance of the ionised calcium concentration in the ECF. Calcium fluxes are also important mediators of hormonal effects on target organs through several intracellular signalling pathways, such as the phosphoinositide and cyclic adenosine monophosphate systems. The cytoplasmic calcium concentration is kept down by a series of calcium pumps, which concentrate calcium within the intracellular storage sites or extrude from the cells the calcium which flows in by diffusion.

The physiology of calcium metabolism is primarily directed towards the maintenance of the concentration of ionised calcium in the ECF. This is protected and maintained by a feedback loop through calcium receptors in the parathyroid glands, which control the secretion of parathyroid hormone. This hormone increases the renal tubular reabsorption of calcium, promotes intestinal calcium absorption by stimulating the renal production of 1,25-dihyroxycolecaliferol [1,25$(OH)_2$D], and, if necessary, resorbs bone.

However, the integrity of the system depends critically on vitamin D status; if there is a deficiency of vitamin D, the loss of its calcaemic action leads to a decrease in the ionised calcium and secondary hyperparathyroidism and hypophosphataemia. This is why experimental vitamin D deficiency results in rickets and osteomalacia whereas calcium deficiency gives rise to osteoporosis.

## DETERMINANTS OF CALCIUM BALANCE

### Calcium absorption

Ingested calcium mixes with digestive juice calcium in the proximal small intestine from where it is absorbed by a process, which has an active saturable component and a diffusion component. At low calcium intakes calcium is mainly absorbed by active (transcellular) transport, but at higher intakes an increasing proportion of calcium is absorbed by simple (paracellular) diffusion. The unabsorbed component appears in the faeces together with the unabsorbed component of digestive juice calcium known as endogenous faecal calcium. Thus, the faeces contain unabsorbed dietary calcium and unreabsorbed digestive juice calcium.

True absorbed calcium is the total calcium absorbed from the calcium pool in the intestines and therefore contains both dietary and digestive juice components. Net absorbed calcium is the difference between dietary calcium and faecal calcium and is numerically the same as true absorbed calcium minus endogenous faecal calcium.

At zero calcium intake, all the faecal calcium is endogenous and represents the digestive juice calcium which has not been reabsorbed; net absorbed calcium at this intake is therefore negative to the extent of about 200 mg (5 mmol). The relationships between calcium intake and calcium absorbed and excreted

calcium calculated from 210 balance experiments in 81 subjects. Equilibrium is reached at an intake of 520 mg, which rises to 840 mg when skin losses of 60 mg are added and to 1100 mg when menopausal loss is included. The curvilinear relationship between intestinal calcium absorption and calcium intake can be made linear by using the logarithm of calcium intake to yield the equation: Caa = 174 loge Cai -909 ± 71 (SD) mg/day, where Cai represents ingested calcium and Caa net absorbed calcium. The relationship between urinary calcium excretion and calcium intake is given by the equation: Cau = 0.078 Cai + 137 ± 11.2 (SD) mg/day, where Cau is urinary calcium and Cai calcium intake. True absorption is an inverse function of calcium intake, falling from some 70 per cent at very low intakes to about 35 per cent at high intakes. per cent net absorption is negative at low intakes, becomes positive as intake increases, reaches a peak of about 30 per cent at an intake of about 400 mg, and then falls off as the intake increases. The two lines converge as intake rises because the endogenous faecal component (which separates them) becomes proportionately smaller.

Many factors influence the availability of calcium for absorption and the absorptive mechanism itself. The former includes substances, which form insoluble complexes with calcium, such as the phosphate ion. The relatively high calcium-phosphate ratio of 2.2 in human milk compared with 0.77 in cow milk may be a factor in the higher absorption of calcium from human milk than cow milk.

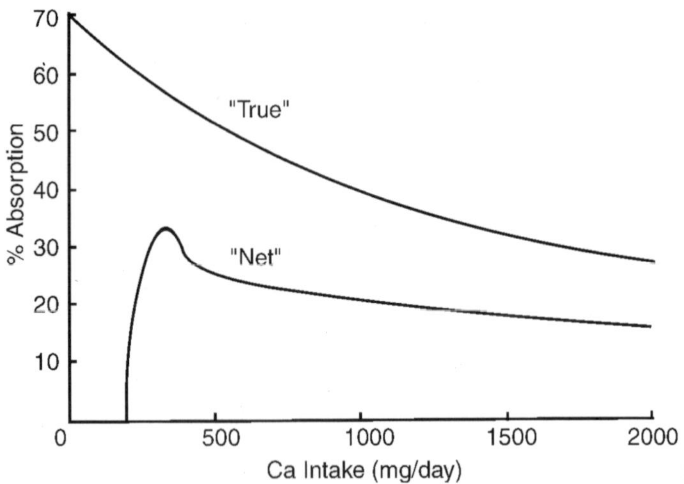


**Fig.** True and Net Calcium Absorption as per cents of Calcium intake

Intestinal calcium absorption is mainly controlled by the serum concentration of 1,25$(OH)_2$D. The activity of the 1-a-hydroxylase, which catalyses 1,25$(OH)_2$D production from 25-hydroxycolecalciferol (25OHD) in the kidneys, is negatively related to the plasma calcium and phosphate concentrations and positively to plasma parathyroid hormone. Thus the inverse relationship between calcium intake and fractional absorption described above is enhanced by the inverse relationship between dietary calcium and serum $1,25(OH)_2D$. Phytates, present in the husks of many cereals as well as in nuts, seeds, and legumes, can form insoluble calcium phytate salts in the gastrointestinal tract. Excess oxalates can precipitate calcium in the bowel but are not an important factor in most diets.

**Note:** The great differences between these functions at low calcium intakes and their progressive convergence as calcium intake increases.

### Urinary Calcium

Urinary calcium is the fraction of the filtered plasma water calcium, which is not reabsorbed in the renal tubules. At a normal glomerular filtration rate of 120 ml/min and ultrafiltrable calcium of 6.4 mg/100 ml (1.60 mmol/l), the filtered load of calcium is about 8 mg/min (0.20 mmol/min) or 11.6 g/day (290 mmol/day). Because the usual 24-hour calcium excretion in developed countries is about 160-200 mg (4-5 mmol), it follows that 98-99 per cent of the filtered calcium is usually reabsorbed in the renal tubules.

However, calcium excretion is extremely sensitive to changes in filtered load. A decrease in plasma water calcium of only 0.17 mg/100 ml (0.043 mmol/l), which is barely detectable, was sufficient to account for a decrease in urinary calcium of 63 mg (1.51 mmol) when 27 subjects changed from a normal- to a low-calcium diet.

This very sensitive renal response to calcium deprivation combines with the inverse relationship between calcium intake and absorption to stabilise the plasma ionised calcium concentration and to preserve the equilibrium between calcium entering and leaving the ECF over a wide range of calcium intakes. However, there is always a significant obligatory loss of calcium in the urine (as there is in the faeces), even on a low calcium intake, simply because maintenance of the plasma ionised calcium and, therefore, of the filtered load, prevents total elimination of the calcium from the urine.

The lower limit for urinary calcium in developed countries is about 140 mg (3.5 mmol) but depends on protein and salt intakes. From this obligatory minimum, urinary calcium increases on intake with a slope of about 5-10 per cent. In the graph derived from 210 balance studies referred to above, the relationship between urinary calcium excretion and calcium intake is represented by the line which intersects the absorbed calcium line at an intake of 520 mg.

## CALCIUM REQUIREMENTS

Although it is well established that calcium deficiency causes osteoporosis in experimental animals, the contribution that calcium deficiency makes to osteoporosis in humans is much more controversial, not least because of the great variation in calcium intakes across the world, which does not appear to be associated with any corresponding variation in the prevalence of osteoporosis. This issue is dealt with at greater length below in the section on nutritional factors; in this section we will simply define what is meant by calcium requirement and how it may be calculated. The calcium requirement of an adult is generally recognised to be the intake required to maintain calcium balance and therefore skeletal integrity. The mean calcium requirement of adults is therefore the mean intake at which intake and output are equal, which at present can only be determined by balance studies conducted with sufficient care and over a sufficiently long period to ensure reasonable accuracy and then corrected for insensible losses.

The reputation of the balance technique has been harmed by a few studies with inadequate equilibration times and short collection periods, but this should not be allowed to detract from the value of the meticulous work of those who have collected faecal and urinary samples for weeks or months from subjects on well-defined diets. This meticulous work has produced valuable balance data, which are clearly valid; the mean duration of the balances in the 210 studies from eight publications used in this report was 90 days with a range of 6-480 days. (The four 6-day balances in the series used a non-absorbable marker and are therefore acceptable.)

The usual way of determining mean calcium requirement from balance studies has been by linear regression of calcium output (or calcium balance) on intake and calculation of the mean intake at which intake and output are equal (or balance is zero). This was probably first done in 1939 by Mitchell and Curzon, who arrived at a mean requirement of 9.8 mg/kg/day or about 640 mg (16 mmol) at a mean body weight of 65 kg. The same type of calculation was subsequently used by many other workers who arrived at requirements ranging from 200 mg/day (5 mmol/day) in male Peruvian prisoners to 990 mg (24.75 mmol) in premenopausal women, but most values were about 600 mg (15 mmol) without allowing for insensible losses.

However, this type of simple linear regression yields a higher mean calcium requirement (640 mg in the same 210 balances) than the intercept of absorbed and excreted calcium (520 mg) because it tends to underestimate the negative calcium balance at low intake and overestimate the positive balance at high intake.

A better reflection of biological reality is obtained by deriving calcium output from the functions and then regressing that output on calcium intake. This yields where the negative balance is more severe at low intakes and less positive at high intakes than in the linear model and in which zero balance occurs at 520 mg.

This may well be an appropriate way of calculating the calcium requirement of children and adolescents (and perhaps pregnant and lactating women) who need to be in positive calcium balance and in whom the difference between calcium intake and output is therefore relatively large and measurable by the balance technique. However, in normal adults the difference between calcium intake and output at high calcium intakes represents a very small difference between two large numbers, and this calculation therefore carries too great an error to calculate their requirement.

We are inclined to think that the most satisfactory way of calculating calcium requirement from current data is as the intake at which excreted calcium equals net absorbed calcium, which has the advantage of permitting separate analysis of the effects of changes in calcium absorption and excretion. The addition to this excretion line of an additional obligatory urinary calcium of 30 mg (0.75 mmol) at menopause raises the amount to about 1100 mg, which we suggest is the mean calcium requirement of postmenopausal women.

However, this type of calculation cannot easily be applied to other high-risk populations (such as children) because there are not sufficient published data from these groups to permit a similar analysis of the relationship among calcium intake, absorption, and excretion. An alternative is to estimate how much calcium each population group needs to absorb to meet obligatory calcium losses and desirable calcium retention and then to calculate the intake required to provide this rate of calcium absorption.

## NUTRITIONAL FACTORS AFFECTING

### Sodium

It has been known at least since 1961 that urinary calcium is related to urinary sodium and that sodium administration raises calcium excretion, presumably because sodium competes with calcium for reabsorption in the renal tubules. Regarding the quantitative relationships between the renal handling of sodium and calcium, the filtered load of sodium is about 100 times that of calcium (in molar terms) but the clearance of these two elements is similar at about 1 ml/min, which yields about 99 per cent reabsorption and 1 per cent excretion for both.

However, these are approximations, which conceal the close dependence of urinary sodium on sodium intake and the weaker dependence of urinary calcium on calcium intake. It is an empirical fact that urinary sodium and calcium are significantly related in normal and hypercalciuric subjects on freely chosen diets. The slope of urinary calcium on sodium varies in published work from about 0.6 per cent to 1.2 per cent (in molar terms); a representative figure is about 1 per cent–that is, 100 mmol of sodium (2.3 g) takes out about 1 mmol (40 mg) of calcium.

The biological significance of this relationship is supported by the accelerated osteoporosis induced by feeding salt to rats on low-calcium diets and the effects of salt administration and salt restriction on markers of bone resorption in postmenopausal women. Because salt restriction lowers urinary calcium, it is likely also to lower calcium requirement and, conversely, salt feeding is likely to increase calcium requirement.

**Protein**

The positive effect of dietary protein particularly animal protein on urinary calcium has also been known at least since the 1960s. One study found that 0.85 mg of calcium was lost for each gram of protein in the diet. A meta-analysis of 16 studies in 154 adult humans on protein intakes up to 200 g found that 1.2 mg of calcium was lost in the urine for every 1g rise in dietary protein.

A small but more focussed study showed a rise of 40 mg in urinary calcium when dietary animal protein was raised from 40 to 80 g (*i.e.*, within the physiological range). This ratio of urinary calcium to dietary protein ratio (1mg to 1g) is a representative value, which we have adopted. This means that a 40g reduction in animal protein intake from 60 to 20 g (or from the developed to the developing world would reduce calcium requirement by the same amount as a 2.3g reduction in dietary sodium, *i.e.* from 840 to 600 mg. How animal protein exerts its effect on calcium excretion is not fully understood. A rise in glomerular filtration rate in response to protein has been suggested as one factor but this is unlikely to be important in the steady state. The major mechanisms are thought to be the effect of the acid load contained in animal proteins and the complexing of calcium in the renal tubules by sulphate and phosphate ions released by protein metabolism.

Urinary calcium is significantly related to urinary phosphate (as well as to urinary sodium), particularly in subjects on restricted calcium intakes or in the fasting state, and most of the phosphorus in the urine of people on Western-style diets comes from animal protein in the diet. Similar considerations apply to urinary sulphate but it is probably less important than the phosphate ion because the association constant for calcium sulphate is lower than that for calcium phosphate. The empirical observation that each 1 g of protein results in 1 mg of calcium in the urine agrees very well with the phosphorus content of animal protein (about 1 per cent by weight) and the observed relationship between calcium and phosphate in the urine.

**Vitamin D**

One of the first observations made on vitamin D after it had been identified in 1918 was that it promoted calcium absorption. It is now well established that vitamin D (synthesised in the skin under the influence of sunlight) is converted to 25OHD in the liver and then to $1,25(OH)_2D$ in the kidneys and that the latter metabolite controls calcium absorption. However, plasma 25OHD closely reflects vitamin D nutritional status and because it is the substrate for the renal enzyme which produces 1,25(OH)$_2$D, it could have an indirect effect on calcium absorption. The plasma level of 1,25-(OH)$_2$D is principally regulated is through increased gene expression of the 1-a-hydroxylase (CYP1a) and not by increased 25OHD levels. This has been seen consistently in animal studies, and the high calcium absorption and high plasma 1,25-(OH) $_2$D observed in Gambian mothers is consistent with this type of adaptation. However, increasing latitude may compromise vitamin D synthesis to the degree that 25OHD levels are no longer sufficient to sustain adequate 1,25-(OH)$_2$D levels and efficient intestinal calcium absorption, although this theory remains unproved. Regardless of the mechanism of compromised vitamin D homeostasis, the differences in calcium absorption efficiency have a major effect on theoretical calcium requirement, which shows that an increase in calcium absorption of as little as 10 per cent reduces the intercept of excreted and absorbed calcium (and therefore calcium requirement) from 840 to 680 mg.

# 9

# Good Health: Food and Nutrition

## NUTRITION AND HEALTH

Continuing to reduce cardiovascular disease and the prevention of cancer and health problems associated with overweight and obesity are currently the most important challenges facing nutrition policy. Prescriptions for a healthier, and in the WHO global strategy on diet, physical activity and health. A healthy diet and regular physical activity can reduce the incidence of cardiovascular disease and cancer and prevent increases in overweight, obesity and type 2 diabetes.

The nutritional needs and health problems change throughout the life cycle. The risk of developing chronic diseases can be influenced at all ages. Health-promoting and preventive nutrition work must take a comprehensive approach to the human life cycle and to different needs at the various stages of life.

The foundation for health and disease is laid already in utero. The mother's nutrition during pregnancy has consequences not only for the child's health as a newborn, but also for its health later in life. In other words, the eating habits and nutrition of pregnant women and women of childbearing age have consequences not only for themselves but for the next generation as well. It is important to ensure that women in this stage of life have proper nutrition, and that their intake of folic acid and iron meets recommended levels.

Breastmilk is of great importance to infants' nutrition, immune systems and development. The greatest possible number of infants should be breastfed in accordance with recommendations. Infants and toddlers are in a biologically vulnerable stage of life, and it is essential that baby and toddler food is healthy and safe, and contains the nutrients required to meet their nutritional needs.

Commissioned by the Ministry of Health and Care Services and completed in the spring of 2005, the action plan for infant and toddler nutrition identifies measures designed to achieve these objectives. Eating habits established during childhood and adolescence, have an impact on the risk of disease later in life. Food and drinks are important indicators of social and cultural identity for everyone, and perhaps particularly for adolescents. The physiological need for nutrients is greater during adolescence than during childhood, and high-quality diet is important. Given society's obsession with perfect bodies, many young people feel pressured to lose weight, and eating disorders are a problem. Children and adolescents are an important target group for health-promoting nutrition work. People who have developed diet-related diseases may benefit greatly from dietary measures to improve their condition. Most chronic diseases have their onset during adulthood. The need for certain nutrients increases with age. Many elderly people experience a loss of appetite and some eat too little, becoming undernourished and frailer than need be. Settling in a new country that has a different culture and language can lead to changes in diet, physical activity and health. Dietary changes, including a higher intake of fats and sugar and a lower intake of vegetables, fruits, lentils and beans, have been documented. Immigrants from non-Western countries differ in many ways, and there are substantial differences in health among the various groups. Some nutritional problems, such as overweight and obesity, type 2 diabetes, and iron and vitamin D deficiency, occur more often in certain immigrant groups.

## CARDIOVASCULAR DISEASE

*Cardiovascular disease* is the most common cause of death and has a great impact on morbidity. For people under the age of 70, deaths from cardiovascular disease have been reduced by more than half in the past 30 years. A large part of this decline is due to improvements in diet. In particular, decreased consumption of solid fats has improved the blood cholesterol level in the population. There is great potential for prevention of these diseases through reduced dietary intake of solid fats and salt and increased intake of fruits and vegetables. A combination of a healthy diet, regular physical activity and no smoking plays an important part in preventing and treating cardiovascular disease.

## CANCER

*Cancer* is the second most common cause of death and the overall incidence is on the rise. Obesity and physical inactivity are important risk factors for cancer. Diet plays an important role in preventing and treating cancer. A healthy diet with a high intake of fibre-rich foods, fruits and vegetables combined with a low salt intake can help prevent the development of a number of types of cancer. Cancer treatment not only exacts toil on the body mentally and physically, it may also alter or disrupt eating habits. As a consequence, proper nutrition is crucial when undergoing treatment.

## OVERWEIGHT AND OBESITY

*Overweight and obesity* have become increasingly prevalent in population in recent decades, as in other Western countries. All segments of the population are experiencing weight gain, regardless of age, gender or education level. Nevertheless, overweight and obesity are most common in the lower socio-economic strata. Weight gain is the result of an imbalance between energy intake and energy expenditure. Overweight readily occurs when a reduced level of physical activity is combined with easy access to energy-dense foods.

There is a need for viable treatment options for those who become seriously overweight or obese. Obesity is a risk factor for developing type 2 diabetes, cardiovascular disease, certain types of cancer and osteoarthritis of the hips and knees. Overweight and obesity represent a growing pro-blem for individuals and society-at-large, meaning prevention is of tremendous importance.

## DIABETES MELLITUS

*Diabetes mellitus* is the most common metabolic disorder in Norway. Diabetes is a result of a combination of genetic disposition and environmental factors. Overweight, obesity and physical inactivity increase people's risk of developing type 2 diabetes. These days, people are developing diabetes at an increasingly younger age. Diabetes is a contributing factor to cardiovascular disease, stroke, kidney failure, blindness, foot ulcers and amputation.

It is estimated that many people may have undiagnosed diabetes. Among immigrants from the Middle East and the Indian sub-continent, particularly among females, there is a substantial over-representation of type 2 diabetes. Dietary changes, increased physical activity, smoking cessation, controlling high blood pressure and weight loss play important roles in the treatment of type 2 diabetes. The single most important nutrition-related risk-factor of bone fractures is underweight. It is important to prevent underweight among the elderly. It is also important to ensure an adequate intake of vitamin D and calcium.

## VISION

A healthy diet meets the recommendations for the composition of nutrients, is varied, tasty and in harmony with cultural values. It is the sum of what is consumed, how much and how often, that is decisive in the long run. From a health-promoting and preventive perspective, health is more than the absence of disease. In addition to physical health, it encompasses contentment and well-being.

## STRATEGIC GOALS

*Work in the nutrition sector should contribute to*:

- Reducing the incidence of cardiovascular disease;
- Reducing the incidence of diet-related cancer;
- Halting the increase in overweight and obesity;

- Preventing type 2 diabetes;
- Preventing underweight and malnourishment;
- Strengthening the role of nutrition in treating the sick.

*High-priority initiatives include*:

- Increased consumption of vegetables, fruits, berries and whole-grain products;
- Decreased intake of solid fats;
- Decreased intake of energy-dense, nutrient- poor foods.

Facilitating healthy choices and increasing the health literacy of the population should be given priority in an attempt to achieve these strategic goals.

## INCREASED CONSUMPTION OF FRUITS, VEGETABLES, BERRIES AND WHOLE-GRAIN PRODUCTS

Fruits, berries, vegetables, potatoes and whole-grain products are good sources of fibre, vitamins, minerals and a number of other nutrients. There is substantial documentation to show that a diet rich in fruits, vegetables, and whole-grain products reduces the risk of cardiovascular disease and certain types of cancer. Such a diet is not energy-dense and can reduce the risk of obesity. Consumer surveys, the consump-tion of vegetables increased from 80 gm./day in the 1970s to 110 gm./day in 2002, and there was a corresponding increase in the consumption of fruits and juice from 120 gm./day to 170 gm./ day. Altogether, consumption has risen from 200 gm./day to 280 gm./day during this period.

The consumption of potatoes has declined by half during the same period. Only about 10 per cent of the population has an intake of vegetables and fruits. There are clear social disparities in the consumption of these foods. The intake of grain products has remained relatively stable, but the consumption of whole-grain flour accounts for less than 20 per cent of total consumption. The goal is to increase the consumption of vegetables and fruits throughout the population to an average total intake of fruits and vegetables of at least 400 gm./day by 2009 to meet WHO recommendations.

Meanwhile, another goal is to increase the consumption of whole-grain products and potatoes at the expense of fat-rich potato products.

## REDUCED INTAKE OF SOLID FATS (SATURATED FATS AND TRANS FATS)

Saturated fatty acids, and particularly trans fatty acids, in the diet have a negative effect on blood lipid profiles and increase the risk of coronary heart disease. It is estimated that a reduction in the intake of solid fats can substantially reduce the risk of coronary heart disease. In the 1970s, saturated fats accounted for 17 per cent, while the percentage has fallen to 14 per cent today, according to consumer surveys. The diet's content of trans fatty acids has been reduced from 4 per cent to less than 1 per cent of the diet's total energy content in the past 30 years.

The most important sources of saturated fats and trans fats in the diet are milk, dairy products, meat and meat products. Bread products, biscuits and cakes can also contain trans fats. The intake of solid fats should be limited to 10 per cent of total energy intake. By promoting the consumption of foods that are low in fat and foods that contain unsaturated fats, the intake of solid fats as well as the total fat intake can be reduced. The goal is to further reduce the consumption of solid fats to 12 per cent.

## REDUCED INTAKE OF ENERGY-DENSE, NUTRIENT-POOR FOODS

A diet rich in energy-dense, nutrient-poor foods is linked to an increased risk of overweight and obesity, type 2 diabetes and caries. This type of diet can also result in a low intake of vitamins and minerals. A consumer surveys, over the past 30 years, total sugar consumption has risen slightly to 15 per cent of energy intake.

Sugar consumption patterns have changed, and the consumption of soft drinks and sweets has increased in particular. The sugar intake of children and adolescents has climbed sharply and is considerably higher than desired levels. Dietary studies among 13-year-olds reveal that sugar accounted for 13 per cent of their energy intake in 1993 and 18 per cent in 2000.

On average, they drank 4–5 dl of sugared soft drinks and fruit drinks a day, and ate 40–45 g of sweets a day. Sugared fruit drinks, soft drinks, and sweets accounted for 65 per cent of 13-year-olds' total sugar intake. Added sugar comprises sucrose, fructose, starch hydrolysate and other isolated sugars, which are used either in their pure form, as components of other food products or in cooking. Added sugar should not exceed 10 per cent of total energy intake. Another goal is to reduce the consumption of sugared soft drinks from some 85 litres per person per year to 60 litres per person annually, corresponding to the level of con-sumption in 1990. An additional goal is to reduce the consumption of sweets, sugared, nutrient-poor beverages, snack foods and fat-rich potato products.

## DIET FOR WOMEN

With the way they are conditioned, women end up doing more or less work equivalent to men. However, the kind of recognition they get is pretty less compared to what men get. Many women feel bad when they even put on one pound of weight. They go on crash diet and try and reduce their weight to make it to normal. But fact is many women don't even realise that they are too skinny to go on diets that make them thinner. Iron deficiency in women is definitely a big cause of worry for many women. We do not teach you special kinds of diets, instead as suggested, be discussing about what foods are advised for women, and what are not.

*What Foods to Avoid*, gives a detail of what type of foods should be avoided, and why. Actually, avoiding bad foods is half the job done to stay healthy. And when you know what foods you avoid, you should also be worried about what gives you a healthy structure and figure. Most of the body weight is constituted by bone weight.

Hence it is important that take foods that give loads of calcium to your body. *Nutrition for Healthy Bones*, will help you understand how to build up healthy bones, and a healthy life.

## PREGNANCY DIET

Though not always, many a woman is always in two minds whenever she is confronted with a new situation. The same is the case when a woman gets pregnant. Unfortunately one cannot say that all pregnant women know how to take care of their health during this important time.

## NUTRITION DURING PREGNANCY

A stable diet is a critical component of good health always in an individual's life. All through pregnancy, diet is still more significant. The foods that one consumes are the chief suppliers of the nutrients for one's baby. As the baby develops, one will require more of the majority of nutrients.

Prior to becoming pregnant is the most excellent time to commence eating a beneficial diet. Eating correctly prior to becoming pregnant can assist an individual in ensuring that both she and her baby start off with the nutrients that both require.

### Supplement

Folic acid is a kind of vitamin that is crucial to the development of the baby, particularly all through the initial months of pregnancy. Not receiving sufficient folic acid in one's diet prior to one becoming pregnant and initially in pregnancy augments the threat of birth flaws, for example neural tube imperfection. Receiving good health care ahead of one becoming pregnant will assist an individual all through one's pregnancy.

Pregnant women are occasionally worried about gaining surplus weight. However, it should be borne in mind that one's diet is the foremost source of energy for the baby. That signifies one has to consume more while pregnant.

When an individual is pregnant, she requires approximately 300 calories additionally everyday day than she generally consumes. The amount of weight a woman puts on during pregnancy is dependent on her weight prior to pregnancy.

A beneficial gain for the majority of women is between 25 and 35 pounds. If a woman is obese, she should put on less, but certain weight gain is usual. If a woman is underweight, she should put on additional weight. The initial move in the direction of healthy eating is to take into account the foods in one's everyday diet.

*Additional Nutrients*:

- Pregnant women may require additional nutrients and these may consist of iron, folic acid and calcium.
- They can be made available as single pills or as an amalgamated pill.
- Occasionally a prenatal vitamin has all that one requires.
- In order to avert neural tube flaws, a woman ought to receive 0.4 mg. of folic acid every day ahead of and all through pregnancy.
- It should be taken for one month ahead of pregnancy and throughout the initial three months of pregnancy.

Women who have had a child with a spine or skull blemish are more liable to have one more child with this trouble. These women require greater amounts of folic acid-4 mg. every day. Milk and additional dairy products are the most excellent sources of calcium in one's diet.

However, several women have indications, for example bloating, diarrhoea, gas and indigestion subsequent to drinking milk or consuming dairy products. This is referred to as lactose intolerance. If a pregnant woman is lactose intolerant, she should ensure that she is receiving adequate calcium.

## DIET FOR HEALTHY WEIGHT GAIN DURING PREGNANCY

Acquiring the correct quantity of weight all through pregnancy by consuming a nourishing, stable diet is an excellent sign that the baby is receiving all the nutrients he or she requires and is developing at a healthy rate. It is not essential to consume for two in pregnancy. It's a reality that pregnant women require additional calories from nutrient-rich foods to aid the growth of her baby, but a pregnant woman commonly should consume just 100 to 300 more calories than she did ahead of becoming pregnant to fulfil the requirements of the developing baby.

It is imperative for a pregnant woman to take the advice of the health care provider on the amount of weight she should put on for the period of pregnancy. A woman of standard weight ahead of pregnancy should put on 25 to 35 pounds for the period of pregnancy. Women who are underweight should put on 28-40 pounds for the period of pregnancy. Obese women may require putting on just 15-25 pounds during pregnancy.

*Ideal weight gain*:

- Generally, one should put on approximately 2 to 4 pounds all through the initial three months of pregnancy and 1 pound a week for the rest of the pregnancy period.
- If an individual is anticipating twins she should put on 35 to 45 pounds for the period of her pregnancy.
- This would be a typical of 1 ½ pounds for every week following the normal weight increase in the initial three months.

### The Additional Weight is Distributed in the Following Manner

For the baby it is 8 pounds, for the placenta 2-3 pounds, for amniotic fluid 2-3 pounds, for breast tissue 2-3 pounds, blood supply 4 pounds, fat reserves for delivery and breastfeeding 5-9 pounds and for uterus increase 2-5 pounds. This makes for a total weight of 25 to 30 pounds.

It is by no means risk-free to shed weight for the period of pregnancy since both the mother and the baby require the appropriate nutrients so as to be healthy. In order to gain the required weight during pregnancy one should consume five to six minor, regular meals everyday. One should stock swift, trouble-free snacks on hand, for example nuts, raisins, cheese and crackers, dried fruit, in addition to ice cream or yogurt. It is imperative to apply peanut butter on toast, crackers, apples, bananas, or celery.

A single tablespoon of creamy peanut butter will make available approximately 100 calories and 7gm. of protein. One should include nonfat powdered milk in foods for example mashed potatoes, scrambled eggs plus hot cereal.

It is crucial to include condiments in one's meal, for example, butter or margarine, cream cheese, gravy, sour cream as well as cheese. Certainly, patterns of weight increase all through pregnancy differ. It's usual to put on less if an individual is heavier at the time of pregnancy and it is normal to put on extra weight if an individual is expecting twins or triplets or if an individual is underweight prior to becoming pregnant.

## WHAT FOODS TO AVOID

Eating proportionate meals is vital at all times, but it is especially crucial when one is pregnant. There are important nutrients, vitamins and minerals that a growing baby requires. The majority of foods are harmless; nonetheless, there are certain foods that one ought to stay away from during pregnancy.

Raw seafood and exceptional or undercooked beef or poultry should be shunned due to the danger of infectivity with coliform bacteria, toxoplasmosis, and salmonella.

Deli meats have been acknowledged to be infected with Listeria, which can trigger miscarriage. Listeria has the capacity to traverse the placenta and may contaminate the baby resulting in contamination or blood poisoning, which can be critical. If a pregnant woman is contemplating to eat deli meats, she should ensure to reheat the meat until it is steaming.

*Avoiding fish*:

- Fish that has high quantities of mercury ought to be avoided.
- Mercury ingested during pregnancy has been associated with developmental hindrance and brain harm.
- Examples of these kinds of fish comprise: shark, swordfish, king mackerel and tilefish.
- Canned, chunk light tuna usually contain less quantities of mercury in comparison to other tuna, but still should only be consumed in restraint.
- Some kinds of fish employed in sushi should also be shunned because of high concentration of mercury.

Frozen, smoked seafood frequently described as lox, nova style, kippered, or jerky should be shunned since they could be infected with Listeria. Preserved or shelf-safe smoked seafood is considered safe for consumption.

Individuals who are pregnant should shun fish from polluted lakes and rivers that may be subjected to high quantities of polychlorinated biphyenyls. Most of seafood borne sickness is attributable to undercooked shellfish, which comprise oysters, clams, and mussels. Cooking assists in averting several kinds of infection, but it does not thwart the algae-related illness that is linked to red tides. Uncooked shellfish create apprehension for everyone and they should be shunned in general all through pregnancy.

Uncooked eggs or any foods that has uncooked eggs should be shunned due to the possible exposure to salmonella. Several home-produced Caesar dressings, mayonnaise, home-produced ice cream or custards, and Hollandaise sauces may be prepared with uncooked eggs. If the recipe is cooked at certain stage, this will reduce the contact with salmonella. Commercially produced ice cream, dressings and eggnog are prepared with pasteurized eggs and do not augment the threat of salmonella. Restaurants also are supposed to be utilizing pasteurized eggs in whichever recipe that is made with uncooked eggs, for example Hollandaise sauce or dressings.

Imported soft cheese may have bacteria recognized as Listeria, which can trigger miscarriage. Listeria has the capacity to traverse the placenta and can contaminate the baby resulting in infection or blood poisoning that can be life-

intimidating. Pregnant women should keep away from soft cheese for example, brie, camembert, Roquefort, feta, gorgonzola and Mexican type cheeses that comprise queso blanco and queso fresco.

## IRON DEFICIENCY ANAEMIA IN WOMEN

Iron insufficiency anaemia—a shortage of iron in the blood affects a large number of women globally. Iron is a vital nutrient in pregnancy; hence it's imperative to be certain that pregnant women have an ample ingestion. There are three major causes that an adequate iron ingestion to thwart anaemia is vital. First, iron is indispensable for the development of maternal and foetal hoemoglobin, the oxygen-transporting constituent of blood.

As a woman's blood volume swells by 25 to 40 per cent in pregnancy, and the baby is producing blood cells, as well, the requirement for iron rises putting the mother in danger of anaemia. Second, in the final trimester, the baby extracts from the mother a quantity of the iron reserves that it will require in the initial four to six months of life. Third, the augmented blood volume and iron stores aids the mother's body adjust, to certain extent, to the blood loss that takes place in childbirth.

*Maternal iron deficiency anaemia*:

- Maternal iron deficiency anaemia is linked to an augmented frequency of anaemia in the baby in the initial year of life, in addition to anaemia and reduced iron reserves in the mother.
- Pregnant women with iron deficiency anaemia, chiefly in the first and second trimesters, have an augmented danger for early delivery and for delivering a low-birth weight baby.

The majority of doctors suggest iron supplements for pregnant mothers. In general, an every day 60 mg. iron supplement is recommended to check anaemia, although the suggested quantity of iron in pregnancy is 30 mg. every day. It is for the reason that iron from supplements is not completely assimilated. Receiving 60 mg. of iron daily will make certain that a pregnant woman in reality assimilated the suggested daily quantity of iron.

Iron supplements are appropriately assimilated if taken with foods enriched with vitamin C, for example orange, grapefruit, or tomato juice. Absorption is weakened if one takes them with antacids or foods containing calcium for example milk and cheese. Iron supplements occasionally trigger upset stomach, constipation, or nausea.

If such a condition arises one can obtain most of the iron an individual requires from iron-rich foods, for example organ meats like liver red meat, egg yolks, and legumes such as dried peas and beans. Iron deficiency anaemia in pregnant women and in babies in the aftermath of delivery is without difficulty avoidable by the consumption of a stable, wholesome, iron-rich diet and taking iron supplements as stipulated by one's doctor. Iron deficiency anemia is linked to psychomotor and cognitive defects in children. Iron deficiency anaemia in pregnancy has been connected with augmented danger for low birth weight, preterm delivery, and prenatal death. Recent studies entail that maternal iron deficiency anaemia may be related to postpartum melancholy and inferior performance on mental and psychomotor tests in children.

## ANTI AGING NUTRITION

Although ageing is unavoidable, physical decay is not. More than a few of the external manifestations of growing old can be decelerated - and life can even be protracted - by sustaining a wise and meaningful approach to diet. As individuals grow old, their bodies' process nutrients less competently, leading to the requirement for individuals to enhance their nutrient ingestion. For instance, Vitamin D is a nutrient necessary for the deterrence of osteoporosis. The human body produces vitamin D when the skin is subjected to sunlight, but when individuals are in their 70s their bodies manufacture merely 40 per cent of it. An ample quantity of vitamin D for people in their 20s is 200 IU; for individuals who are grown-up, 400 IU to 600 IU is required for performing the identical amount of work.

*Requirement related to age*:

- The requirement for B vitamins rises with age also.
- Three B vitamins—folic acid, vitamin B6 and vitamin B12—are crucial for maintaining levels of a compound described as homocysteine at a low level in the blood; if permitted to increase, homocysteine plays a part in heart-disease threat and probably memory loss, as indicated by studies in the relevant sphere.
- When individuals age it is imperative for them to augment their B6 amount from 2 mg to 5 mg; augment B12 in due course from 2 mcg to 10 mcg.
- Women ought to receive 400 mcg of folic acid every day; pregnant women ought to ingest 800 mcg everyday in order to thwart neural-tube flaws in the foetus.

Women, specifically, should be conscious that their calcium ingestion should augment as they age to avert osteoporosis. Individuals who eat diets rich in fresh fruits and vegetables have reduced ailment rates, additional energy and less danger for weight gain that can result in health troubles in comparison to those who omit these foods.

With the omission of avocados, olives and coconuts, fresh fruits and vegetables are devoid of fat, cholesterol or sodium. Fresh fruits and vegetables are furthermore rich in fibre. Eight servings of fruits and vegetables consumed everyday offers roughly 27 gm. of fibre, which is well inside the everyday requirement of 25 gm. to 35 gm.. Foods rich in fibre reduce an individual's threat for developing age-linked ailments for example heart disease, cancer, diabetes and hypertension. Foods rich in fibre are moreover reduced in calories, nonetheless satisfying; consequently they assist in filling up individuals without filling him or her. Fresh fruits and vegetables are rich in nutrients, making available sufficient quantities of calcium, iron, magnesium, vitamin C, beta carotene and folic acid, and they are short in calories. Fruits and vegetables also contain longevity-boosting compounds referred to as antioxidants which comprise vitamins C and E in addition to beta carotene. Antioxidants resist free radicals, oxygen fragments that strike and harm cell membranes, life-supporting proteins and even genetic code of cells that trigger aging and ailments.

Diets high in antioxidants check ailment and untimely aging. Antioxidants, moreover, invigourate the immune system and defend the nervous system and brain from the oxidative harm connected with age-linked memory loss.

## DIET DURING MENOPAUSE

Menopause is the expression employed to signify the cease of the period of probable sexual reproduction, as demonstrated by the termination of menstrual periods. This is completely usual and happens between 45 to 55 years. Menopause does not reduce women's physical capability, sexual energy and capacity to enjoy life. Menopause fetches specific freedoms to female life. Such as no longer they have to be anxious about the monthly bleeding and about birth control.

Still then in this period a woman suffers a great deal of emotional strain. Ovaries discontinue making oestrogen and this result in oestrogen deficiency. This hormonal disparity may trigger short-term symptoms and long term health threat.

*Adhering to a healthy diet*:

- Sticking to a healthy diet can be beneficial for vitality in general and this in the process assists in providing a woman with better resistance against any troubles during menopause.
- Hot flushes can be diminished by acquiring vitamin E rich foods similar to wheat germ, nuts, eggs and olive oil.
- Vitamin A, D, calcium, phosphorous and magnesium can assist in checking osteoporosis.
- Fish, drumstick leaves, ragi and dairy products are outstanding suppliers of calcium. During menopause women should shun consuming uncooked bran, which hinders calcium absorption and should reduce the consumption of tea, coffee which advances the excretion of calcium.

Many women gain weight which augments the blood cholesterol level. To regulate body weight and blood cholesterol one should choose low fat dairy foods and reduce the consumption of saturated fats such as butter and cheese. Studies indicate that substances from plants identified as phytoestrogens can assist in diminishing the acuteness of hot flushes and additional indications of menopause. Phytoestrogens, which imitate human oestrogen, are obtained chiefly from soybeans and alfalfa sprouts. Soya bean flour can be combined with wheat flour for making bread. Additional soya foods are soymilk, tofu, as well as soy sauce. Carrot in addition to beet root juice is considered to be extremely helpful in menopausal maladies. Oats, corn, barley, brown rice, whole wheat are as well outstanding sources of phytoestrogens.

Frequent exercise is necessary in this period. This stage is to be considered as a usual period in a women's life. Nonetheless the family members ought to understand that this stage in the life of a woman requires a great deal of thought, attention and sympathy to make the daily life stress free. A nourishing diet can not only diminish the indications of menopause, but also bring about an improved lifestyle and augmented energy levels, enabling one to do the types of activities that will support an improved body and an improved lifestyle in general. Foods rich in calcium and supplements are an excellent suggestion if one intends to lead a vigourous way of life during menopause. Calcium is mainly helpful when used with additional vitamins and minerals such as magnesium and vitamin D, which supports superior skeletal health.

## NUTRITION FOR HEALTHY BONES

Healthy bones provide the body with power and firmness to defend the internal organs from damage. Significant as the skeleton is, it accounts for merely around 12 per cent of a human being's entire body weight.

Bones are living tissues and are continuously experiencing remodeling since old bone tissue gets worn-out and fresh bone is produced. A subtle equilibrium has to be kept between these two procedures. If that equilibrium is disrupted, problems can take place, including brittle bones and osteoporosis.

*Ensuring healthy bones needs*:

- Frequent physical exercise and a nourishing, stable diet are equally vital.
- Evading threat factors similar to smoking and strain also add to healthy bones.
- Every individual can do a bit to shape the health of their bones.
- By indulging in weight-bearing physical work out one can promote bone mineralization.
- By eating correctly one can make certain that the essential nutrients are obtainable for bone metabolism.

- These major nutrients are Calcium and Vitamin D.

Calcium is essential for strong teeth and bones and furthermore, plays a vital part in a variety of bodily systems, for example, the health and performance of nerves and muscle tissue. Superior sources of calcium comprise dairy foods and leafy green vegetables, even though calcium from milk and milk products is more effortlessly assimilated and present in larger quantities. Individuals at various life phases require dissimilar quantities of calcium. Adolescents, young children in addition to elderly women all have bigger than normal necessities. Calcium is one of the vital nutrients required for healthy growth of bone.

Ample calcium ingestion is crucial for the accom-plishment of peak bone mass in the late teen. This is the maximum stage of bone strength which takes place at cease of growth, and consequently results in tough healthy bones, which will prolong the consequences of ageing on the skeleton. It is vital to have a proportionate diet with sufficient quantities of dairy products, which are the principal sources of foods high in calcium.

Vitamin D is the broad name for a cluster of steroid-like substances with anti-rachitic action. Vitamin D is obtained only from animals and there are simply some foods which have vitamin D like oily fish, fish oils, butter and eggs. Different from other vitamins, individuals can in reality produce vitamin D in their bodies as an outcome of contact to sunlight, on condition that ingestion of ascorbic acid is sufficient. The two major members of this vitamin cluster are ergocalciferol or vitamin D2 and cholecalciferol or vitamin D3. Vitamin D is necessary for the assimilation of calcium and phosphorus from the small intestine, their re-assimilation in the kidneys, and the mineralization procedure of the bones. It therefore promotes healthy bone development. It, furthermore performs a vital role in the appropriate working of muscles, nerves, blood clotting, cell growth and energy utilization.

## BREAST CANCER DIET

When an individual is coping with breast cancer, appropriate nutrition becomes especially vital. Nonetheless, a proportionate diet and breast cancer treatment may not be effective simultaneously. The side effects from breast cancer treatments, together with the emotional stress of being afflicted by the disease can make it tough for patients to eat. By pursuing recommen-dations to deal with the side effects when eating; selecting beneficial foods to eat; and drawing assistance and support from others, breast cancer patients can preserve a well-balanced diet during cure and recuperation. While taking into account the diet in breast cancer treatment, one should initiate a hunt for cancer-combating nutrients. Foods with such nutrients should assist in satisfying the palate of the breast cancer patient. One may start by looking for foods that are rich in selenium.

*Selenium effective in fighting cancer*:

- Selenium is equally an indispensable natural mineral and a helpful cancer-fighting antioxidant.
- Foods rich in selenium require being an ingredient of a diet for breast cancer treatment.
- Selenium aids to fortify the immune system, and helps in easing the action of the thyroid. It also assists in stimulating specific enzymes.
- One can acquire a required ingestion of selenium by consuming tuna, eggs, wheat grain, chicken, liver, garlic as well as Brazil nuts.

The benefits of selenium make it suitable for addition in the diet for breast cancer cure. Studies indicate a connection between the capacity of selenium to initiate the action of specific enzymes and the mineral's ability to defend against cancer threats.

An every day ingestion of no less than 70 microgm. of selenium should be the aim of every woman who is concerned with regard to her diet for breast cancer treatment. If an individual consumes a quantity far higher than 100 microgm. every day, then this surplus quantity of selenium can trigger nausea, awful breath, skin complaints, giddiness, feebleness and cold indications.

Ingestion of above 60 microgm. of selenium every day is unsuitable for pregnant women. An excessive ingestion of selenium seems connected with birth problems. However, certain women can include extra selenium to a diet in breast cancer treatment.

One more nutrient that should be an ingredient of every diet in breast cancer treatment is indole-3-carbinol, a chemical that is as well described as 13C. This phytochemical, a crucial component of the chemical composition of broccoli and additional cruciferous vegetables has been revealed to be a natural means of averting specific cancers.

The useful 13C utilizes three dissimilar means for supplying its beneficial effects. Initially, 13C disrupts the cancer cell phase; a broken up cycle checks cell division. Second, 13C checks the development of blood vessels in the tumor; with no blood vessels, the tumor cells can not obtain required nutrients. Third, 13C work in a way that is capable of preparing the phase for the death of the cancer cells. The maximum worth of 13C stems from the anticipated product formed when an individual has consumed a diet high in 13C.

## HEALTH DIETS FOR PATIENTS

When taking care of various health issues, one has to be extremely careful about one's diet. Doctors advise medicines mentioning what kind of diet should be taken with it. If this diet isn't followed carefully, medicines do not do the complete job.

## DIET FOR CANCER

A strict diet is advised for Cancer because some foods directly affect cancer maturity. Fat, especially saturated fats do more harm than any one can imagine. Hence diets for Cancer should increase as much as only 55gm. of Fat intake daily.

## DIET FOR GOUT

Gout is one type of arthritis and is called metabolic arthritis. It is one of the worst types of arthritis. Gout makes sodium urate crystals deposit on the particular cartilage of joints and tendon tissues. It might even cause stones in kidneys. Rich Carbohydrate diet is advised for people who suffer from Gout. Protein intake should be very limited as well.

## DIET DURING ACID REFLUX

When someone feels heartburn, or suddenly realises that he or she gets food back into their mouths, they should suspect Acid Reflux. Gastric juices that contain acids are pushed back from stomach to esophagus, and this condition is called acid reflux. Diet for acid reflux starts off with taking smaller meals, more than three times a day. And the diet is all given in the substance called diet during acid reflux.

## DIET DURING DIARRHOEA

Diarrhoea is one of the most irritating health problems. It could be cause by contaminated food or even climate change. And importantly one should not stop diarrhea because it is nature's way of eliminating virus.

## DIET FOR CONSTIPATION

Constipation is the exact opposite situation of diarrhoea. While you struggle to control defecating in diarrhoea, Constipation doesn't allow easy defecating. Fibre is the most suggested diet for constipation. And make sure you find the correct sources of Fibre from the substance.

## DIET FOR OBESE

United States suffers with an ever increasing population of obese people. Though obesity doesn't kill right away, one needs to be specially aware of what it can do to ones body. Obesity isn't a disease but a condition which definitely leads to disease over a period of time. Fat is the mean reason behind obesity.

So, if you think and find that you are growing in weight regularly, you should first consult your doctor. One can be called obese when is unable to see their toes, when they stand straight. All you need to do is avoid food, and you lose weight. But why should any one take food for weight loss? All foods play an important role in the way we act and think daily. Hence if we do not have foods over a period of time, it is imperative that we are not as good as when we have enough food in our bellies. However, we need to understand that certain foods with too much of fat in them, make us fatter, and certain foods have lesser amounts of fat. Hence, taking food that has lesser amounts of fat helps.

## LOW CARB DIETS

Food, in general, contains proteins, carbohydrates, fat, minerals, water and other nutrients. In all these we proteins are digested for various activities performed inside the body. Carbohydrates provide energy required for the body to do various physical activities. Fat helps our body in many ways, and it acts as a substitute for carbs. So when carbs fall short, fat is burnt to provide energy. That's how low carb diets help.

## SAFE SWEETENERS AND FAT BURNERS

If you crave for that sweet taste and can't get adjusted to not having sugar in your tea and coffee, then sweeteners help you out. These small tablets contain sucralose or saccharin apart from various other ingredients. Importantly they add lesser amounts of calories to your body. Fat burners are dangerous if not taken under a doctor's advice. They simulate burning of excessive calories in your body, and their effect is felt immediately.

## HEALTHY EATING

Healthy eating should be made a daily routine and cannot be taken easy. Healthy eating guildelines provide apart from few easy tips for weight loss, with an substance especially for new moms who want to shed weight.

# LOW CARB DIETS—HOW THEY WORK?

Low carb diets are anchored in the principle that a diet extremely low in carbohydrate results in a decrease in the body's insulin production, leading to fat and protein stores being utilized as its major energy source.

## OBJECTIVE

- The objective of low carbohydrate diets is to compel the body to utilize fat as its chief energy source.
- When this takes place an individual produces "ketone bodies" to stimulate parts of the body that cannot utilize fat as an energy source—the brain, and red blood cells, specifically.
- When this occurs an individual is said to be in a condition of ketosis—typified by stinking breath and side effects for example sickness and exhaustion.

In essence an individual eliminates practically all carbohydrate from his or her diet and increases the protein and fat ingestion. Hence one reduces the consumption of pasta, bread, rice in addition to alcohol, and consumes unrestricted quantities of meat, cheese in addition to butter.

In the short term, the majority of individuals who follow low carb diets do lose weight and they lose it extremely fast. Nonetheless, most of the weight loss happens from loss of water as well as muscle tissue, not fat which one requires to lose to avoid the surplus weight.

In addition, if an individual is attempting to lose weight on a permanent basis, losing valuable lean muscle tissue is similar to damaging one's own body. Even when an individual is relaxing, muscle tissue is metabolically active, and burns calories. A reduction in the quantity of muscle tissue an individual possesses will result in a reduction in the number of calories an individual requires every day to preserve one's weight, making it a great deal tough to keep one's weight under check when one discontinues pursuing the low carb diet. Persons are fascinated by low carb diets since weight loss is extremely fast, and individuals love to observe immediate results on the weighing machine. However, low carb diet is not a very healthy choice. Crucial vitamins and nutrients are obtained from a balanced diet and low carbohydrate diets are definitely not balanced.

One can simply obtain a lot of vital nutrients from fruit, vegetables and grains and low carb diets merely permit extremely small quantities of fruit and vegetables which is certainly not sufficient to offer an individual his or her suggested every day allowance. The crucial point these low carb diets expresses is that carbohydrates advance insulin production, which in the process leads to weight gain. Hence by decreasing carbohydrate ingestion, individuals will shed weight.

The reality is that by consuming a low carb diet, individuals do not offer sufficient carbohydrates to his or her body for every day function. Consequently it will begin burning the stored carbohydrates known as glycogen for energy. When a person's body commences burning glycogen, water is discharged. Consequently the severe early drop of weight at the start is merely water one loses as a consequence of burning glycogen.

## SAFE SWEETENERS

Widespread obesity and diabetes promoted the expansion of the artificial sweetener industry. Increasing number of people are endeavoring to shed weight or trying to preserve a healthy weight. Sweeteners can be discovered in nearly all chewing gum, diet pop as well as drinks, light yogurt in addition to various frozen ice cream. If a product is labelled sugar free, it is extremely probable that sweeteners are added to them.

*Types of sweeteness are*:

- Nutritive Sweeteners make available calories to the diet at approximately four calories for every gm., akin to the usual carbohydrate individuals acquire from food.
- Instances of nutritive sweeteners comprise white and brown table sugars as well as molasses, honey in addition to syrups.
- Besides, sugar alcohols obtained from fruits or commercially prepared are as well nutritive sweeteners.
- The majority of widespread sugar alcohols comprise sorbitol, mannitol, xylitol as well as maltitol.
- Every nutritive sweetener supplies calories to the body and may well have an effect on one's blood glucose.
- Nonnutritive sweeteners are the real artificial sweeteners.
- They do not supply calories and will not affect blood glucose.
- These consist of, saccharin, neotame, aspartame, sucralose, stevia and acesulfame potassium.

The safest thing to do is to keep away from all synthetic and chemical sweetener substitutes. They boast of no food value, deceive the body into believing it is consuming something sweet, and they have by-products of damaging poisonous side effects.

Foods having saccharin no more carry a warning maintaining that the utilization of this product may perhaps be dangerous to one's health accompanied by the assertion that such foods have saccharin which has been revealed to trigger cancer in laboratory animals. This caution was removed following indications that saccharin no longer has been associated with cancer in human beings.

Saccharin may possibly be there in drugs in large amounts. Intake of the suggested every day dosage of chewable aspirin or acetaminophen tablets in a child of school going age would make available roughly the similar quantity of saccharin enclosed in one can of a diet soft drink. This quantity, comparative to the body weight of a child younger than 9 or 10 years and consumed for extended duration would be regarded as excessive use, as characterized in a key scientific report.

In this report, heavy utilization of artificial sweeteners was connected with a considerably augmented danger for the growth of bladder cancer. Acesulfame Potassium which was permitted for utilization as a harmless artificial sweetener is an offshoot of acetoacetic acid. Regrettably, a number of probable troubles connected with the application of acesulfame have been brought up. They are centred mainly on animal studies because experiments on humans continue to be limited. Aspartame, a dipeptide of aspartic acid and a methyl ester of phenylalanine, is permitted for utilization in pharmaceutical products and is being employed more and more in chewable tablets and sugar-free formulations.

**FAT BURNERS**

Ripped Fuel, ProBURN, Thermo-Cuts, Metabolift, OptiBurn and Hydroxycut are promoted as fat-burning supplements that will enable an individual acquire a lean shape in a rapid manner. In reality, these fat burners do have a propensity to augment the pace at which a person uses up calories, but as with every product that promises marvel, it is essential for an individual to exercise caution prior to use and care should be taken while using them.

A fat burner that an individual selects will more or less at all times have two basic ingredients, namely, ephedrine and caffeine. Ephedrine is a bronchodilator, which is available as asthma medicine or cold medication to augment the body's capacity to carry oxygen into the bloodstream. Additional oxygen in the bloodstream offers individuals the capability to generate more energy in the cells.

More significantly for fat burning, ephedrine is a stimulant that enhances heart rate and blood pressure, thereby stimulating the body during workouts at the gym. In addition, ephedrine has a propensity to hinder appetite and perform as a diuretic. Synephrine, norephedrine, and pseudoephedrine are all related to ephedrine that offers comparable results. Individuals who drink coffee are aware of caffeine's invigourating ability, and packing caffeine collectively with ephedrine augments the thermogenic or heat-producing effect inside the body. Caffeine in addition shows on labels as kola nut extract, guarana paste, and maté leaves. Studies have revealed that adding aspirin to the ephedrine, caffeine pile additionally boosts the thermogenic effect, thus advancing improved weight loss. Whenever the internal temperature of the body is raised, individuals automatically burn more calories and this characteristically leads to weight loss and fat loss in particular. White willow bark is a source of salicin, the primary component of aspirin, and each of these expressions might as well become evident on labels. Products having the ephedrine, caffeine, aspirin stack or its chemical counterparts are time and again described as ECAs.

Lure of fat burners:

- Fat burners are appealing since they have an effect on the body just about straight away.
- When individuals check out these stimulant-based products, they generally experience something immediately and it is the effect of the stimulant.
- This acts as a major reason for people clinging to such products.

The trouble is fat burners shouldn't be used simply by everyone. Not every individual reacts positively to stimulants and individuals on aspirin or heart medicine or an additional kind of asthma medicine or people who are caffeine responsive are likely to undergo quick or irregular heart rate. A number of individuals have trouble breathing or experience panic attacks, which liberates endorphins, thus aggravating the effect of the stimulants. Often it has been found that many products contain excessive or reduced amounts of ephedrine than declared on the label.

## WEIGHT LOSS AFTER PREGNANCY

- Weight gain in pregnancy is beneficial and normal, but a number of women desire to go back to their pre-pregnancy bodies.
- But one should exercise prudence when losing one's baby weight.
- Clearly as it is ideal to gain weight gradually and progressively during one's pregnancy, one should be slow and stable in losing weight following one's pregnancy.

One excellent manner to shake off pregnancy weight is to breastfeed. One should at all times combine breast-feeding with additional types of post pregnancy weight loss. One of the grounds that an individual's body gains weight during pregnancy is to assist in storing the caloric energy it expends to breastfeed one's baby which is approximately 200 to 500 additional calories every day. Hence one should take the benefit of losing calories in the manner the body naturally planned and that is through breastfeeding.

*Benefits of exercise*:

- There are numerous advantages of exercising in the aftermath of pregnancy.
- It enables individuals to shed those additional pounds gained during pregnancy, ease post pregnancy complications and, not like dieting; it won't hinder one's breast-feeding.

It's vital that one should work one's way into exercising once more. Exercise should be done six weeks subsequent to a vaginal birth and eight weeks following a c-section. It is suggested that individuals should indulge in low-impact workout, for example, walking, swimming or yoga. Exercises for duration of ten minutes should be attempted initially and subsequently enhanced when an individual feels more certain. One should place a 30-minute curb on one's exercise time and stop instantly if one begins to experience giddiness or runs out of breath. There are numerous exercise schedules ideal for the post birth stage that can be done at home. Yoga activities are ideal for work outs at home.

Besides exercising, a healthful diet is the most excellent manner of losing one's pregnancy weight. One should consult a doctor regarding what foods are vital for the long-lasting health of both the baby and the mother. One should concentrate on nutrition and not on weight-loss diets. Walking is one of the finest exercises available and it doesn't even necessitate particular equipment.

All one requires is a fine pair of shoes, bright weather and one's baby, naturally. This exercise is planned to commence six to eight weeks after giving birth and is centered on the baby's requirements for stimulation. Pregnancy and weight increase are closely linked. They are related to each other and it's useful for the concerned mother.

Hence, while making an attempt to shed those additional pounds gained during pregnancy one should be reasonable and should not give thought to extremes such as no junk food splurges and no superstar diets. Stable nutrition together with exercise is the most ideal and beneficial manner of retrieving one's pre-pregnancy body.

## EATING TIPS DURING HOLIDAYS

During holidays individuals should concentrate on weight preservation instead of weight loss. If an individual is overweight and desires to shed weight, the holidays are the perfect time for doing so. Preservation of an individual's present weight can go a long way in motivating an individual to make good use of the holiday season.

One should not set impractical goals in this regard and end up in failure. It is imperative not to take vows on dieting. Prospect of food curbs can instigate one to overeat during the holidays. Moreover, restraining diets don't succeed eventually. They augment the loss of lean body mass in contrast to fat, decelerate one's metabolism, enhance worry, dejection, food fixation, and overeating, and make weight re-gain more possible.

*Physically active*:

- During the holiday season it is crucial for one to be physically active each day.
- Physical exercise, particularly aerobic activities such as vigourous walking, jogging, bicycling, roller blading, and swimming can assist in alleviating stress, control appetite, and burn up additional calories from holiday eating.

One should consume a light snack prior to leaving for holiday parties. It is not a helpful idea to turn up at a party hungry. Not only will an individual be inclined to eat too much, but will also be less likely to refuse to give in to the lure of eating the higher fat and higher calorie foods.

During the holiday season it is vital to chalk out a plan. One should deliberate upon where one will be, the persons who will be there, what foods will be accessible, what foods one actually prefers against those that one could possibly remain without and what are one's individual causes to eat too much and how one can restrict them.

When an individual has taken into consideration all of these things, he or she should create a plan of action. It's much trouble free to cope up with a tricky social eating condition if an individual has previously planned for it.

One should take measures to shun frivolous eating. While several foods are more calorie-intense in comparison to others, no food will make a person put on weight unless one consumes excessive amounts of it. One should make an attempt to diminish the fat in holiday recipes.

There are an abundance of low fat and low calorie alternates that are astonishingly delicious. One can attempt employing applesauce instead of oil in one's preferred holiday breads or utilize egg alternates instead of whole eggs. One should select one's beverages prudently. Alcohol is high in calories. Liquors, sweet wines as well as sweet mixed drinks have 150-450 calories in every glass. In comparison, water and diet sodas are calorie-free.

If an individual prefers to drink, he or she should opt for light wines and beers, and utilize non-alcoholic mixers for example water and diet soda. One should get pleasure from good friends and family. Even though food can be a big component of the season, it doesn't have to be the focal point. One can afford to eat in excess for a day or two since overeating in a day or two won't make or cut into one's eating plan.

## TIPS FOR EASY WEIGHT LOSS

For numerous individuals weight loss is a prolonged attempt.

*The following tips will help individuals in reducing their weight in an effective manner*:

- It's nothing novel, but exercise is possibly the most vital indicator whether an individual will be successful at long-term weight loss and weight loss preservation. In order for exercise to be useful in weight loss, one should plan no less than five-30 minute sessions every week.
- There is considerable weight loss advantages associated with weight lifting. The greater muscle tissue an individual possesses, the greater calories he or she will burn. Unlike fat, muscle is an active tissue. Consequently, muscle burns a considerable number of calories every day for its own preservation.
- Food diary
  - Maintenance of a food diary can be an immense advantage in successful weight loss.
  - One should dedicate some time each day to note down what one has consumed together with it its quantity, one's level of hunger before eating, and any thoughts or feeling prevailing at the time.
- A food record can offer a substantial degree of self- awareness. It can recognize feelings and behaviours that prompt overeating, promote

greater consciousness of portion sizes, and assist an individual in determining his or her individual food triggers. One may examine any pattern that surfaces from one's food diary and distinguish where one might be capable of making more beneficial alterations. A food diary makes available an additional advantage of keeping an individual alert and dedicated to his or her objectives.

- Numerous individuals achieve greater success at long term weight loss when their purpose alters from desiring to be thinner to desiring to be in good health. One should alter one's attitude to dwell on choosing foods that will assist one's body's health rather than be concerned about foods that will have an effect on one's body's weight.
- Frequently overeating is prompted by strain, monotony, isolation, irritation, dejection and additional emotions. One should find out means to cope up with emotions devoid of food and is a considerable ability that will greatly assist long-term weight control.
- A considerable solution in long term weight control arrives from getting support and assistance from others.
- An individual should be careful of the quantities of food he or she eats at a sitting. One should be able to focus on one's hunger level and discontinue eating when one feels contentedly full, not overfed.
- It is vital to understand that the more rapidly weight is lost, the more probable the loss is occurring from water and muscle, not fat. As muscle tissue is vital in keeping the metabolism high, losing it in reality results in a reduction in the quantity of calories individuals can lose every day without putting on weight. Fat loss is ideally accomplished when weight is lost gradually. One should attempt for a weight loss of just 1-2 pounds every week.
- Eating unhurriedly is one technique that can assist individuals in losing weight. That's for the reason that from the time one starts eating it takes the brain 20 minutes to initiate signaling feelings of completeness. Rapid eaters frequently consume further than their right level of fullness prior to the 20 minute signal has had an opportunity to develop.

## HEALTHY EATING GUIDELINES

Eating is a vital component in the life of individuals. Food should be pleasant in addition to offering a suitable equilibrium of nutrients as unconsumed food will supply no nourishment by any means. All foods make available a number of nutrients and add to the taste, smell, colour, texture and delight of a meal. Taking time to unwind while eating and to split a meal with acquaintances and family is a significant part of getting pleasure from meals.

*Combination of foods*:

- No single food makes available all the nutrients necessary for the body to stay healthy.
- A combination of dissimilar foods is crucial to be eaten all through life.
- Choosing foods for a beneficial diet doesn't imply that one has to give up one's preferred foods.

Diversity is vital also in making fruit in addition to vegetables, as well as foods akin to bread, breakfast cereals, rice, pasta and potatoes the major part of the meal. Snacks in addition to meals add up towards the balance.

Food supplies the energy required to keep the body energetic and working properly. Every individual requires a dissimilar quantity of energy and hence every person is different in the quantity of food he or she should consume. Women are likely to require less energy than men. Older adults are likely to require a lesser quantity of energy than adolescents and young adults. The more dynamic an individual, the greater is his or energy requirements. A beneficial weight is best accomplished and preserved by both being actually active and by not consuming additional calories than those that are expended.

Not consuming sufficiently for the body's requirements could result in underweight and weakness. Eating too much can trigger overweight, which can cause ill health together with heart disease, high blood pressure or diabetes. One should consume abundance of foods rich in starch and fibre. Foods akin to bread, additional cereals as well as potatoes are full of starch and can be excellent sources of fibre. Starches as well as fibre are names for clusters of carbohydrates.

There are diverse kinds of starch as well as fibre and these are obtained only from plants or foods made from plants. The majority of people do not consume an adequate amount of the starchy, fibre-rich foods similar to bread, potatoes, rice and pasta and require eating them in proper quantities.

Whole-grain cereal foods are predominantly high in insoluble fibre, which assists in checking constipation. Soluble fibre in fruit, pulses in addition to vegetables is capable of assisting in the decrease in the quantity of cholesterol in the blood. One should consume lots of fruit and vegetables in order to ensure good health. There is ample proof that diets high in fruits as well as vegetables diminish the danger of developing chronic ailments, for example, coronary heart disease and perhaps some cancers, in life later on.

## FOOD ITEMS

How healthy you are depends on what food items you eat. In fact, it is the combination of foods, that makes your diet, and in turn health. So what you eat should be chosen very carefully. If you don't realise what you are eating, then you don't realise what you are inviting into your body.

## FISH

It is called sea vegetable in India, and is consumed even by practicing Brahmins. Fish is one of the best foods, offering variety in your food, gives you good taste and health as well. Fish Oil, Omega 3 Fatty Acids are one of the most important nutrients that fish give you. If you are missing out on fish, you should either be advised by a doctor, or else you've never tasted it.

## SEEDS AND NUTS

Fish, seeds and nuts will compete with all the meats in the world to give all the requisite nutrients to your body. Actually nuts and seeds can be called as a vegetarian's meat. Apart from offer enough fibre, they give your body disease fighting energy, improving your immune system.

## GARLIC

Think medicinal herb, think garlic. Garlic has been used over ages and eons as a medicine. Induce it into your food, you are fighting accumulation in your arteries and cholesterol as well. But if you are taking it too much, it results in a stomach upset. So use it, but carefully.

## SOY

Why is soy included in every diet regimen? Simply because, it is the only vegetable that contains more proteins than carbohydrates. So if you are on a low-carb diet, soy is your best mate, because that's how it helps you fight weight gain.

## TEA AND COFFEE

Ah! Who doesn't love them. Every body knows that tea and coffee taken daily will help you enjoy your life, keep you active. However, keep a check on the amount of coffee you take.

## CHOCOLATES AND OTHERS

Chocolate has been called a delicious sin. So indulge with it carefully and make sure you use it only for the best purposes. Of course, give it to some one you love because chocolates contain flavanoids that turn on your moods. Just check out each food, and the next time you have them, you know what you are taking.

## FLAX SEED BENEFITS FOR HEART DISEASE PATIENTS

Flax is cultivated both for seed as well as for fibre. Different portions of the plant have been utilized to produce fabric, medicines, paper, dye, fishing nets in addition to soap. A vegetable oil known as linseed oil or flaxseed oil is produced by the seeds.

Flax seeds are somewhat bigger than sesame seeds and contain a rigid shell that is smooth and glossy. Their colour varies from deep amber to reddish brown conditional on whether the flax is of the golden or brown type. While whole flaxseeds include a soft crunch, the nutrients in grounded seeds are more effortlessly assimilated.

*Health advantages*:

- There are numerous health advantages to be achieved when eating flax seed as part of a healthy diet.
- A large number of individuals are preferring to incorporate flax seed in their diet due to its role in combating health conditions, for example, diabetes, cancer, menopause and arthritis.
- Possibly the most remarkable of these health advantages is the role of flax seed in effectively combating heart disease.

Flax seed has excessive quantities of the essential fatty acid Alpha-Linolenic Acid or ALA. Essential fatty acids are necessary for human health but cannot be produced by the body and ought to be acquired from food. ALA fits in to a cluster of fatty acids referred to as omega-3 fatty acids. Omega-3 fatty acids are normally obtained from fatty fish such as salmon. Omega-3 fatty acids help the heart by presenting some level of defence against coronary heart disease.

Omega-3 fatty acids are as well vital since they are building blocks of human cell membranes and they play a vital part in a number of functions inside the body. Omega-3 fatty acids also aid in diminishing inflammation. Flax seed and flax seed oil have been revealed to assist increase HDL-cholesterol or the "good" cholesterol while reducing LDL-cholesterol or the Bad cholesterol levels. Other advantages demonstrate that flax seed may as well assist in reducing blood triglyceride and blood pressure. It may in addition keep platelets from turning out to be sticky hence diminishing the possibility of a heart attack

Flax seed is principally a good source of lignans. Lignan is a kind of antioxidant obtained from a diversity of plants. These potent antioxidants work all over the human body to eliminate free radicals. Free radicals can harm tissue and are considered to play a part in the pathology of numerous ailments. Lignans also make available an excellent source of fibre. Since the external hull of the flax seed is exceedingly hard to digest, it is usually suggested that one should crush or mill the whole flax seed to obtain the maximum nutritional advantage. Flax seed can be crushed with a reasonably priced coffee grinder or obtained pre-ground or milled. Flax seed is recognizable by the nutty flavour it imparts to a range of dishes. The seeds can be supplemented with almost every food.

## NUTS IN DIET

Individuals who are averse to eating nuts because of their excessive fat content may be encouraged by recent studies on nuts which show that though nuts are rich in calories and approximately 80 per cent of their calories come from fat, nuts are nutrient intense.

Nuts have the essential fatty acids, linoleic and linolenic acids, which are crucial for development, blood pressure control, healthy skin as well as hair, immune response in addition to blood clotting. Besides, the fats in nuts generally have unsaturated fats, particularly monounsaturated fat. This kind of fat does not increase blood cholesterol intensity like saturated fats. Monounsaturated fats have the extra advantage of increasing high-density lipoprotein, the "good" cholesterol. Nuts also make available one of the most excellent natural sources of Vitamin E, an antioxidant, and are high in protein, magnesium, dietary fibre, copper, potassium, phosphorus, selenium as well as folate.

*Nuts are helpful in Reducing heart disease threat*:

- It's long been acknowledged that dietary practice influences the threat factors of heart disease.
- A number of major nutrition studies have linked frequent nut use, particularly almonds, walnuts, hazelnuts in addition to macadamias, with a diminished threat of heart disease of 30-50 per cent
- It is believed that nuts can assist in decreasing the build-up of plaque in blood vessels by reducing the "bad" cholesterol levels.
- The antioxidant traits of nuts rich in vitamin E content may also have a say in the decrease of heart disease.
- Besides cholesterol, nuts can be useful in controlling high blood pressure.

Nuts can be utilized in combination with vegetable dishes as well as salads or added to pastas and casseroles for a crispy touch. The most significant point to keep in mind is that nuts should be eaten with restraint. The following are a few guidelines on how to integrate nuts into one's diet without having to bother about the calories: One can diminish the serving size by slicing or cutting the nuts into pieces.

Nuts can be roasted at 350° F for 5 to 10 minutes to draw out the flavour. One can extract the cheese from pasta while utilizing nuts. It is advisable to opt for diminished quantities of lean meats, poultry and fish, when nuts are being used with them. It is preferable to select fat-free dressing for the salad while utilizing nuts.

One can mix nuts with cereals or dried fruits to prepare a healthful snack that is wonderful to savor. It is recommended that one should opt for pre-portion nutty snacks instead of consuming them from a big jar or bag.

When incorporating nuts in one's diet, one should make certain to consider them as ingredient of the meat, fish, poultry, dry beans, eggs and nuts group. As far as portion size is concerned 1/3 cup of nuts is equivalent to one ounce of meat.

## BENEFITS OF GARLIC IN HEART DISEASE PATIENT

Garlic has been utilized as a medication for ages. Numerous researches have in addition confirmed the utilization of garlic for well-being and health. A number of studies imply that garlic may decrease levels of cholesterol, triglycerides or fatty materials and plaque accumulation in the arteries.

If individuals are fond of including additional garlic to their diet, there are definite tactics for cooking it to obtain its utmost advantage. Individuals are advised to be cautious of garlic supplements that are available in the market. Even though consumption of moderate amounts of garlic in food is not likely to be detrimental to health, taking excessive garlic in the shape of supplements can give rise to indications, for example, giddiness or fainting, stomach pain and sickness. In addition, garlic supplements may not be a prudent selection for everybody. Like every vitamin, mineral or herbal supplements, garlic supplements too can trigger adverse reactions if taken with other medicines.

Hence it is advisable for individuals to seek the help of a doctor before using garlic supplements for enhancing their garlic ingestion. The precise procedure by which garlic may be benefiting the body is yet to be comprehended. A number of the substances present in garlic, for example, sulfur-containing compounds, have been connected with definite health advantages.

- Garlic contains adenosine which may help in the deterrence of blood clots.
- Garlic is also known to contain certain substances that assist in the deterrence of blood clots and also aids in reducing cholesterol.
- Organic sulfide compounds present in garlic may aid in reducing cholesterol and thwart cancer.
- Sulfur-containing amino acids such as S-allylcysteine in garlic may assist in reducing cholesterol.
- Certain studies have indicated considerable heart- linked advantages of garlic. Garlic has the antioxidants Vitamin A, Vitamin C as well as selenium and the use of garlic helps in the decline in plaque and deterrence of additional plaque accumulation which in turn diminishes the threat of atherosclerosis or hardening of the arteries.

Studies have revealed that garlic helps in maintaining elasticity or flexibility of the major artery, *i.e.*, the aorta that pumps blood from the heart to the other parts of the body. Garlic seems to present the utmost health benefits when it has been permitted to remain in the crushed state for 10 to 15 minutes after being squashed or crushed. Throughout this time, sulfur-containing compounds are formed.

Preferably, garlic is then ingested as an unprocessed flavouring on food. A number of health specialists even advocate that garlic cloves be chewed raw for maximum result. Nonetheless, other experts caution that consumption of excessive garlic can result in stomach trouble or heartburn. Consequently, cooking the garlic lightly after it has been preserved in a crushed state for a while could be the most excellent tactic.

## BENEFITS OF SOY

A considerable number of studies back the assertion that soy ingestion can assist an individual in losing weight. Soy protein makes available low-fat high-quality protein in comparison to several additional protein sources. It can assist individuals in developing lean muscle mass. In conjunction with exercise and a beneficial diet, soy protein makes an outstanding collaborator in a profitable weight loss plan. Soy protein assists an individual in feeling fuller for an extended period. New medical researches confirm soy protein assists individuals in feeling less hungry, and aids individuals in feeling full for a greater duration of time. Consumption of soy might work by triggering one's stomach to transmit a message to the brain indicating that one is full. This aids in diminishing the desire to snack between meals and late at night which are the two main reasons of weight gain.

*Soy has more protein than carbs*:

- Soybeans are the lone vegetable that has more protein than carbs.
- As a low-carb food that occurs naturally, soy is the ideal supplement to any weight loss plan, incorporating well-liked "low-carb" as well as "high-protein" diets.

Not only is soy protein depleted in carbs and fat, but it in addition has a low-glycemic index which implies it won't trigger a fast increase in blood sugar levels after ingestion. This averts excess discharge of insulin that results in the unnecessary consequence of amassing additional sugar in one's bloodstream as body fat. Steady blood sugar and insulin levels signify fewer hunger yearning and fewer calories being accumulated as fat.

Soy protein is the lone plant protein that is an absolute protein, which implies it contains all nine essential amino acids in the correct balance to cater to the body's requirements.

This signifies that individuals obtain the top quality protein accessible, with less fat and fewer calories than the majority of meats. Soy protein has important nutritional traits that sustain energy, stamina, and sports activities. Soy protein is plentiful in "branched-chain amino acids" which the body can utilize as "fuel" to generate energy. As an absolute protein, soy assists in developing and preserving lean muscle mass. Soy may aid promote the discharge of specific anabolic hormones that advance muscle formation. Soy may assist in prolonging stamina levels for the duration of exercise.

Soy is also known to assist in enhancing recuperation time and decrease post-exercise exhaustion. Soy is in addition is useful in promoting a healthy cardiovascular system that is vital for exercising or an energetic lifestyle. Studies confirm that soy reduces total cholesterol, the "bad" LDL cholesterol, triglycerides, and might in addition increase good HDL cholesterol levels. Research indicates that diets at a low level in saturated fat and cholesterol that comprise 25 gm. of soy protein daily may diminish the threat of heart disease.

## POMEGRANATE JUICE AND ITS BENEFITS

The pomegranate is approximately the size of a normal orange or apple. It is dark red to brownish in shade with a hard skin. The parts of the fruit that can be eaten are the seeds and the succulent transparent scarlet red pulp. Generally the pomegranate's flavour is covered in the seeds. The essence of these juicy seeds is subtle, sweet, and strong. The seeds are sheathed in the membrane which is white and malleable with an exceedingly unpleasant taste. The pomegranate has been recognized since long as the "jewel of winter".

*Health advantages*:

- Pomegranates have as well been in recent times preferred for their health advantages.
- The pomegranate has a great possibility for disease-combating antioxidants.
- Latest studies imply that pomegranate juice may possibly have nearly three times the antioxidant capability compared with the similar amount of green tea or red wine.
- It is in addition fairly rich in potassium as well as fibre, and has Vitamin C and niacin.
- Pomegranate juice has been utilized to deal with swelling, painful throats, in addition to rheumatism.
- One garden-fresh pomegranate has 0.1 gm. of saturated, monounsaturated, and polyunsaturated fats, 105 calories, 27 gm. of carbohydrates, 0 cholesterol, 0.9 gm. of dietary fibre, 5 mg. of sodium, 0.9 mg. of manganese, 0.5 gm. of fat, and 2 gm. of protein.

Researchers have discovered that pomegranate juice is effective in treating prostate cancer cells. The juice is acknowledged to be plentiful in antioxidants that give rise to the vibrant colours of fruits and vegetables. These antioxidants also destroy cells that causes cancer and additional such ailments. One more study implies that pomegranate juice may perhaps in addition assist in combating heart disease. At present, there is scientific proof for the wild fruit's curative potential.

The antioxidants in the juice may as well aid in reducing the development of fat accumulation on artery walls. The pink or red-flowered sort incorporates the majority of the widespread and popular commercial types of pomegranates. In shape the fruit is round oblate or obviate. The external skin differs in depth. The external and internal colour too differs from off-white to a purplish or lively crimson colour. The seeds of the pomegranate in addition differ in size as well as hardness.

Some fruits more or less appear to be seedless, while others are approximately unfit for human consumption since the seeds are very big and hard. Nonetheless, individuals in search of a wonderful tasting, sweet, and juicy pomegranate, should opt for ones that are white or pinkish in colour. The dark red to brownish fruits are frequently bitterer and contain bigger, harder seeds. Wonderful is certainly the most extensively grown pomegranate in the U.S. This type is big and intense purplish-red with a shiny look.

## TEA AND ITS HEALTH BENEFITS

Tea prevents heart disease, reduces cholesterol as well as prevents a number of kinds of cancer while defending skin in addition to fortifying bones and teeth. What's more tea contains almost no calories; no fat and no salt and two cups of genuine tea are as plentiful in flavonoids as a helping of vegetables. One should drink tea that is strong and newly prepared, since studies confirm that bottled in addition to powdered types can be less helpful. An everyday quantity of four to six cups can yield immense benefits for the human body.

*Benefits of tea are:*

- Several of the most convincing studies related to tea links tea to reduced threat of stroke, high cholesterol and heart disease.
- A number of clinical experiments in addition to sizeable population studies have established that habitual tea drinkers are 44 per cent less expected to experience a heart attack than the common population, and those who have suffered attacks have greater chances of revival.
- Studies indicate that black tea seems to restore blood-vessel harm in individuals who have coronary-artery disease.
- Studies also reveal that regular tea-drinking considerably reduced LDL cholesterol or the bad type without diminishing useful HDL cholesterol.

Tea aids in checking sunburn as well as skin cancer. Researches indicate that consumption of hot black tea seems to defend against squamous-cell carcinoma. Putting on tea could be truly as helpful since studies reveal that green-tea compounds in skin lotions may defend against, and even undo sun harm.

Both experimental and large-population surveys imply black or green tea diminishes the threat of a numbers of cancers, especially, stomach and colorectal. Further studies indicate improved bone-density capacity among tea drinkers, perhaps because of the fluoride in tea, together with the catechins. Tea has been revealed to curb bacterial increase in the mouth, and it aids in checking cavities.

Green tea was the initial tea analysed for its cancer-combating advantages. New studies reveal that any tea obtained from the leaf of a warm-weather perennial referred to as Camellia sinensis has comparable cancer-combating traits. This consists of all green, black as well as red or oolong teas. The leaves of this tree have chemicals named polyphenols, which provide tea its antioxidant characteristics. The amount of processing decides whether a tea will be green, black or red. Green tea is slightly processed. They are just steamed swiftly prior to packaging. Black as well as red teas are moderately dried, compressed and fermented. The duration of fermentation, which causes the leaves to blacken, decides whether the tea will be red or black. No matter what the processing technique is, all teas have polyphenols.

Polyphenols, like additional antioxidants, assist in safeguarding cells from the usual, but harmful, physiological procedure referred to as "oxidative stress". even though oxygen is central to life, it's in addition integrated into reactive substances identified as free radicals. These can harm the cells in the body and have been concerned with the sluggish chain reaction of harm causing heart disease in addition to cancer.

## COFFEE-ANTIOXIDANTS AND HEALTH BENEFITS

An individual's daily cup of coffee could in reality be of immense benefit to his or her health. The tannins in addition to antioxidants that occur naturally in coffee are recognized to combat free radicals and additional attacks on the body. Coffee which contains a number of defensive antioxidants is also known to diminish the threat of asthma attacks. Antioxidants are chemical compounds that defend the body's cells from the harmful consequences of oxidation. They assist in sustaining the immune system, and as a result, may reduce the threat of both cancer as well as heart disease. It is thought that the caffeine in coffee assists in enhancing the blood circulation inside the heart and arteries. One study demonstrates that in an evaluation among a variety of food groups, coffee had 64 per cent of the overall antioxidant ingestion. Coffee could in addition decrease the threat of gallstones by 45 per cent and cirrhosis of the liver by 80 per cent. A new study corroborates the presence of an inverse association between coffee ingestion and liver cirrhosis; even though studies have not been able to conclude which element in the coffee is responsible for generating the defensive effect.

*Coffee is Helping asthma victims*:

- An additional advantage of coffee is a 25 per cent decrease in the commencement of bouts among asthma victims.
- This recurring disease causes the airways to shut because of swelling, resulting in shortness of breath, coughing, tightness in the chest in addition to wheezing.
- One of the compounds in coffee, named theophylline, functions as a bronchodilator, which reduces these hazardous symptoms.
- Individuals with a headache continuing all through the day will find coffee extremely useful in relieving them of their discomfort.
- The caffeine in coffee has been acknowledged to assist in curing such types of headaches.

Generally, doctors suggest consumption of 2 to 4 cups of coffee every day, which is regarded as a sensible and reasonable quantity. Certainly, individuals are all dissimilar, and a number of them may prefer to drink more and several may wish to drink less, according to their personal way of life, routine, and health concerns. An 8 ounce cup of coffee contains roughly 75mg. of caffeine.

As large amounts of caffeine in coffee can be harmful for one's health, it is vital not to go beyond the suggested 300mg. of caffeine every day. Researches indicate that the ingestion of coffee is connected with diminished threat of specific cancers, Parkinson's disease, kidney stones and hepatic diseases. As far has health hazards of coffee consumption is concerned, nothing by any means has been established against coffee when consumed in an amount not in excess of four cups on a daily basis.

## HEALTH BENEFITS OF REISHI

Reishi is a type of mushroom generally found in the coastal regions of China. It is also grown in Taiwan, Korea, North America, and Japan. Reishi is known as the "herb of spiritual potency", or *hing zhi*. They are usually discovered on the bases of fallen trees and decaying logs.

Reishi can be found in six different types of colour, but red mushrooms are commonly utilized for medicinal purposes in Asia and North America. The fruiting portion of the mushroom is generally used for medicinal purposes. Reishi is made use of to cure asthma, coughs, debility and exhaustion, along with sleeplessness. Polysaccharides, coumarin, sterols, mannitol, and triterpenoids labelled ganoderic acids are the chief elements of the mushroom.

Ganoderic acids can be capable of reducing cholesterol and blood pressure apart from hindering blood platelets from joining together. Although it has not yet been established, these acids may also aid in the treatment of hepatitis B that is chronic in nature, sickness associated with altitude, cancer, and diabetes mellitus. It flourishes in thickly wooded mountains where humidity is high and sunlight is not particularly strong.

It is not often found because it grows chiefly on the parched trunks of dead plum, guercus serrata or pasonia trees.

Among 10,000 such mature trees, possibly 2 or 3 will have Reishi development. Consequently it is exceedingly in short supply. Its scarcity can be attributed to the hard outer husks of its spores that make germination almost impracticable.

There are several types of Reishi, namely, *Akashiba* (red reishi), *Kuroshiba* (black reishi), *Aoshiba* (blue reishi), *Shiroshiba* (white reishi), *Kishiba* (yellow reishi), *Murasakishiba* (purple reishi). Reishi is considered as an ideal medicine since its wide-ranging qualities can be effective for healing as well as precautionary purposes. It yields outstanding results when made use of by a person who is vulnerable to ailment in the pre-ailment phase. Reishi mushroom is specifically helpful for persons with asthma in addition to other respiratory ailments. Reishi is known to have a curing effect on the lungs and is beneficial for respiratory power in addition to coughing.

*Benefits of Reishi are*:

- Reishi is known to expand longevity, enhance youthful energy and vigour.
- It also helps in improving blood circulation by eradicating thrombi in the blood streams.
- This accounts for improved vigour of a person. Use of Reishi checks degeneration of body and mind.
- Reishi is indeed well known for its versatility.
- It has also been found that Reishi possesses traits that help in dealing with cholesterosis and coronary deficiency along with effectively enhancing the nervous system.
- The use of Reishi has also proved beneficial in treating chronic bronchitis and hepatitis.
- Reishi also assists in developing the leukocytopenia and reticuloendothelial system.

As far as Reishi is concerned the success rate of healing a number of ailments are highly impressive. For instance, allergy associated with chronic bronchitis, which is among the toughest to heal, has a recuperation rate of 60 per cent to 97.7 per cent when treated with Reishi.

## CHOCOLATES—ARE THEY GOOD FOR HEALTH ?

Since centuries, chocolate has been extremely appreciated by individuals of all ages because of its unique taste. Several experts have observed that chocolates are harmful and excessive consumption frequently leads to tooth decay. A number of medical professionals have affirmed that chocolates have sugar substances and therefore enhance the level of calories in the body and augment the sugar concentration in the blood.

But, it has been in recent times established that chocolates are beneficial for the health since they have numerous advantages. Chocolates have antioxidants. Consequently they destroy the free radicals and hinder the oxidization of lipids into the body. The antioxidants are a condensed type of flavonoids.

*Benefits of chocolates are*:

- The antioxidants in chocolate assist in the anti-ageing procedure.
- As indicated by recent studies if individuals eat chocolates he or she is diminishing the possibility of heart troubles.
- Chocolate is an anti-inflammatory means as well.
- Chocolate has cocoa butter to a certain degree and these aids in salvaging the exhausted elasticity in the body.
- In addition to these traits, chocolate functions as a remarkable medicine for depression. Many advocate that individuals eat a chocolate any time he or she feels like consuming it. One can actually spend one's time in an exceedingly attractive manner and stop thinking about all the tribulations of life when one savors tasty chocolate.

Chocolate has in excess of 300 chemicals, and has been the focus of several studies by universities as well as other scientific institutes

### Some of the Beneficial Effects of Chocolates

Cacao, the main ingredient of chocolate, has antibacterial agents that combat tooth decay. Obviously, this is neutralized by the excessive amount of sugar present in milk chocolate. The aroma of chocolate may augment theta brain waves, giving rise to relaxation. Chocolate has phenyl ethylamine, a docile mood elevator. The cocoa butter in chocolate has oleic acid, a mono-unsaturated fat which may possibly increase good cholesterol.

It has been found that consumption of a cup of hot chocolate prior to meals may in reality reduce appetite. It has been observed that people who consume chocolate live a year longer in comparison to those who don't. The flavanoids in chocolate may assist in keeping blood vessels elastic. It has been revealed that chocolate augments antioxidant levels in the blood. The carbohydrates in chocolate increase serotonin concentrations in the brain leading to a feeling of happiness.

There are numerous misconceptions about the effects of chocolate on the human body. Contrary to popular perception studies confirm that chocolate is not a contributing factor in acne. The stimulants caffeine and bromine are present in cacao in such little amounts that they don't result in nervous excitability. Unlike widespread belief chocolate is not addictive. Chocolate has stearic acid, a neutral fat which doesn't increase bad cholesterol.

**HEALTH BENEFITS OF YOGURT**

Consumption of yogurt on a daily basis is exceedingly beneficial for the body. For individuals trying to increase their protein, calcium and dairy intake, yogurt is a nourishing alternative.

Yogurt is not only a delicious snack including fruits on the bottom, it has immense health advantages.

It is an outstanding source of calcium, protein, riboflavin and vitamin B 12. When yogurt is contrasted to milk, yogurt has greater amounts of calcium as well as protein because of the additional cultures in the yogurt. Yogurt ought to have active and living cultures in order to be yogurt. Cultures are made up of distinctive living microorganisms which are responsible for numerous health as well as nutritional advantages of yogurt.

*Yogurts are wed for enhancing natural resistance*:

- It enhances natural resistance and contains a good quantity of phosphorus as well as 88 per cent water.
- Individuals with a threat of osteoporosis ought to consume no less than one helping of yogurt every day.
- It has as well been asserted that yogurt may defend against certain kinds of cancer but more studies have to be conducted.

There are three kinds of yogurt, namely regular or whole milk, low-fat and skim. Low-fat and skim yogurt are beneficial for individuals who are on a cholesterol reducing diet or simply trying to maintain their weights. These types of yogurt do not increase blood cholesterol concentrations.

A number of individuals have problems digesting lactose, a carbohydrate in milk as well as milk products, due to the lack of enzyme lactase in the body. Live yogurt cultures yield lactase and split down the lactose.

Yogurt is a beneficial way to obtain the calcium the body requires, for the individuals who can not endure milk products.Additional advantages of live as well as active cultures in the yogurt are that they may assist in improving the immune system. They promote the appropriate type of bacteria to grow in the gut. These bacteria aid in digesting food and foil stomach infections. In addition, they facilitate to offer respite from vaginal infections. Yogurt must be stocked in the refrigerator since it is a fresh dairy product. Yogurt treated with heat has a greater shelf life but it does not provide the nutritional advantages akin to the yogurt with live cultures since heat processing damages the cultures.

To obtain the maximum health advantages from yogurt, there ought to be a live and active cultures stamp on the label. Yogurt is quite popular and ingested in nearly all areas of the world. People in several regions utilize lots of yogurt in their food. In certain countries people generally consume yogurt, plain devoid of sugar together with major dishes akin to stuffed cabbage as well as spinach. Some people also make yogurt drinks made with plain yogurt, salt and water. Many people eat yogurt with fried vegetables for example eggplant or zucchini.

## KEYS TO A HEALTHY DIET

Developing healthy eating habits isn't as confusing or as restrictive as many people imagine. The first principle of a healthy diet is simply to eat a wide variety of foods. This is important because different foods make different nutritional contributions. Secondly, fruits, vegetables, grains, and legumes—foods high in complex carbohydrates, fibre, vitamins, and minerals, low in fat, and free of cholesterol—should make up the bulk of the calories you consume. The rest should come from low-fat dairy products, lean meat and poultry, and fish. You should also try to maintain a balance between calorie intake and calorie expenditure—that is, don't eat more food than your body can utilize. Otherwise, you will gain weight.

The more active you are, therefore, the more you can eat and still maintain this balance. Following these three basic steps doesn't mean that you have to give up your favourite foods. As long as your overall diet is balanced and rich in nutrients and fibre, there is nothing wrong with an occasional cheeseburger. Just be sure to limit how frequently you eat such foods, and try to eat small portions of them.

You can also view healthy eating as an opportunity to expand your range of choices by trying foods—especially vegetables, whole grains, or fruits—that you don't normally eat. A healthy diet doesn't have to mean eating foods that are bland or unappealing.

*The following basic guidelines are what you need to know to construct a healthy diet*:

- Eat plenty of high-fibre foods—that is, fruits, vegetables, beans, and whole grains. These are the"good" carbohydrates-nutritious, filling, and relatively low in calories. They should supply the 20 to 30 gm. of dietary fibre you need each day, which slows the absorption of carbohydrates, so there's less effect on insulin and blood sugar, and provides other health benefits as well. Such foods also provide important vitamins, minerals, and phytochemicals.

- Make sure to include green, orange, and yellow fruits and vegetables-such as broccoli, carrots, cantaloupe, and citrus fruits. The antioxidants and other nutrients in these foods may help protect against developing certain types of cancer and other diseases. Eat five or more servings a day.
- Limit your intake of sugary foods, refined-grain products such as white bread, and salty snack foods. Sugar, our No.1 additive, is added to a vast array of foods. Just one daily 12-ounce can of soda can add up to 16 pounds over the course of a year. Many sugary foods are also high in fat, so they're calorie-dense.
- Cut down on animal fat. It's rich in saturated fat, which boosts blood cholesterol levels and has other adverse health effects. Choose lean meats, skinless poultry, and nonfat or low-fat or nonfat dairy products.
- Cut way down on trans fats, supplied by hydrogenated vegetable oils used in most processed foods in the supermarket and in many fast foods.
- Eat more fish and nuts, which contain healthy unsaturated fats. Substitute olive or canola oil for butter or stick margarine.
- Keep portions moderate, especially of high-calorie foods. In recent years serving sizes have ballooned, particularly in restaurants. Choose a starter instead of an entrée, split a dish with a friend, and don't order supersized anything.
- Keep your cholesterol intake below 300 mg. per day. Cholesterol is found only in animal products, such as meats, poultry, dairy products, and egg yolks.
- Eat a variety of foods. Don't try to fill your nutrient requirements by eating the same foods day in, day out. It is possible that not every essential nutrient has been identified, and so eating a wide assortment of foods helps to ensure that you will get all the necessary nutrients. In addition, this will limit your exposure to any pesticides or toxic substances that may be present in one particular food.
- Maintain an adequate calcium intake. Calcium is essential for strong bones and teeth. Get your calcium from low-fat sources, such as skim milk and low-fat yogurt. If you can't get the optimal amount from foods, take supplements.
- Try to get your vitamins and minerals from foods, not from supplements. Supplements cannot substitute for a healthy diet, which supplies nutrients and other compounds besides vitamins and minerals. Foods also provide the "synergy" that many nutrients require to be efficiently used in the body.

- Maintain a desirable weight. Balance energy intake with energy output. Exercise and other physical activity are essential.
- If you drink alcohol, do so in moderation. That is one drink a day for women, two a day for men. A drink is defined as 12 ounces of beer, 4 ounces of wine, or 1.5 ounces of 80-proof spirits. Excess alcohol consumption leads to a variety of health problems. And alcoholic beverages can add many calories to your diet without supplying nutrients.

## CONCLUSION

This chapter presents recommendations for high-priority measures to promote proper nutrition in the years ahead. The National Council for Nutrition, an independent council appointed by the Ministry of Health and Care Services in 2003, has formulated overall health and diet objectives. These are based on nutrition-related challenges and the vision of a healthy diet for lifelong good health.

The nutrition policy is rooted in health policy and builds on the following three documents: recommendations for nutrition and physical activity 2005, which presents updated scientific information on which intake of nutrients is best. Prescriptions for a healthier, which sets outs strategies for nutrition and public health work in a 10-year perspective; and the Global strategy on diet, physical activity and health adopted by the World Health Organization in May 2004. Social disparities in health are a major challenge for nutrition policy. Eating habits and levels of physical activity vary greatly throughout the population according to education and income.

Segments of the population with low income and little education eat more energy-dense foods and fewer vegetables than high-income, highly-educated segments of the population. Reducing social disparities in health is a primary goal in nutrition work.

The efforts to encourage a healthy diet are linked to the goal of preventing health problems and promoting good health. Eliminating or reducing the scope of diet-related health problems is of utmost importance.

At the same time, the role of nutrition in treatment merits more attention. The efforts to promote good health through a healthy diet must have a global perspective. Sustainable food production is an aim in food and nutrition policy. A sustainable diet is both healthy, and takes environmental issues like production, processing and transport into account. Promoting a healthy diet requires efforts in a number of sectors. Food and food culture form an important frame-work for day-to-day life. It is vital to ensure that dietary recommendations are based on reliable, up-to-date information.

The National Council for Nutrition attaches great importance to issuing recommendations to the population and the health authorities that are based on solid scientific documentation. Knowledge about the relation between diet and health is comprehensive and growing, but much remains to be learned and new questions continue to emerge. Public health services and social services at all levels must be provided by competent personnel, whether dealing with the prevention or the treatment of diet-related health problems. Schools and day-care centres are key arenas for promoting a healthy diet for children and adolescents.

There are huge economic interests at stake in the food and beverage industry, and reconciling commercial interests and the interests of nutrition can be challenging. The authorities should promote cooperation with industrial players in order to promote healthy diet through the production, and supply of foods. As voluntary organizations also play an important role in nutrition work, the National Council for Nutrition aspires to promote strong alliances for good health.

The National Council for Nutrition's main concern is nutrition as it relates to diet. The Food Safety Authority is responsible for inspecting food production and sales to ensure that food is safe and healthy and complies with regulations. Determining what is necessary for food to be healthy and safe requires knowledge in a broad range of fields. Both the National Council for Nutrition and the Food Safety Authority's Scientific Committee for Food Safety play important roles in this process. Among other tasks, the Scientific Committee carries out risk assessments on foods and food components.

## OVEREATING

All agree that excessive indulgence in alcoholics is harmful physically, mentally and morally. We condemn the too free use of tea and coffee and nearly all other excesses. However, intemperate eating is considered respectable. A large part of our social life consists in partaking of too much food. Medical text-books say that we must eat great quantities of food to maintain strength and health. Humanity views the subject of eating from the wrong angle, and it will perhaps be many years before the majority gets the right point of view. We should eat to live, but most of us eat to die. Benjamin Franklin said that we dig our graves with our teeth.

Men and women band themselves into societies and associations for the purpose of decreasing or doing away with the use of tobacco and alcoholic drinks. They advocate temperance and even abstinence in the use of those things which do not appeal to their own senses; but most of them are far from temperate in their eating. They have very keen vision when searching for weaknesses and faults in others, but are quite near-sighted regarding their own.

Is excessive indulgence in liquor any worse than overeating? Not according to nature's answer. The inebriate deteriorates and so does the glutton. Both cause race deterioration. Gluttony is more common than inebriety and is responsible for more ills. Gluttony is often the cause of the tea, coffee, alcohol and drug habits. Overeating often causes so much irritation that food does not satisfy the cravings, and then drugs are used.

Improper eating, chiefly overeating, causes most of the ills to which man is heir. If people would learn to be moderate in all things disease and early death would be very rare. It is quite important to combine foods properly, but the worst combinations of food eaten in moderation are harmless, as compared to the damage done by overeating of the best foods. Overeating is with us from the cradle to the grave. It shortens our days and fills them with woe.

There is a hoary belief that a pregnant woman must eat for two. The mothers have generally obeyed this dictum. The result is that women suffer greatly during pregnancy and at childbirth. The morning sickness, the aching back, the headache, the swollen legs and all of the discomforts and diseases from which civilized woman suffers during this period are mostly due to improper eating. Pregnancy and childbirth are physiologic and are devoid of any great amount of discomfort, pain or danger when women lead normal lives. The overeating affects both mother and child.

The mothers are often injured or lose their lives during childbirth. Sometimes labour is so protracted that the child dies and at other times the baby is so large that it can not be born naturally. The mother's suffering is frequently very great. In fact, it is at times so great that it is like a threatening storm cloud to many women, and some of them refuse to become mothers for this reason.

Babies born of normal mothers, who have lived moderately on a non-stimulating diet during gestation, are small. They rarely weigh more than six pounds. Their bones are flexible. The skull can easily be moulded because the bones are very cartilaginous. The result is that childbirth is rapid and practically devoid of pain. However, there are very few normal mothers, and consequently normal babies are also rare. A heavy baby is never healthy.

Its growth has been forced by excessive maternal feeding. It is no hardier than other growing things which result from hot-house methods. Such babies show early signs of catarrhal afflictions, indigestion or skin disease. Their bodies are filled with poisons before they are born. Mothers who overeat invariably overfeed their babies. And why should they do otherwise? Family, friends and physicians give the same advice: The mother must eat much to be able to feed the child, and the child must be fed frequently in order to grow. It sounds very plausible, but it does not work well in practice.

Why are babies cross? Why do they soon show catarrhal symptoms? Why do they vomit so much? Why are they so subject to stomach and intestinal disorders? Why do they have skin eruptions? Because they are overfed. The diseases of babies are almost entirely of digestive origin, and in nearly every instance overfeeding is the cause.

Statistics show that about one-fifth of the babies born die before they are one year old. In nearly every instance the parents are to blame. One's intentions may be good, but good intentions coupled with wrong actions are deadly to infants. Oscar Wilde wrote, "We kill the thing we love." Parental love too often takes the form of indulging them and so it happens that hundreds of thousands of little ones are placed in their coffins annually through love.

Each year about 280,000 babies under one year of age perish in the United States, according to estimates based on census figures. Outside of accidental deaths, which are but a small per cent, the mortality should be practically nil. It is natural for children to be well, and healthy children do not die. If an army of about 280,000 of our men and women were to perish in a spectacular manner each year it would cause such sorrow and indignation that a remedy would soon be found. But we are so accustomed to the procession of little caskets to the grave that it hardly arouses comment. It costs too much in every way to produce life to waste it so lavishly.

Why do little children suffer so much from eruptive diseases, whooping cough, tonsilitis, adenoids, diphtheria and numerous other diseases? Because they are overfed. The younger the child the greater is the per cent of disease due to wrong feeding. In adult life overeating and eating improperly otherwise are still the principal causes of disease. But during adult life the causation of disease is more complex than in childhood, for the senses have been more fully developed and instead of confining our physical sins to overeating we fall prey to the abuse of various appetites and passions. Vigourous adults are often the victims of pneumonia, typhoid fever and tuberculosis. Overeating is chiefly to blame, not the bacteria which are given as the principal cause.

Rheumatism, kidney disease and diseases that manifest in hardening of the various tissues, all being forms of degeneration, are quite common. Again, the principal cause is overeating. There are a great number of people who live many years without any special disease, but who are always on the brink of being ill. They are full-blooded and too corpulent.

Although they are often considered successful, they are never fully efficient either physically or mentally. They do not know what good health is, but they are so accustomed to their state of toleration that they consider themselves healthy. They are rather proud of their stoutness and their friends mistake their precarious condition for health. These people often die suddenly, and friends and acquaintances are very much surprised. No healthy man dies suddenly and unexpectedly except by accident.

Instead of growing old gracefully, in possession of our senses and faculties, we die prematurely or go into physical and mental decay. Bleary eyes, pettiness, childishness and lost mental faculties are no part of nature's plan for advanced years. Those manifestations result from man's improvement on nature! From birth to death we are victims of this terrible ogre of overeating. It deprives us of friends and relatives. It takes away our strength and health.

It makes us mentally inefficient and cowardly. At last it deprives us of life when our work is not half done and our days should not be half run. How is it possible, you may ask, that this is true? Of course, overeating is not the only cause, but it is the overwhelming one. It is the basic cause. Aided by other bad habits it conquers us.

We are what we are because of our parentage, plus what we eat, drink, breathe and think, and the eating largely influences the other factors of life. Cholera infantum causes the death of many babies. It never occurs in babies who are fed moderately on natural, clean food, not to exceed three or four times a day. The child is cross.

The mother thinks that it is cross because it is hungry and accordingly feeds. The real cause of the irritability is the overfeeding that has already taken place. The baby has had so much milk that it is unable to digest all of it. A part of the milk spoils in the digestive tract. This fermented material is partly absorbed and irritates the whole system. A part of it remains in the alimentary tract where it acts as a direct local irritant to the intestines. When these are irritated, the blood-vessels begin to pour out their serum to soothe the bowels and the result is diarrhoea. The sick child is fed often. Digestive power is practically absent.

The additional food given ferments and more serum has to be thrown out to protect the intestinal walls. Soon there is a well established case of cholera infantum.

If only enough food had been given to satisfy bodily requirements, none of the milk would have spoiled in the alimentary tract. If all feeding had been stopped as soon as the child became irritable and pinched looking about the mouth and nose, and all the water desired had been given and the child kept warm, there would have been no serious disease. In these cases, the less food given the quicker the recoveries and the fewer the fatalities.

Another common disease of childhood is adenoids. To talk of these maladies as diseases is rather misleading, for they are merely symptoms of perverted nutrition, but we are compelled to make the best of our medical language. Adenoids are due to indigestion.

The indigestion is due to overeating. This is how it comes about: A child eats more than can be digested, generally bolting the food, which is often of a mushy character. The excessive amount of food cannot be digested, and as the intestines and the stomach are moist and have a temperature of 100 degrees Fahrenheit, fermentation soon takes place.

Some of the results of fermentation in the alimentary tract are acids, gases and bacterial poisons. These deleterious substances are absorbed into the bloodstream and go to all parts of the body, acting as irritants. We do not know why they cause adenoids in one child and catarrh in another. It is easy enough to say that children are predisposed that way, which is no information at all.

It seems that all of us have some weak point, and here disease has a tendency to localize. What part the sympathetic nervous system plays, we do not know. Glandular tissue is rather unstable and therefore it becomes diseased easily and adenoids are therefore quite frequent. A coated tongue, or an irritated tongue, both due to indigestion, is a concomitant of adenoids. Such diseases do not merely happen. There are good reasons for their appearance. They are not reflections on the child, but they are on the parents who should have the right knowledge and should take time and pains enough to educate and train the child into health. Tuberculosis is one of the results of ruined nutrition. First there is overeating.

This causes indigestion. The irritating products of food fermenting in the alimentary tract are taken up by the blood. The blood goes to the lungs where it irritates the delicate mucous membrane. In self-protection it begins to secrete an excess of mucus and if the irritation is great enough, pus. The various bacteria are incidental. The tubercular bacillus is never able to gain a foothold in healthy lungs, but after degeneration of lung-tissue has taken place the lungs furnish a splendid home for this bacillus. The tubercular bacillus is a scavenger and therefore does not thrive in healthy bodies. It is the result of disease, not the cause.

Tubercular subjects never have healthy digestive organs. Unfortunately, nearly all of them are persuaded to eat many times more food than they can digest, and thus they have no opportunity to recover, for the overfeeding ruins the digestive and assimilative powers beyond recuperative ability. A large per cent of the human race perish miserably from this disease, which results principally from the ingestion of too much food. The liberal use of such devitalized foods as sterilized milk, refined sugar and finely bolted wheat flour is doubtless a great factor in so reducing bodily resistance that the system falls an easy prey to disease. Too little breathing and poor, devitalized air are also important factors.

There are many causes of rheumatism, but overeating is the chief and it is very doubtful if a case of rheumatism can develop without this main cause. Exposure is often given as the cause, but a healthy man with a clean body does not become rheumatic. Rheumatism is due to internal filth. A filthy alimentary tract makes filthy blood. Some say that the poison in rheumatism is uric acid, and perhaps it is, but there are no uric acid deposits in the body of a prudent eater. The elimination in this disease is imperfect. The skin, the kidneys, the bowels and the lungs do not throw out the debris as they should. Perhaps only one or two of these organs are acting inadequately. The debris is stored up in the system.

Why do the organs of elimination fail to act? Because so much work is thrust upon them that they grow weary and worn; also, a part of the material furnished them is the product of decay in the alimentary tract, and they can not thrive on poor material. Too much food is eaten. An excess of nutritive material, poorly digested, is absorbed. And so we come back to the principal cause, overeating. When the eliminative organs fail to perform their function, the waste is deposited in those parts of the body which are weakened. The irritation from these foreign substances causes inflammation and the result is pain. The extent to which this depositing of material will go is well emphasized in some cases of multiple articular rheumatism, or arthritis deformans, where the deposits are so great that many of the joints become fixed. We could review all the diseases, and nearly every time we would come back to disturbed nutrition as the principal factor, and this is true of not only physical ills, but the mental ones as well.

Various foods do not combine well, still if they are eaten in moderation they do but little harm. If we overeat, the evil results are bound to manifest, no matter how good the food, though it sometimes takes years before they are perceptible. The effects are cumulative.

Each day there is a little fermentation with absorption of the poisonous products. Each day the body degenerates a little. The time always comes when the body can continue its work no longer, and then the individual must choose between reform on one hand and suffering or death on the other.

It is very difficult to convince people that they eat too much. Indeed, the average person is a small eater, in his own estimation. We have been educated into consuming such vast quantities of food that we hardly know what moderation is. In the past, physiologists and observers have watched the amount of food that people could coax down and this they have called the normal amount of food. This is far from the truth. The average American eats at least two times as much as he can digest, assimilate and use to advantage. Many eat three and four times too much. However, nature is very tolerant for a while.

Most of us start out with a fair amount of resistance and are thus enabled to live to the age of forty or fifty in spite of abuses. If we could only dispense with our excesses, we could double or treble our life span, live better, get more enjoyment out of life and give the world more and better work than we can under present conditions.

There is much talk of food shortage. The amount of food consumed and wasted annually in the United States is enough to feed 200,000,000 people. Even with our present knowledge we can easily produce twice as much per acre as we are averaging, and we are tilling only about one-fourth of the land that could be made productive. If we use our brains there is little danger of starving. What is needed now is not more food, but intelligent distribution and consumption of what we produce. We hear of cases of undernourishment. This doubtless occurs at times in the congested parts of great centres of populations. But there are not so many cases suffering from want of the proper quantity of food as from want of quality of food. Bread of finely bolted white flour is starvation food, no matter how great the quantity, unless other food rich in organic salts is also eaten.

The overeating habit is so common and comes on so insidiously that the sufferers do not realise that they are eating to excess. The resultant discomforts are blamed on other things. Babies are fed every two hours or oftener. They should be fed but three or at most four times a day, and never at night. When able to eat solid foods they get three meals a day and generally two or more lunches.

Some children seem to be lunching at all times. They have fruit or bread and butter with jelly or jam in the hand almost all the time. They are encouraged to eat much and often to produce growth and strength. This kind of feeding often does produce large children, heavy in weight, but they are not healthy. Sad to relate, the excess causes disease and death. Such frequent feeding allows the digestive organs no rest. The overwork imposed upon them and the fermentation cause irritation.

This irritation manifests in a constant and almost irresistible desire for food, as does the consumption of much alcohol cause a desire for more alcohol, as the use of morphine or cocaine produces a dominating and ruinous appetite for more of these drugs. These appetites grow by what they feed upon. Man ceases to be master and becomes the abject slave of his abnormal cravings.

Slaves of alcohol and the various habit-forming drugs generally lack the strength of body and mind to assert themselves and to regain mastery of themselves. Coffee and tea have their victims, though they are generally not very firmly enslaved. No one realises how he is bound by his cravings for an excessive amount of food until he tries to break the bonds. Such people may eat moderately for days, perhaps for weeks, and then the old appetite reasserts itself in all its strength and unless the sufferer has a very strong will a food debauch follows.

We have seen men go from one restaurant to another, consuming enormous quantities of food to efface the awful craving, just as men go from one saloon to another to satisfy their desire for alcohol. The gluttons often look with the greatest contempt upon the slaves of liquor. But what is the difference? No matter what appetite, what habit, what passion has gained the mastery, we are slaves.

The important thing is to keep out of slavery, or break the bonds and regain freedom. Those who eat to excess often eat more than three times a day. They take a little candy now, a little fruit then, or they go to the drug store for a glass of malted milk or buttermilk, which they call drinks, or they take a dish of ice cream. The housewife nibbles at cake or bread. If a person is in fair health and wishes to evolve into self-mastery and good health, he should make up his mind never to eat more than three times a day. Nothing but plain water should enter his mouth except at meal times. Next he should limit the number of substances eaten at a meal. The breakfast and lunch should each consist of no more than two or three varieties of food. The dinner should not exceed five or six varieties, and if that many are eaten, they should be compatible. Less would be be better.

The less variety we have, the better the food digests. Also, eating ten or twelve or more kinds of food, as many people do, always leads to overeating. A little of this added to a little of that soon makes a too great total. It is easy to eat all one should of a certain substance of food and feel satisfied, and then change off to something else and before one is through one has eaten three or four times as much as necessary. If the meal is to consist of starch there is no great objection to a small amount of bread, potatoes, rice, macaroni and chestnuts. However, a normal person does not need to coax food down by using great variety.

Those who mix their foods this way invariably overeat. Besides, the various starches require different periods for digestion. Rice is more easily disposed of than bread. Each new item stimulates the desire for more food. It is best, when having potatoes, to have no other starchy food in that meal; or when bread is eaten, to have no potatoes or other starchy food. The habit of eating meat, potatoes and bread in the same meal is very common and causes much disease.

Next the searcher for health should teach himself to eat foods that are natural, cooked simply, and with a minimum amount of seasoning and dressing. The various spices and sauces irritate the digestive organs and create a craving for an excessive amount of food.

The food should be changed as little as possible because such denatured foods as white flour, polished rice, pasteurized milk, and many of the canned fruits and vegetables are so lacking in the natural salts that they do not satisfy one's desire for organic salts. Overeating results. Preserves, jellies and jams are open to the same objection. They cause an abnormal desire for food. Therefore, they should be used seldom and very sparingly.

So long as apples, oranges, figs, dates, raisins, sweet prunes and various other fruits can be had, there is no excuse for the consumption of great quantities of the heavily sugared concoctions which are now so popular. Simplicity and naturalness are great aids in breaking away from food slavery.

## DAILY FOOD INTAKE

It is generally believed that the more we eat the better. Physicians say that it is necessary to eat heartily when well to retain health and strength. When ill it is necessary to consume much food to regain lost health and strength. "Eat all you can of nourishing food", is a common free prescription, and it sounds very reasonable. The physicians of today are not to blame for this belief in overeating, for they were taught thus at college, and very few men in any line do original thinking. It has been a racial belief for centuries and no one now living is responsible.

When a physician advocates what he honestly believes he is doing his best, "and angels can do no more". When a child loses its appetite, the parents worry, for they think that it is very harmful for young people to go without food for a few meals. A lost appetite is nature's signal to quit eating, and it should always be heeded. If it is, it will prevent much disease and suffering and will save many lives. The present-day mode of preparing food leads to overeating. The sense of taste is ruined by the stimulants put into the food.

Dishes are so numerous and so temptingly made that more is eaten than can be digested and assimilated. Refined sugar, salt, the various spices, pickles, sauces and preserves all lead to overeating because of stimulation. The same is true of alcohol taken immediately before meals. If we only give nature a chance, and are perfectly frank and honest with ourselves, she will guard us against the overconsumption of food.

Those who eat but few varieties of plain food at a meal are not sorely tempted to overeat. But when one savory dish is served after another it takes much will power to be moderate. People generally have had more than sufficient before the last course is served. However, the various dishes have different flavours and for this reason the palate is overwhelmed and accepts more food than is good for us.

Men who like to call their work scientific, figure on the amount of food we need to furnish a certain number of heat units—calories. Heat, of course, is a form of energy. Basing the body's food requirements on heat units expended does not solve the problem. The more food that is ingested, the more heat units must be manufactured, and often so much food is taken that the body is compelled to go into the heating business. Then we have fevers.

A large part of the heat is given off by the skin. Those who overeat are compelled to do a great deal of radiating. This excessive amount of fuel taken into the system in the form of food, wears out the body. It gives a result of food need that is at least twice as great as necessary. Experience is the only correct guide to food requirements, and each individual has to settle the matter for himself. The human body is not exactly a chemical laboratory, nor is it an engine which can be fed so much fuel with the resultant production of such and such an amount of heat and energy. Some bodies are more efficient than others. It is among human beings as among the lower animals, some require more food than others. We need enough food to repair the waste, to perform our work and to furnish heat. Every muscle contraction uses up a little energy. Every breath deprives us of heat and carries away carbon dioxide, the latter being formed by oxidation of tissues in the body.

Every minute we lose heat by radiation from the skin. Every thought requires a small amount of food. If we worry, the leak of nervous energy is tremendous, but at the same time we put ourselves in position where we are unable to replenish our stock, for worry ruins digestion. All this expenditure of energy and loss of heat must be made up for by the food intake. Only a small amount of surplus food can be stored in the body. Some fat can be stored as fat. Some starch and sugar can be put aside as either glycogen—animal sugar—or be changed into fat.

This storing of excess food is very limited, except in cases of obesity, which is a disease. Overeating invariably causes disease. It may take two or three years, yes even twenty or thirty years, before the overeating results in serious illness, but the results are certain, and in the meanwhile the individual is never up to par. He can use neither body nor mind to the best advantage. To emphasize and emphasize these remarks, we shall copy a few diet lists, which their authors consider reasonable and correct for the average person for one day, and we shall give our comments.

*The first is taken from Kirke's Physiology, which has been used extensively as a text-book in medical colleges*:

- 340 gm. lean uncooked meat,
- 600 gm. bread,
- 90 gm. butter,
- 28 gm. cheese,
- 225 gm. potatoes, and
- 225 gm. carrots.

An ounce contains 28.3 gm.; a pound, 453 gm.. It is easy to figure these quantities of food in ounces or pounds, which give a better idea to the average person. It is self-evident that this is too much food.

Over twelve ounces of lean, uncooked meat, over twenty-one ounces of bread, almost one-half of a pound each of potatoes and carrots, about an ounce of cheese and over three ounces of butter make enough food for two days, even for a big eater. He who tries to live up to a diet of this kind is sure to suffer disease and early death.

The average loaf of bread weighs about fourteen ounces. Here we are told to devour one-half of a pound of carrots, one-half of a pound of potatoes, three-fourths of a pound of lean raw meat, which loses some weight in cooking, a loaf and one-half of bread, besides butter and cheese. The vast majority of people cannot eat more than one-third of this amount and retain efficiency and health, but many eat even more.

The next table is taken from Dr. I. Burney Yeo's book on diet, and is given as the food required daily by a "well nourished worker":

- 151.3 gm. meat,
- 48.1 gm. white of egg,
- 450.0 gm. bread,
- 500.0 gm. milk,
- 1065.9 gm. beer,
- 60.2 gm. suet,
- 30.0 gm. butter,
- 70.0 gm. starch,
- 17.0 gm. sugar, and
- 4.9 gm. salt.

This worker is too well fed. Often those who are so well fed are poorly nourished, for the excessive amount of food ruins the nutrition, after which the food is poorly digested and assimilated.

This worker eats so much that he will be compelled to do manual labour all his days, for such feeding prevents effective thinking. The following daily average diet is taken from *Diet and Dietetics*, by A. Gauthier, a well known authority on the subject of the nutritive needs of the body. Mr. Gauthier averaged the daily food intake of the inhabitants of Paris for the ten years from 1890 to 1899, inclusive.

*He takes it for granted that this is the average daily food requirement for a person*:

- 420.0 gm. bread and cakes,
- 216.0 gm. boned meat,
- 24.1 gm. eggs (weighed with shell),
- 8.1 gm. cheese (dry or cream),
- 28.0 gm. butter, oil, etc.,
- 70.0 gm. fresh fruit,
- 250.0 gm. green vegetables,
- 40.0 gm. dried vegetables,
- 100.0 gm. potatoes, rice,
- 40.0 gm. sugar,
- 20.0 gm. salt,
- 213.0 C. C. milk, and
- 557.0 C. C. of various alcoholics, containing, 9.5 C. C. of pure alcohol.

So long as the Parisians consume such quantities of food they will continue to suffer and die before they reach one-half of the age that should be theirs. The French eat no more than do other people, in fact, they seem moderate in their food intake as compared with some of the Germans, English and Americans, but they eat too much for their physical and mental good. The lists given are from sources that command the respect of the medical profession. They are the orthodox and popular opinions.

It would be an easy matter to give many more tables, but they agree so closely that it would be a waste of time and space. Quantitative tables from vegetarian sources are not so common. The vegetarians say that meat eating is wrong, being contrary to nature.

Whether they are right or wrong, they make the same mistakes that the orthodox prescribers do, that is, they advocate overeating. Medical textbooks prescribe a too abundant supply of starch and meat in particular. The vegetarians prescribe a superabundance of starch. Read the magazines advocating vegetarianism and note their menus, giving numerous cereals, tubers, peas, beans, lentils, as well as other vegetables, for the same meal. It is as easy to overeat of nuts and protein in leguminous vegetables as it is to overeat of meat. Starch poisoning is as bad as meat poisoning and the results are equally fatal.

*The following are suggestions offered by a fruitarian. They give the food intake for two days*:

- 120 gm. shelled peanuts, raw,
- 1000 gm. apples,
- 500 gm. unfermented whole-wheat bread,
- 120 gm. shelled filberts,
- 450 gm. raisins, and
- 800 gm. bananas.

In the first day's menu it will be noted that over two pounds of apples and over one pound of whole wheat bread are recommended, also over four ounces of raw peanuts. The writer says that this food should preferably be taken in two meals. There are very few people with enough digestive and assimilative power to care for more than one-half of a pound of whole-wheat bread twice a day, especially when taken with raw peanuts, which are rather hard to digest.

The trouble is made worse by the addition of more than one pound of apples to each meal, for when apples in large quantities are eaten with liberal amounts of starch, the tendency for the food to ferment is so strong that only a very few escape. Gas is produced in great quantities, which is both unnatural and unpleasant. Neither stomach nor bowels manufacture any perceptible amount of gas if they are in good condition and a moderate amount of food is taken.

Whole-wheat bread digests easily enough when eaten in moderation, but it is very difficult to digest when as much as eight ounces are taken at a meal. One can accustom the body to accept this amount of food, but it is never required under ordinary conditions and the results in the long run are bad.

The food prescribed for the second day is more easily digested, but it is too much. Raisins are a splendid force food, but no ordinary individual needs a pound of raisins in one day, in addition to about one and three-fourths pounds of bananas, which are also a force food and are about as nourishing as the same amount of Irish potatoes.

In all my reading it has not been my good fortune to find a diet table for healthy people, giving moderate quantities of food. Diet lists seem scientific, so they appeal to the mind that has not learned to think of the subject from the correct point of view. Quantitative diet tables are worthless, for one person may need more than another.

Some are short and some are tall. Some are naturally slender and others of stocky build. There is as much difference in people's food needs as there is in their appearance. To try to fit the same quantity and even kind of food to all is as senseless as it would be to dress all in garments of identical size and cut. If we eat in moderation it does not make much difference what we eat, provided our diet contains either raw fruits or raw vegetables enough to furnish the various mineral salts and the food is fairly well prepared. There are combinations that are not ideal, but they do very little harm if there is no overeating. People who are moderate in their eating generally relish simple foods. Unfortunately, there is but little moderation in eating. From childhood on the suggestion that it is necessary to eat liberally is ever before us. Medical men, grandparents, parents and neighbours think and talk alike. If the parents believe in moderation, the neighbours kindly give lunches to the children. It is really difficult to raise children right, especially in towns and cities.

After such training we learn to believe in overeating and we pass the belief on to the next generation, as it has in the past been handed down from generation to generation.

Finally we die, many of us martyrs to overconsumption of food. Ask any healer of intelligence who has thrown off the blinders put on at college and who has allowed himself to think without fear, and he will tell you that at least nine-tenths of our ills come from improper eating habits. It is not difficult to make up menus of compatible foods. No one knows how much another should eat, and he who prepares quantitative diet tables for the multitude must fail.

However, every individual of ordinary intelligence can quickly learn his own food requirements and the key thereto is given by nature. It is not well to think of one's self much or often. It is not well to be introspective, but everyone should get acquainted with himself, learning to know himself well enough to treat himself with due consideration. We are taught kindness to others. We need to be taught kindness to ourselves. The average person ought to be able to learn his normal food requirements within three or four months, and a shorter time will often suffice.

*The following observations will prove helpful to the careful reader*:

- Food should have a pleasant taste while it is being eaten, but should not taste afterwards. If it does it is a sign of indigestion following overeating, or else it indicates improper combinations or very poor cooking. Perhaps food was taken when there was no desire for it, which is always a mistake. Perhaps too many foods were combined in the meal. Or it may be that there was not enough mouth preparation. It is generally due to overeating. Cabbage, onions, cucumbers and various other foods which often repeat, will not do so when properly prepared and eaten in moderation, if other conditions are right.
- Formation of gas and gas in the bowels are indications of overeating. More food is taken than can be digested. A part of it ferments and gas is a product of fermentation. A very small amount of gas in the alimentary tract is natural, but when there is belching or rumbling of gas in the intestines it is a sign of indigestion, which may be so mild that the individual is not aware of it, or it may be so bad that he can think of little else. When there is formation of much gas it is always necessary to reduce the food intake, and to give special attention to the mastication of all starch-containing aliments. Also, if starches and sour fruits have been combined habitually, this combination should be given up. Starch digests in an alkaline medium, and if it is taken with much acid by those whose digestive powers are weak, the result is fermentation instead of digestion.
- People should never eat enough to experience a feeling of languor. They should quit eating before they feel full. If there is a desire to sleep after meals, too much food has been ingested. When drowsiness possesses us after meals we have eaten so much that the digestive organs require so much blood that there is not enough left for the brain. This is a hint that if we have work or study that requires exceptional clearness of mind, we should eat very moderately or not at all immediately before. The digestive organs appropriate the needed amount of blood and the brain refuses to do its best when deprived of its normal supply of oxygen and nourishment.

Serpents, some beasts of prey and savages devour such large quantities of food at times that they go into a stupor. There is no excuse for our patterning after them now that a supply of food is easily obtained at all times. A bad taste in the mouth is usually a sign of overeating. It comes from the decomposition following a too liberal food intake. If water has a bad taste in the morning or at any other time, it indicates overeating. It may be due to a filthy mouth or the use of alcohol.

Heartburn is also due to overeating, and so is hiccough; both come from fermentation of food in the alimentary tract. A heavily coated tongue in the morning indicates excessive food intake. If the tongue is what is known as a dirty grey colour it shows that the owner has been overeating for years. The normal mucous membrane is clean and pink. The mucous membrane of the mouth, stomach and the first part of the bowels should not be compelled to act as an organ of excretion, for the normal function is secretory and absorptive.

However, when so much food is eaten that the skin, lungs, kidneys and lower bowel cannot throw off all the waste and excess, the mucous membrane in the upper part of the alimentary tract must assist. The result is a coated tongue, but the tongue is in no worse condition than the mucous membrane of the stomach. A coated tongue indicates overcrowded nutrition and is nature's request to reduce the food intake. How much? Enough to clean the tongue. If the coating is chronic it may take several months before the tongue becomes clean.

A muddy skin, perhaps pimply, is another sign of overeating. It shows that the food intake is so great that the body tries to eliminate too many of the solids through the skin, which becomes irritated from this cause and the too acid state of the system and then there is inflammation. Many forms of eczema and a great many other skin diseases are caused by stomach disorders and an overcrowded nutrition. There is a limit to the skin's excretory ability, and when this is exceeded skin diseases ensue. Some of the so-called incurable skin diseases get well in a short time on a proper diet without any local treatment.

Dull eyes and a greenish tinge of the whites of the eyes point toward digestive disturbances due to an oversupply of food. The green colour comes from bile thrown into the blood when the liver is overworked. The liver is never overtaxed unless the consumption of food is excessive. Another very common sign of too generous feeding is catarrh, and it does not matter where the catarrh is located. It is true that there are other causes of catarrh, in fact, anything that irritates the mucous membrane any length of time will cause it, but an overcrowded nutrition causes the ordinary cases.

It is the same old story: The mucous membrane is forced to take on the function of eliminating superfluous matter, which has been taken into the system in the form of food. Many people dedicate their lives to the act of turning a superabundance of food into waste, and as a result they overwork their bodies so that they are never well physically and seldom efficient mentally. Many people, especially women, say that if they miss a meal or get it later than usual, they suffer from headache.

This indicates that the feeding is wrong, generally too generous and often too stimulating. A normal person can miss a dozen meals without a sign of a headache. To repeat: No one can tell how much another should eat, but everyone can learn for himself what the proper amount of food is. Enough is given to help solve the problem. The interpretations presented are not the popular ones, but they are true for they give good results when acted upon. If bad results follow a meal there has been overeating, either at the last meal or previously. Undermasticating usually accompanies overeating and causes further trouble. Those who masticate thoroughly are generally quite moderate in their food intake. Many say that they eat so much because they enjoy their food so. He who eats too rapidly or in excess does not know what true enjoyment of food is. Excessive eating causes food poisoning, and food poisoning blunts all the special senses. To have normal smell, taste, hearing and vision one must be clean through and through, and those who are surfeited with food are not clean internally.

The average individual does not know the natural taste of most foods. He seasons them so highly that the normal taste is hidden or destroyed. Those who wish to know the exquisite flavour of such common foods as onions, carrots, cabbage, apples and oranges must eat them without seasoning or dressing for a while. To get real enjoyment from food it is necessary to eat slowly and in moderation.

We know both from personal experience and from the experience of others that seasoning is not necessary. Instead of giving the foods better flavour, they taste inferior. A little salt will harm no one, but the constant use of much seasoning leads to irritation of the digestive organs and to overeating. Salt taken in excess also helps to bring on premature aging. It is splendid for pickling and preserving, but health and life in abundance are the only preservatives needed for the body.

Refined sugar should be classed among the condiments. People who live normally lose the desire for it. Grapefruit, for instance, tastes better when eaten plain than when sugar is added.

People who sleep seven or eight hours and wake up feeling unrefreshed are suffering from the ingestion of too much food. A food poisoned individual can not be properly rested. To get sweet sleep and feel restored it is necessary to have clean blood and a sweet alimentary tract. Much has been said about overeating. Once in a while a person will habitually undereat, but such cases are exceedingly rare. To undereat is foolish.

At all times we must use good sense. It is a subject upon which no fixed rules can be promulgated. Be guided by the feelings, for perfect health is impossible to those who lack balance. Those who think they need scientific direction may take one of the orthodox diet tables. If it contains alcoholics, remove them from the list. Then partake of about one-third of the starch recommended, and about one-third of the protein. Use more fresh fruit and fresh vegetables than listed. Instead of eating bread made from white flour, use whole wheat bread. Do not try to eat everything given on the scientific diet list each day. For instance, rice, potatoes and bread are given in many of these tables. Select one of these starches one day, another the next day, etc. If one-third of the amount recommended is too much, and it sometimes is, reduce still further. Please bear in mind that the orthodox way, the so-called scientific way, has been tried over a long period of time and it has given very poor results. Moderation has always given good results and always will.

## CLASSIFICATION OF FOODS

Food is anything which, when taken into the body under proper conditions, is broken down and taken into the blood and utilized for building, repairing or the production of heat or energy. There are various forms of foods, which can be divided into two classes: First, nitrogenous foods or proteins. Second, carbonaceous foods, under which caption come the sugars, starches and fats. Salts and water are not usually classified as foods, though they should be, for life is impossible without either.

The chief proteins are: First, the albuminoids, which are represented by the albumin in eggs, the casein in milk and cheese, the myosin of muscle and the gluten of wheat. Second, the gelatinoids, which are represented by the ossein of bones, which can be made into glue, and the collogen of tendons. Third, nitrogen extractives, which are the chief ingredients in beef tea. They are easily removed from flesh by soaking it while raw in cold water.

They are rich in flavour and are stimulating. They have absolutely no food value. Beef tea, and other related extracts, are not foods. They are stimulants. In truth they are of no value, and those who purchase such preparations pay a high price and get nothing in return. The sugars and starches are grouped under the name of carbohydrates, which means that they are a combination of water and carbon. There are various forms of sugar. About 4 per cent of milk is milk sugar, which agrees better with the young than any other kind of sugar. It is not so soluble in water as the refined cane sugar, and therefore not so sweet, but it is fully as nourishing. Honey is a mixture of various kinds of sugars. Cane sugar is taken principally from sugar beets and sugarcane.

There is no chemical difference between the products of canes and beets. Sugars can not be utilized by the blood until it has changed them into other forms of sugar. The use of sugar is rapidly increasing. Several centuries ago it was used as a drug. It was doubtless as effective as a curing agent as our drugs are today. Until within the last sixty or seventy years it has not been used as a staple food. Now it is one of our chief foods. Not so very long ago but ten pounds of sugar per capita were used annually, but now we are consuming about ninety pounds each annually, that is, about four ounces per day. Many people look upon sugar as a flavouring, which it is in a measure, but it is also one of our most concentrated foods.

That this great consumption of sugar is harmful there is no doubt. Physicians who practiced when the use of sugar was increasing very rapidly called attention to the increasing decay of teeth. Sugar, as it appears upon the table is an unsatisfied compound. It does not appear in concentrated form in nature, but mixed with vegetable and mineral matters, and when the pure sugar is put into solution it seeks these matters.

It is especially hungry for calcium and will therefore rob the bones, the teeth and the blood of this important salt, if it can not be had otherwise. The most noticeable effect is the decay of the teeth. We have read considerable literature of late blaming sugar for producing many diseases, among them tuberculosis and cancer.

Improper feeding is the chief cause of these diseases, but to blame sugar for all ills of that kind is far from arriving at the truth. Cancer and tuberculosis killed vast numbers of people before sugar was used as a staple. If we wish to get at the root of any trouble, it is necessary for us to bury our prejudices and be broad minded. People who eat much sugar should also partake liberally of fresh raw fruits and vegetables, in order to supply the salts in which sugar is deficient.

Lump sugar is practically pure, and therefore a poorer substance of diet than any other form of sugar, for man can not live on carbon without salts. Grape sugar and fruit sugar are the same chemically. Another name for them is dextrose, and in the form of dextrose sugar is ready to be taken up by the blood. Children like sweets, but it is just as easy to give them the sweet fruits, such as good figs, dates and raisins, as it is to give them commercial sugar and candy, and it is much better for their health.

Children who get used to the sweet fruits do not care very much for candies. The sugar in these fruits is not concentrated enough to be an irritant and it contains the salts needed by the body. Hence it does not rob the body of any of its necessary constituents.

Because the fruit sugar, taken in fruit form, is not so concentrated and irritating as the common sugar, the child is satisfied with less. Sugar is an irritant of the mucous membrane and therefore stimulates the appetite. This is true only when it is taken in excess in its artificial form, and it does not matter whether it is sugar, jelly or jam. For this reason jellies and jams should be used sparingly, because it is not necessary to stimulate the appetite. Those who resort to stimulation overeat. When much sugar is taken, it not only irritates the stomach, but it even inflames this organ. Sugar is a preservative, and like all other preservatives it delays digestion, if taken in great quantities, and four ounces per day make a great quantity. The digestive organs rebel if they are given as much of sugar as they will tolerate of starch. When taken in excess sugar ferments easily, producing much gas, which is followed by serious results.

Sugar is changed into forms less sweet by acids and heat. The ferment invertin also acts upon sugars. Sugar is a valuable food, but we are abusing it, and therefore it is doing us physical harm. The quantity should be reduced, and families who are using four ounces per person per day, as statistics indicate that most are doing, should reduce the intake to about one-third of this amount. It would be well to take as much of the sugar as possible in the form of sweet fruits.

It is a fact that sugar is easy to digest and that one can soon get energy from it, but feeding is not merely a question of giving digestible aliments, but a question of using foods that are beneficial in the long run. The moderate use of this food is all right, but excess is always bad.

Starches need more change than sugars before they can be absorbed by the blood, but they give better results. Chemically there is but small difference between starch and sugar. The starch must be changed into dextrose, a form of sugar, before it can be utilized by the body. The human body contains a small amount of a substance called glycogen, which is an animal starch or sugar. This glycogen is burned. Sugar is a force food. It combines with oxygen and gives heat and energy.

The waste product is carbonic acid gas, which is carried by the blood to the lungs and then exhaled. Honey and maple sugar are good foods, but overconsumption is harmful. Sugar eating is largely a habit. Because the sugar has so much of the life and so many of the necessary salts removed in its refinement it is a good food only when taken in small quantities. Nature demands of us that we do not get too refined in our habits, for excessive refinement is followed by decay. It is easy to overcome the tendency to overeat of sugar.

Some spoil the most delicious watermelon by heaping sugar or salt, or both, upon it. In this way the flavour is lost. There is not a raw fruit on the market which is as finely flavoured after it has been sugared as it was before. True, those who have ruined their sense of taste object to the tartness and natural acidity of various foods, but they are not judges and can not be until they have regained a normal taste, which can only be done by living on natural foods for a while.

Fats are obtained most plentifully from nuts, legumes, dairy products and animal foods. They are the most concentrated of all foods, yielding over twice the amount of heat or energy that we can obtain from the same weight of pure sugar, starch or protein. Many who think they are moderate eaters consume enough butter to put them in the glutton class. Salts are present in all natural foods of which we partake. Water is indispensable, for the body has to have fluids in order to perform its functions. Foods are burned in the body. They are valuable in proportion to the completeness with which they are digested and assimilated and the ease with which this process is accomplished.

It takes energy to digest food and if the food is very indigestible it takes too much energy. The following remarks on digestibility are according to the best knowledge we have on the subject: As a general rule, the protein of meat and fish is more completely and more quickly digested than the protein in vegetable foods.

The reason is that the vegetable protein is found in cells which are protected by the indigestible cellulose which covers each cell. This covering is not always broken and then the digestive juices are practically powerless. The legumes, which are rich in protein, are comparatively hard to digest. If properly prepared and eaten, they give little or no trouble, but they are generally cooked soft and the mastication is slighted. The result is fermentation. Beans, peas and lentils should be very well chewed, and eaten in moderation, for they are rich both in starch and protein.

Nuts are as a rule not as completely digested as meats and animal fats, and the principal reason is that they are eaten too rapidly and masticated too little. Nuts properly masticated, taken in correct combinations and amounts agree very well. It is not necessary, as many believe, to salt them in order to prevent indigestion.

Compositions and fuel values of various foods which have been grouped for the sake of convenience, for the foods in each group are quite similar. These are not complete, for to list every food would take too much space. We have simply selected a representative list from the various classes of foods. Under flesh are given fish, meats and eggs. Under succulent vegetables are given both root and top vegetables, because of their similarity.

Nuts, cereals, legumes, tubers and fruits are each grouped because it is easy to gain an understanding of them in this way. Milk is given a rather long part of its own because of its great importance in the morning of life. Allow us to repeat that it is impossible to figure out the calories in a given amount of food and then give enough food to furnish so many calories and thus obtain good results. We have already given the key to the amount of food to eat, and it is the only kind of key that works well. However, it is very helpful to have a knowledge of food values.

The calorie is the unit of heat, and heat is convertible into energy. A calorie is the heat required to raise the temperature of one kilogram of water one degree C. To translate into common terms, it is the heat required to raise one pound of water four degrees F.

- One pound of protein produces 1,860 calories.
- One pound of sugar produces 1,860 calories.
- One pound of starch produces 1,860 calories.
- One pound of oil or fat produces 4,220 calories.

For the scientific facts regarding foods we have consulted various works, especially the following: *Diet and Dietetics*, by Gauthier; *Foods*, by Tibbles; *Food Inspection and Analyses*, by Leach; *Foods and Their Adulteration*, by Wiley; *Commercial Organic Analysis*, by Allan. However, we are most indebted to the numerous bulletins issued by the U.S. Department of Agriculture. All who make a study of foods and their value owe a great debt to W.O. Atwater and Chas. D. Wood, who have worked so long and faithfully to increase our knowledge regarding foods.

As we consider the various groups of foods, directions are given for the best way of cooking, but no fancy cooking is considered. Those who wish fancy, indigestible dishes should consult the popular cook books. The women have it in their power to raise the health standard fifty to one hundred per cent by cooking for health instead of catering to spoiled palates, and by learning to combine foods more sensibly than they have in the past. The art of cooking has made its appeal almost entirely to the palate. This art is not on as high level as the science of cooking, which gives foods that build healthy bodies. The right way of cooking is simpler, quicker and easier than the conventional method, and gives food that is superior in flavour. After the normal taste has been ruined, it takes a few months to acquire a natural taste again so that good foods will be enjoyed.

## FLESH FOODS

The food value of meat depends on the amount of fat and protein it contains. Lean meat may contain less than four hundred calories per pound, while very fat meat may contain more than one thousand five hundred calories.

| | Water | Pro-tein | Fat | Carbohy-drates | Ash | Calories per lb. |
|---|---|---|---|---|---|---|
| Beef, average | 72.03 | 21.42 | 5.41 .. | 1.14 | .. | |
| Veal, lean | 78.84 | 19.86 | .82 | .. | .50 | .. |
| Mutton, average | 75.99 | 17.11 | 5.77 .. | 1.33 | .. | |
| Pork, average fat | 47.40 | 14.54 | 37.34 .. | .72 .. | | |
| Pork, average lean | 72.57 | 20.25 | 6.81 .. | 1.10 .. | | |
| Rabbit | 66.80 | 22.22 | 9.76 .. | 1.17 .. | | |
| Chicken, fat | 70.06 | 9.59 | 9.34 .. | .91 .. | | |
| Turkey | 65.60 | 24.70 | 8.50 .. | 1.20 .. | | |

| | | | | | | |
|---|---|---|---|---|---|---|
| Goose | 38.02 | 15.91 | 45.59 .. | .49 | .. | |
| Pigeon | 75.10 | 22.90 | 1.00 .. | 1.00 | .. | |
| Duck, wild | 69.89 | 25.49 | 3.69 .. | .93 | .. | |
| Black bass | 76.7 | 20.4 | 1.7 | .. | 1.2 | 450 |
| Sea bass | 79.3 | 18.8 | .5 | .. | 1.4 | 370 |
| Cod, steaks | 82. | 16.3 | .3 | .. | .9 | 315 |
| Halibut, steaks | 75.4 | 18.3 | 5.2 . | . | 1.1 | 560 |
| Herring | 74.67 | 114.55 | 9.03 .. | 1.78 | .. | |
| Mackerel | 73.4 | 18.2 | 7.1 | .. | 1.3 | 640 |
| Perch, white | 75.7 | 19.1 | 4.0 | .. | 1.2 | 525 |
| Pickerel | 79.8 | 18.6 | .5 | .. | 1.1 | 365 |
| Salmon | 71.4 | 19.9 | 7.4 | .. | 1.3 | 680 |
| Salmon trout | 69.1 | 18.2 | 11.4 .. | 1.3 | 820 | |
| Shad | 70.6 | 18.6 | 9.5 | .. | 1.3 | 745 |
| Sturgeon | 78.7 | 18.0 | 1.9 | .. | 1.4 | 415 |
| Trout, brook | 77.8 | 18.9 | 2.1 | .. | 1.2 | 440 |
| Clams, long | 85.8 | 8.6 | 1.0 | 2.00 | 2.6 | 240 |
| Clams, round | 86.2 | 6.5 | .4 | 4.20 | 2.7 | 215 |
| Lobster | 79.2 | 16.4 | 1.8 | .40 | 2.2 | 390 |
| Oyster in shell | 86.9 | 6.2 | 1.2 | 3.70 | 2.0 | 230 |

These foods are eaten because they are rich in protein. Protein is the great builder and repairer of the body. It forms the framework for both bone and muscle. We can get along very well without starch or sugar or fat, but it is absolutely necessary to have proteid foods. They are the only ones that contain nitrogen, which is essential to animal life.

Nitrogenous foods are used not only to build and repair, but in the end they are burned, supplying as much heat as the same weight of sugar or starch. Proteid foods are generally taken to excess. To most people they are very palatable, and they are generally prepared in a manner that renders rapid eating easy.

Besides, meats contain flavouring and stimulating principles, called extractives, which increase the desire for them. The consequence is that those who eat meat often have a tendency to eat too much. Excessive meat eating often leads to consumption of large quantities of liquor.

Stimulants crave company. As will be noted, most fish and meat contain about 20 per cent of protein, while about 75 per cent is water. The fatter the meat, the less water it contains, and the more fuel value it has. The leaner the meat, the more watery the animal, and the more easily is the flesh digested. Beef is fatter than veal and harder to digest. Also, the flesh of old animals is more highly flavoured than that of the young ones, because it contains more salts. For this reason people who have a tendency to the formation of foreign deposits, as is the case with those who have rheumatism and gout or hardening of the arteries, should take the flesh of young animals when it is obtainable. In the past we have been taught to partake of excessive amounts of protein. The prescribed amount for the average adult has been about five ounces.

If we were to obtain all the protein from meat, this would necessitate eating about twenty-five ounces of meat daily. However, inasmuch as there is considerable protein in the cereals and milk, and a little in most fruits and vegetables, a pound of meat would probably suffice under the old plan. A few physicians have known that such an intake of protein is excessive, and now the physiologists are learning the same.

It has lately been determined experimentally that the body needs only about an ounce of protein daily, which will be supplied by about five ounces of flesh. Three or four ounces of flesh daily make a liberal allowance, for it is supplemented by protein in other foods.Workers eat large quantities of flesh because they think they need a great deal. The fact is that very little more protein is needed by those who do hard physical labour than by brain workers. The extra energy needed calls for more carbohydrates, not for protein. When the organism is supplied with sugar, starch and fat, or one of these, the protein of the body is saved, only a very small amount being used to replace the waste through wear and tear.

Though protein can be burned in the body, it is not an economical fuel, either from a physiological or financial standpoint. The energy obtained from flesh costs much more than the same amount of energy obtained from carbonaceous foods. Ten acres of ground well cultivated can raise enough cereals and vegetables to support a number of people, but if this amount of land is used for raising animals, it will support but a few.

The protein obtained from peas, beans and lentils is cheap, but these foods do not appeal to the popular palate as much as flesh. Meat immediately after being killed is soft. After a while it goes into a state of rigidity known as rigor mortis. Then it begins to soften again. This third stage is really a form of decay, called ripening. It is believed that the lactic acid formed is one of the principal agents producing this softening. Some people enjoy their meats, especially that of fowls and game, ripe enough to deserve the name of rotten.

The ripening produces many chemical changes in the meat, which give the flesh more flavour. Consequently those who indulge are very apt to overeat. It is a fact that those who eat much flesh go into degeneration more quickly than those who are moderate flesh eaters and depend largely on the vegetable kingdom for food. If an excess of good meat causes degeneration, there is no reason to doubt that partaking of overripe foods is even worse. All meat contains waste.

If the flesh comes from healthy animals and is eaten in moderation this waste is so small that it will cause no inconvenience, for a healthy body is able to take care of it. If too much is eaten, the results are serious. Overeating of flesh is followed by excessive production of urea and uric acid products. Some of these may be deposited in various parts of the body, while the urea is mostly excreted by the kidneys. The kidneys do not thrive under overwork any more than other organs. The vast majority of cases of diabetes and Bright's disease are caused by overworking the digestive organs. Too much food is absorbed into the blood and the excretory organs have to work overtime to get rid of the excess. Meats are easily spoiled.

They should be kept in a cold place and not very long. Fresh meat and fish are more easily digested than those which are salted, or preserved in any other way. Pickled meats should be used rarely The same is true of fish. Ptomaines, or animal poisons, form easily in flesh foods. These are very dangerous, and it is not safe to eat tainted flesh, even after it is cooked. Fish decomposes quickly and fish poisoning is probably even more severe than meat poisoning.

Fish should be killed immediately after it is caught, for experiments have shown that the flesh of fish kept captive after the manner of fishers degenerates very rapidly. Fish should be eaten while fresh. Even when the best precautions have been taken, it is somewhat risky to partake of fish that has been shipped from afar.

Flesh foods are more easily and completely digested than the protein derived from the vegetable kingdom. From the table it will be noted that some fish is fat and some is lean. The ones containing more than 5 per cent of fat should be considered fat fish. These are somewhat harder to digest than the lean ones, but they are more nutritious. Shell fish is generally low in food value and if taken as nourishment is very expensive. However, most people eat this food for its flavour.

## COOKING FLESH FOODS

Cooking is an art that should be learned according to correct principles. Every physician should be a good cook. He should be able to go into the kitchen and show the housewife how to prepare foods properly. Medical men who are well versed in food preparation and able to make good food prescriptions have no need of drugs.

The flesh of animals is composed of fibres. These fibres are surrounded by connective tissue which is tough. The cooking softens and breaks down these tissues, thus rendering it easier for the digestive juices to penetrate and dissolve them. That is, proper cooking does this. Poor cooking generally renders the meats indigestible. The simpler the cooking, the more digestible will be the food. Flavours are developed in the process, but these are hidden if the meats are highly seasoned.

**"Boiling"**

When meats are boiled they lose muscle sugar, flavouring extracts, organic acids, gelatin, mineral matters and soluble albumin. That is, they lose both flavour and nourishment. Therefore the liquid in which they are cooked should be used. The proper way to boil meat is to plunge it into plain boiling water.

Allow the water to boil hard for ten or fifteen minutes. This coagulates the outer part of the piece of meat. Then lower the temperature of the water to about 180 degrees F. and cook until it suits the taste. If it is allowed to boil at a high temperature a long time, it becomes tough, for the albumin will coagulate throughout. Salt extracts the water from meat. Therefore none of it should be used in boiling.

The meat should be cooked in plain water with no addition. No vegetables and no cereals are to be added. All meats contain some fat, and this comes into the water and acts upon the vegetables and starches, making them indigestible. Season the meat after it is cooked, or better still, let everyone season it to suit the taste after serving. Meats that are to be boiled should never be soaked, for the cold water dissolves out some of the salts and some of the flavouring extracts, as well as a part of the nutritive substances. It is better to simply wash the meat if it does not look fresh and clean enough to appeal to the eye, which it always should be.

**"Stewing"**

If meat is to be stewed, cut into small pieces and stew or simmer at a temperature of about 180 degrees F until it is tender. It is to be stewed in plain water. If a meat and vegetable stew is desired, stew the vegetables in one dish, and the meat in another. When both are done, mix. By cooking thus a stew is made that will not "repeat" if it is properly eaten. Foods should taste while being eaten, not afterwards.

**"Broths"**

If a broth is desired, select lean meat. Either grind it or chop it up fine. There is no objection to soaking the meat in cold water, provided this water is used in making the broth. Use no seasoning. Let it stew or simmer at about 180 degrees F until the strength of the meat is largely in the water. When the broth is done, set it aside to cool. Then skim off all the fat and warm it up and use. One pound of lean meat will produce a quart of quite strong broth.

**"Broiling"**

Cut the meat into desired thickness. Place near intense fire, turning occasionally, until done. Be careful not to burn the flesh. An ordinary steak should be broiled in about ten minutes. Of course, the time depends on the thickness of the cut and whether it is desired rare, medium or well done, and in this let the individual suit himself, for he will digest the meat best the way he enjoys it most.

Beefsteak smothered in onions is a favourite dish. It is not a good way to prepare either the onions or the steak. A better way is to broil both the steak and the onions, or broil the steak, cut the onions in slices about one-half to three-fourths of an inch thick, add a little water and bake them. Beefsteak and onions prepared in this way are both palatable and easy to digest. "Roasting" is just like broiling, that is, cooking a piece of meat before an open fire. Here we use a larger piece of meat and it therefore takes longer. Of old roasting was quite common, but now we seldom roast meat in this country.

**"Baking"**

Here we place the meat in an enclosed oven. Most of our so-called roast meats are baked. The oven for the first ten or fifteen minutes should be very hot, about 400 degrees F. This heat seals the outside of the meat up quite well. Then let the heat be reduced to about 260 degrees F. If it is kept at a high temperature it will produce a tough piece of meat. The time the meat should be in the oven depends upon the size of the piece of meat and how well done it is desired. While baking, some of the juices and a part of the fat escape.

About every fifteen minutes, baste the meat with its own juice. A few minutes before the meat is to be removed from the oven it may be sprinkled with a small amount of salt, and so may broiled and roasted meats a little while before they are done. However, many prefer to season their own foods or eat them without seasoning and they should be allowed to do so.

**"Steaming"**

This is an excellent way of cooking. None of the food value is lost. Put the meat in the steamer and allow it to remain until done. The cheapest and toughest cuts of meat, which are fully as good as the more expensive ones and often better flavoured, can be rendered very tender by steaming. Tough birds can be treated in the same way.

An excellent way to cook an old hen or an old turkey is to steam until tender and then put into a hot oven for a few minutes to brown. Some birds are so tough that they can not be made eatable by either boiling or baking, but steaming makes them tender. It is best to avoid starchy dressings, in fact dressings of all kinds. A well cooked bird needs none, and dressing does not save a poorly cooked one. Most dressings are very difficult to digest.

**"Fireless Cooking"**

Every household should have either a good steamer or a fireless cooker. Both are savers of time and fuel and food. They emancipate the women. Those who have fireless cookers and plan their meals properly do not need to spend much time in the kitchen. Place the meat in the fireless cooker, following the directions which accompany it. However, if they tell you to season the meat, omit this part.

**"Smothering"**

It is a modification of baking. Any kind of meat may be smothered, but it is especially fine for chickens. Take a young bird, separate it into joints, place into a pan, add a pint of boiling water. If chicken is lean put in a little butter, but if fat use no butter. Cover the pan tightly and place in oven and let it bake. A chicken weighing two and one-half pounds when dressed will require baking for one hour and fifteen minutes. Keep the cover on the baking pan until the chicken is done, not raising it even once. Gravy will be found in the pan.

Pressed chicken is very good. Get a hen about a year old. Place it into steamer or fireless cooker until so tender that the flesh readily falls from the bones. Remove the bones, but keep the skin with the meat. Chop it up. Place in dish or jar, salting very lightly. Over the chopped-up meat place a plate and on this a weight, and allow it to press over night. Then it is ready to slice and serve.

This is very convenient for outings. Fish should preferably be baked or broiled. It may also be boiled, but it boils to pieces rather easily and loses a part of its food value. It must be handled with great care. No seasoning is to be used. When served a little salt and drawn butter or oil may be added as dressing.

**"Frying"**

It is an objectionable method of cooking. It is generally held, and with good reason, that when grease at a high temperature is forced into flesh, it becomes very indigestible. In fact the crust formed on the outside of the flesh can not be digested. It is folly to prepare food so that it proves injurious. However, there is a way of using the frying pan so that practically no harm is done. Grease the pan very lightly, just enough to prevent the flesh from sticking. Make the pan very hot and place the meat in it. Turn the meat frequently. Fries may be cooked in this way with good results. The same is true of steaks and chops. Avoid greasy cooking. It is an abomination that helps to kill thousands of people annually.

**"Paper Bag Cooking"**

It is all right if it is convenient. Those who have good steamers or fireless cookers will not find it of special advantage. Brown flour gravies are not fit to eat. If there is any gravy serve it as it comes from the pan without mixing it with flour or other starches. It may be put over the meat or used as dressing for the vegetables. Milk gravies are also to be avoided. Use only the natural gravies. Oysters may be eaten raw or stewed. Stew the oysters in a little water.

Heat the milk and mix. Eat with cooked succulent vegetables and with raw salad vegetables. It is best to leave the crackers out. The oysters themselves contain very little nourishment, but when made into a milk stew the result is very nutritious.

Eggs should be fresh. Some bakers buy spoiled eggs and use them for their fancy cakes and cookies. This is a very objectionable practice and may be one of the reasons that bakers' cookies never taste like those"mother used to make". Eggs take the place of fish, meat or nuts, for they are rich in protein. They may be taken raw, rare or well done. Eggs may be boiled, poached, steamed or baked. Soft boiled eggs require about three and one-half minutes. Hard boiled ones require from fifteen to twenty minutes. The albumin of an egg boiled six or seven minutes is tough. When boiled longer it becomes mellow.

Eggs may be made into omelettes or scrambled, but the pan should be lightly greased and quite hot so that the cooking will be quickly done. Eggs are variously treated for an omelette. Some cooks add nothing but water and this makes a delicate dish. Others use milk, cream or butter, and beat. Bacon is a relish and may be taken occasionally with any other food. It should be well done, fried or broiled until quite crisp.

This is one place where frying is not objectionable. Pork should rarely be used. It is too fat and rich and requires too long to digest. When eaten it should be taken in the simplest of combinations, such as pork and succulent vegetables or juicy fruits, either cooked or raw, and nothing else. Flesh may be eaten more freely in winter than in summer. Meat especially should be eaten very sparingly during hot weather, for it is too stimulating and heating. Nuts, eggs and fish are then better forms in which to take protein.

## FLESH FOODS COMBINATIONS

Flesh foods combine best with the succulent vegetables and the salad vegetables or with juicy fruits. It is more usual to take vegetables with flesh than to take fruit, but those who prefer fruit may take it with equally as good results. Both fruits and vegetables are rich in tissue salts, in which flesh foods are rather deficient.

The succulent vegetables contain some starch and the juicy fruits some sugar, but not enough to do any harm. They both act as fillers. Flesh is quite concentrated and it is customary to take it with other concentrated foods, such as bread and potatoes. As a result too much food is ingested.

It would be a splendid rule to make to avoid bread and potatoes when flesh food is taken, but if this seems too rigid, make it a rule never to eat all three at the same meal. It is best to eat the flesh foods without bread or potatoes, but if starch is desired, take only one kind at a time. Most people crave a certain amount of food as filler, and they have fallen into the habit of using bread and potatoes for this purpose. This is a mistake. Use the juicy fruits and the succulent vegetables for filling purposes and thus get sufficient salts and avoid the many ills that come from eating great quantities of concentrated foods. When possible, have a raw salad vegetable or two with the meat or fish meal. Eat only one concentrated albuminous food at a meal. If you have meat, take no fish, eggs, nuts or cheese.

# Bibliography

A Jayakumar: *Food Security Management : A Comparative Study*, Anmol, Publication, Delhi, 2007.

A Mohamed Abdullah: *Food Security and Gender Inequality*, Abjiheet, Publication, Delhi, 2008.

*Agriculture, Food Security and Rural Development*, Oxford University Press, 2010.

Amalesh Banerjee: *Food Security and Public Distribution System Today*, Kanishka, Publication, Delhi, 2004.

Amita Saxena: *Fisheries Resources and Food Security*, Narendra Publication, Delhi, 2014.

Anshu: *Food Security in India : Challenges of 21st Century*, Kalakriti Offset, Delhi, 2009.

Archana Ruhela: *Agriculture and Food Security*, Oxford Book Company, 2008.

Avanish K. Tiwari and Jeevan Nair: *Food Security and Global Economy*, Pentagon Press, 2009.

B.D. Sharma: *Agriculture Development and Food Security*, Ancient Publishing House, Delhi, 2012.

Basudeb Guha-Khasnobis, Shabd Acharya. S and Benjamin: *Food Security: Indicators, Measurement and the Impact of Trade Openness*, Oxford University, 2008.

Bimal N. Patel and Ranita Nagar: *Food Security Law: Interdisciplinary Perspectives*, Eastern Book Company, 2014.

Biswajit Chatterjee and Asim K. Karmakar: *Food Security in India : A Comprehensive Plan for Sustainable Solution*, Regal Publications, Delhi, 2012.

Brij K. Taimni: *Food Security in 21 Century : Perspective and Vision*, Konark, Publication, Delhi, 2001.

C.H. Hanumantha Rao: *Agriculture, Food Security, Poverty and Environment*, Oxford University Press, 2005.

C.H. Hanumantha Rao: *Agriculture, Food Security, Poverty and Environment*, Oxford University Press, 2006.

Dalip Kumar and Asmi Raza: *Agriculture and Food Security: Contemporary Issues*, Deep and Deep Publication, Delhi, 2011.

Debashis Basu; B Francis Kulirani and B Datta Ray: *Agriculture Food Security Nutrition and Health in North East India*, Mittal Publication, Delhi, 2006.

G.K. Kulkarni and B.N. Pandey: *Bioresources for Food Security and Rural Livelihood*, Narendra Publication, Delhi, 2010.

L. Reddeppa: *Food Security in India*, Kanishka Publication, Delhi, 2011.

M Lakshmi Narasaiah: *Economic Growth and Food Security*, Discovery Publishing House, Delhi, 2008.

M Lakshmi Narasaiah: *Energy and Food Security*, Discovery, Publication, Delhi, 2007.

M. Lakshmi Narasaiah: *Food Security and Irrigation*, Discovery, Publication, Delhi, 2003.

Mrinmoy Datta; Narendra Pratap Singh and Er Dhiman Daschaudhuri: *Climate Change and Food Security*, New India Publication, Agency, 2008.

Opender Koul, G.S. Dhaliwal, Sucheta Khokhar and Ram Singh: *Biopesticides in Environment and Food Security*, Scientific, Publication, Delhi, 2012.

P C Trivedi: *Biotechnology and Food Security*, Pointer, Publication, Delhi, 2008.

Pradeep Chaturvedi: *Food Security and Panchayati Raj*, Concept, Publication, Delhi, 2004.

Pradeep Chaturvedi: *Food Security in South Asia*, Concept, Publication, Delhi, 2002.

R.K. Behl, L. Bona, J. Pauk, W. Merback and A. Veha: *Crop Science and Technology for Food Security Bioenergy and Sustainability*, Agrobios, Publication, Delhi, 2012.

S.R. Sharma and Vijay Kaushik: *Food, Nutrition and Cookery*, Anmol, Publication, Delhi, 2002.

Shashi Kumar: *Biodiversity and Food Security*, Atlantic, Publication, Delhi, 2002.

Shyam Kartik Mishra and Babita Agrawal: *Food Security in India : Policies and Challenges* , New Century Publications, Delhi, 2013.

Subhajyoti Das: *Drinking Water and Food Security in Hard Rock Areas of India* Edited by, Geological Society of India, 2008.

Sudip Chakraborty: *Food Security and Child Labour: The Case of a Hazardous Occupation*, Deep and Deep, Publication, Delhi, 2011.

Sujata K. Dass: *Biotechnology and Food Security*, Isha Books, Delhi, 2004.

Vibha Dhawan: *Agriculture for Food Security and Rural Growth*, TERI Press, 2008.

Vijay S. Vyas: *Food Security in Asian Countries in the Context of Millennium Goals*, Academic Foundation, Delhi, 2005.

# Index